Portraits of Buddhist Women

SUNY series in Buddhist Studies

Matthew Kapstein, Editor

Portraits of Buddhist Women

Stories from the *Saddharmaratnāvaliya*

Translated by

Ranjini Obeyesekere

State University of New York Press

Published by
State University of New York Press, Albany

Printed in the United States of America

For information, address the State University of New York Press,
90 State Street, Suite 700, Albany, NY 12207

Production by Michael Haggett
Marketing by Patrick Durocher

Library of Congress Cataloging-in-Publication Data

Dharmasena, Thera, 13th cent.
[Saddharmaratnavaliya. English Selections]
Portraits of Buddhist women : stories from the Saddharmaratnavaliya / Ranjini Obeyesekere.
p. cm. — (SUNY series in Buddhist studies.)
Includes index.
ISBN 0-7914-5111-9 (alk. paper) — ISBN 0-7914-5112-7 (pbk. : alk. paper)
1. Dhammapadaòòhakathå. 2. Tipiòaka. Suttapiòaka. Khuddakanikåya Dhammapada. 3. Buddhist women—India—History—To 1500. 4. Women—South Asia—Social conditions. I. Obeyesekere, Ranjini. II. Title. III. Series.

BQ1375.D5613 2001
294.3'82322—dc21 2001034164

10 9 8 7 6 5 4 3 2 1

To my mother, now in her ninetieth year—
a source of love and inspiration for four generations.

Contents

Acknowledgments

This book was made possible in part by a generous grant from the National Endowment for the Humanities.

I wish also to thank Prof. G. D. H. Wijewardene of the University of Colombo, Sri Lanka, for his unfailing support and for giving generously of his time to answer innumerable questions on matters of Buddhist philosophy, etymology, and Pali terminology; my friends of the Princeton Research Forum and especially the late Margit Minkin for reading and critically commenting on the stories; my dear friend Anna Szemeredi who helped save the day when my computer crashed as I was desperately trying to get the final printout to the State University of New York Press before catching a plane to Sri Lanka; my husband Gananath Obeyesekere whose request for a "quick translation" of a page of this text first triggered my interest in the Saddharmaratnāvaliya and who then kept urging me to translate more and more of it; and finally, Nancy Ellegate and the editors of the State University of New York Press for putting up with the delays and hassles of long-distance communication.

siyalu denāṭama piṇ aiti vēvā!
[May they all be blessed with much merit!]

Introduction

In 1986 I first began to translate the *Saddharmaratnāvaliya,* [Jewel Garland of The True Doctrine] an important and well-loved Buddhist work from the Sinhala literary canon. The National Endowment for the Humanities generously funded me for a two-year period. I had assumed at the time that I could translate the entire book—a collection of three hundred and sixty stories—in that time. I found out very early that it would be a lifetime project not a two-year one. I decided then to limit myself to a two-volume work. For the first volume I chose to translate the initial fifteen stories of the *Saddharmaratnāvaliya*. They formed an entity as they illustrated the first of the twenty-nine sections of *Dhammapada* [Stanzas of the Doctrine], the *Yamaka vagga* [Twin Verses]. By focusing on this section I was able to illustrate something of the larger structure of the *Saddharmaratnāvaliya* and how it differed from its original, the *Dhammapadattakata*. The author-translator had provided link passages between some of the stories, used others as an emotional and doctrinal counterpoint, and thereby provided a unity lacking in the original. That collection with an Introduction, Notes and Glossary has now been published as *The Jewels of the Doctrine: Stories of the Saddharmaratnāvaliya*, Albany: State University of New York Press, 1991.

This book is intended as a companion volume of more stories from the same work. In the process of selection I became fascinated by the many stories in the text where the central characters were women. I decided then to focus on these stories because they not only illuminate the position of women in the early-medieval Buddhist worlds[1] of India and Sri Lanka but also provide insights into shifting stances over time on issues of sexuality and gender. The complex interplay of Hindu influences from the subcontinent, local folk beliefs

1. I refer here to the period from around the fifth century C.E. (when the *Dhammapadattakata* is believed to have been written) and the thirteenth century C.E. when the *Saddharmaratnāvaliya* was written.

and attitudes, and the worldview of celibate monks as they impinge on the core Buddhist doctrinal positions, surface throughout the stories.

The *Saddharmaratnāvaliya*, henceforth referred to as SR, is believed to be the work of a thirteenth-century scholar-monk, the Elder Dharmasena. It was intended to be a translation of a Pali work, the *Dhammapadattakata* [Commentary on the Dhammapada] henceforth referred to as DA, written around the fifth century C.E. The colophon to the Pali work states however, that the DA was in turn a translation of an even earlier Sinhala text. Thus we have today a text that goes back to a period prior to the fifth century C.E., which has been kept alive, translated, and retranslated at different points in its history, and in the process has come to reflect the changing values and worlds of the translators. Translations, especially of commentarial texts, were often more than close literal transferences of a work. The authors-translators seem to have felt no compunction about adding to or cutting down the original in order to achieve their vision of what the work was intended to be. For example, the fifth-century Pali translator, while acknowledging the original source of his text as a work existing in Sinhala, in Sri Lanka, then dismissively adds, "Because it is in the language of the island it is of no profit or advantage to foreigners. Therefore I shall discard this dialect and its diffuse idioms and translate the work into the pleasing language of the Sacred Texts."[2]

Similarly, in the thirteenth-century retranslation back to Sinhala, the monk, Dharmasēna, states with equal confidence, "We have abandoned the strict Pali method and taken only the themes in composing this work." He adds with mock modesty and in an ironic dig at the fifth-century Pali translator's dismissal of the "style" of the Sinhala original,

> It [this work] may have faults and stylistic shortcomings but ignore them. Be like the swans who separate milk from water even though the milk and water have been mixed together, or like those who acquire learning and skills even from a teacher of low status because it is the acquisition of knowledge with which they are concerned.[3]

He then goes on quite deliberately to indulge in the very kind of "diffuse idioms" his predecessor had so cavaliarly eliminated!

> So consider only its usefulness and apply the healing salve of the *Saddharmaratnāvaliya* to remove the hazy film of Delusion that

2. Burlingame, E. W. *Buddhist Legends: Translated from the original Pali text of The Dhammapada Commentary,* Part I, London, Henley & Boston, 1979, p. 145.
3. Obeyesekere, R. tr. *Jewels of the Doctrine: Stories from the Saddharmaratnāvaliya,* Albany: State University of New York Press, 1991, p. 3.

> clouds the Eye of Wisdom and go happily and with clear sight along the highway of Right Actions to the city of *nirvāṇa*.[4]

The *Saddharmaratnāvaliya* as a result is three times as long as its original, contains expanded descriptions, new and elaborate metaphors, and images drawn from the contemporary world of the author intended to capture the imagination of his thirteenth century audiences. Both translators rework their sources in terms of the feel and flow of their respective languages. Thus in contrast to the terse and restrained telling of the Pali stories the Sinhala work is written in an easy flowing, colorful prose, in the half-colloquial half-literary style still used by Buddhist monks in their sermons. The speaking voice and narrative persona of the author cuts into the text constantly, revealing his humanity and humor, his narrative gifts and above all, the intellectual and psychological subtlety with which he explores and illuminates abstract elements of Buddhist doctrine, relating them to the everyday needs and problems of ordinary people.

It is not surprising then that the connection with the Pali work hardly surfaces in the conciousness of the average Sinhala reader or listener. To them it is essentially a Sinhala Buddhist work, rooted in the culture, the worldview, and the very texture of Sinhala society. This is all the more so because the world of reference of both the Pali and Sinhala works is agrarian, feudal, medieval, and also profoundly Buddhist. In spite of five hundred years of colonial contact, the Buddhist ethical system of most Sinhala villagers even as late as the fifties, was not too far removed from the thirteenth-century world of this text—which perhaps accounts for its popularity in the villages of Sri Lanka. The work was equally revered by generations of scholars and by the native intelligentsia who regarded it as an important literary work that resonated with their Buddhist past.

The stories of the SR were intended to illustrate and illuminate abstract philosophical doctrines for lay audiences. Each story illustrates a specific doctrinal point and refers to a specific verse or verses in the *Dhammapada* text. The opening passage in each story clearly indicates the ethical thrust and the moral point of the story. Other issues that the context of the stories may raise are not necessarily focused on. In that sense these stories are not about women, their social roles, or issues of gender. They are about larger ethical and moral issues. The women are merely characters in the stories.

However, what fascinates a modern reader is that the stories are firmly contextualized in the everday world of their respective authors—one, a Buddhist South Indian monk believed to have lived around the fifth century C.E.

---

4. Ibid.

and the other, a Sinhala monk of the thirteenth century C.E.—and that of their readers-listeners, the agrarian villagers for whom the stories were told. It is this context that throws light on the position of women and their social roles.

The selection of stories for this book is arbitrary and the focus is mine. I begin this collection of stories of "Women in the Saddharmaratnāvaliya" with the story of King Udēnī and end with the story of Soreyya, both males, a strange choice. However, as the author of the SR in his opening comment states, it is the stories of Udēnī's two queens, Sāmāvatī and Māgandi, which are the central element in the Udēnī Cycle. The stories of King Udēnī and the noble merchant Ghōṣaka merely form the background to these two powerful women whose lives illustrate two important aspects of Buddhist Doctrine—"the positive and negative consequences of Acts of Merit and Demerit."

The concluding story of Soreyya is about a man who undergoes a dramatic sex change, becomes a woman, marries and has children, and then changes back into a man. It is an unusual story of the shifts of gender identities and provides insights into the social and psychological changes that such a transference entails.

The *Udēnī Cycle,* as I have termed it, not only contains the stories of Sāmāvatī and Māgandi but there are also several other very dynamic women who often control and direct the lives of the male "heroes" or rather "counterparts." Udēnī's mother, the queen, when faced with the terrible trauma of being carried off by a bird acts with intelligence and good sense and saves her life and that of her child. Again, when rescued by the hermit it is her survival instinct for herself and her child that makes her decide to seduce the hermit and ensure his continued support. When she later hears of the death of her husband, King Parantapa, she sends her son back to regain his kingdom. Fully aware that the people at court might not believe his claim she takes care to give him identifying objects such as a cape and a ring and to tell him the identities and names of ministers she knew at the time.

Similarly, in the story of Ghōṣaka the most dynamic character is his wife. It is she who intelligently and with considerable foresight takes control of both of their lives and directs their destinies. During the early years of his life Ghōṣaka is the victim of his *karma,* abandoned as an infant and left to die—a consequence of his own attempts to abandon his child in a past life. Thereafter, for most of his life things happen to Ghōṣaka or he is the victim of other's actions. However, from the moment he meets the woman who later becomes his wife, *she* takes control of his life and fortunes. She not only saves his life by exchanging the death warrant he unwittingly carries for another letter but she does so in such a manner that her own desires are fulfilled. She successfully saves his life, gets herself chosen as his bride, and even arranges for a palace to be constructed for the two of them to live in! Throughout the story it is she who assesses the possible dangers to her husband's life and fortunes and acts accordingly. For example, when she finally leaves with her husband to visit her father-in-law, anticipating the possibility of their being disinherited by his father, she shrewdly orders that the tribute they had collected from a hundred villages to take to him, be left instead in her parental home! At the father's deathbed when he is about to disinherit Ghōṣaka, his adopted son, it is her timely performance of unmitigated grief that precipitates the father's death and changes Ghōṣaka's future.

Not only does she direct the course of their lives but she is fully aware of her clearly superior intelligence and of the role she has played in her husband's fortunes—hence her condescending smile when she greets him on his return, a little dizzy with circumambulating the city and with the high honors showered on him! His reaction is childish and simpleminded—threatening to kill her for what he perceives as an insult. When she tells him the reason for her smile and the servant confirms the truth of what she says, Ghōṣaka (in the SR translator's version) expresses no gratitude but exclaims about his own past Acts of Merit. However, in the DA version, Ghōṣaka's comment is: "How great was my presumption! But since I have escaped from so terrible a death I must no longer live the life of heedlessness." He then goes on to establish alms-halls for the poor and the blind. The humility and willingness to accept the truth of his wife's claim is eliminated in the later version. That absence perhaps says something about shifts in monks' attitudes toward the role of women that might have occurred between the fifth and thirteenth centuries.

THE NARRATIVE STRUCTURE

In deciding to translate the "Udēnī Cycle" in full (summarizing only a few segments of the repetitive attempts on the life of the young Ghōṣaka), I realized that I could also illustrate the complex structure of Buddhist narratives. The "Udēnī Cycle" is a group of interrelated stories. As often happens with Buddhist narratives there is more than one central character. A single story can thus extend into a series of stories about several characters each of whom become the central character of their particular story. What prevents them from being individual stories is that there are several links that tangentially connect one or other though certainly not all to each other. (See diagram.)

This particular group of stories provides a good illustration of what Paula Richman describes as the pattern of "branch stories" in Buddhist narratives.[5]

5. Richman, Paula, *Women, Branch Stories and Religious Rhetoric in a Tamil Buddhist Text,* Syracuse, NY 1988.

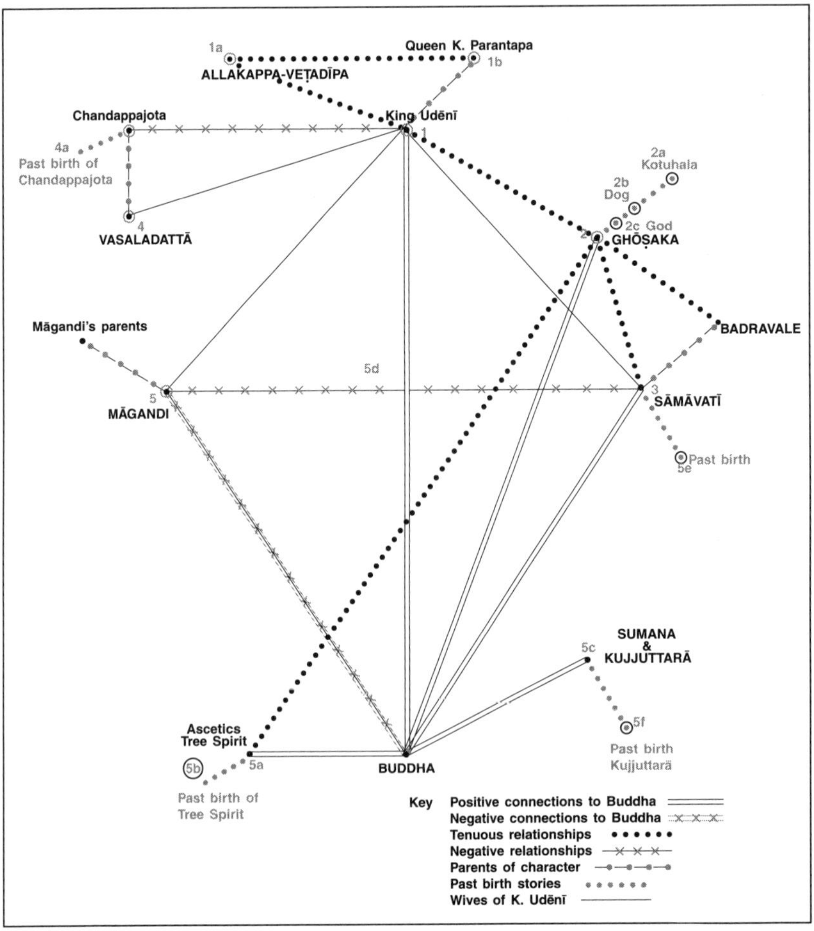

Instead of a main plot and subplots connected to a central character or theme we have a collection of stories that do not necessarily lead one into the other in either a linear or a cyclic structure. Nor is there a timeline since they move from the present into the past or future births or from past into present or future births and cover time periods that shift back and forth over several rebirths spread out over aeons. They *are* linked however, though tenuously. The link is not so much a central protagonist—the Udēnī Cycle for example, has several protagonists in its several branch stories—but rather by cross-references to events and incidents as they occasionally surface in one or other story. There is no overarching unity. Sometimes the Buddha connects one or two of the stories by stressing the *karmic* causal links that have operated in past rebirths. At other times the links occur in the body of later stories and become an important catalyst in the movement of the plot.

The Udēnī Cycle starts well before the birth of King Udēnī and extends into the past births not only of important characters such as Sāmāvatī but also of marginal characters like Kujjuttarā and the Tree Deity. In between we have the individual stories of Sāmāvatī and Māgandi that are linked on the one hand to King Udēnī as they become his queens and on the other, in their relationships to the Buddha—the one devotional, the other antagonistic.

Most editors of the SR divide the cycle into five main stories because statements such as "This is the birth story of King Udēnī" or "This is the birth story of Sāmāvatī" provide dividing markers at the end of each of the five sections. I too have marked these five sections for convenience:

(1) the story of King Udēnī, (2) the story of the noble merchant Ghōṣaka, (3) the story of Sāmāvatī, (4) the story of Vāsuladattā, and (5) the story of Māgandi.

Connected to the five main stories are several branch stories. I have identified and numbered them not because such divisions exist in the text but in order to discuss the larger narrative structure and the cross-connections within it. Thus there are several "branch" stories within the five main ones. The story of King Udēnī (1) begins with the story of the two ascetics (1a) who help him to finally regain his kingdom. The story of Ghōṣaka that follows begins with stories of three of his former births (marked 2a, 2b, and 2c). The story of Sāmāvatī is placed within the story of Ghōṣaka but separately identified and marked (3).Vāsuladattā's story is (4) and that of her father's past birth marked as [4a]. There are five stories included in the Māgandi story. They are identified as [5a] the story of the ascetics, [5b] the story of the past birth of the Tree Spirit, [5c] the story of Sumana and Kujjuttarā, [5d] the main story of the rivalry between Māgandi and Sāmāvatī and the Buddha, [5e] the past birth story of Sāmāvatī, and [5f] the past birth stories of Kujjuttarā.

Apart from the tenuous links that interconnect different characters within these different stories there are certain distinguishing features that suggest that they *were* meant to be read as a group. While other stories of the SR and the DA also have similar "branch stories," none of them are as complex or as extended or interlinked as this one. Several of them do have link passages that connect one story to the next but such links are most often thematic or intended as a balancing device to illustrate a doctrinal point. For example, the Maṭṭakundalī story is linked to the Nāgasēna story that follows it in this manner:

> To increase the faith of the faithful we related the story of Maṭṭakundalī, describing what joys and blessings he obtained merely by the power of his serene thoughts. Now, in order to encourage those

> same good men in the practice of the Doctrine we shall relate the story of the Senior Monk Nāgasēna.[6]

Except for such introductory links these two stories are separate and distinct and have no internal connection to each other.

Individual stories in the SR can also be identified by a certain pattern. They are framed by an introductory comment that states the moral or ethical doctrine (based on a verse from the Dhammapada text) which the story is intended to illustrate, and they end with a concluding sermon. The sermon is given either by the Buddha who appears as a character within the story or by the author of the text who was himself a monk. Thus an introductory statement and a concluding sermon frame each separate story in this text. This is so with all the other stories I have translated in this collection. In the Udēnī Cycle the introductory comment appears at the start of the Allakappa/Veṭhadīpa story (1a) and the concluding sermon occurs only after the past birth story of Kujjuttarā (5f). Thus most editors of both the DA and the SR tend to treat this group of stories as a large, unwieldy, but loosely structured unit. Both the major and the minor stories in the cycle can and are read or related as individual stories. But they are clearly connected not necessarily *to each other* but to *one or another*. They are often related as individual stories but are to be *read* as a unit—not in the Aristotelian sense of "unity" but in the Buddhist narrative tradition that Richman [1988] describes.

Sāmāvatī, King Udēnī's queen, not King Udēnī, is the central figure in the cycle. She represents the Buddhist ideal of compassion. Unlike Ghōṣaka's wife who is intelligent, worldy wise, and willing to use whatever is in her power to achieve success and fortune for her husband and herself—even if it means hastening her father-in-law's death—Sāmāvatī is the ideal of Buddhist womanhood.

She is a dutiful daughter. In spite of her sheltered, wealthy upbringing she willingly suffers the humiliation of begging at an alms-hall when their fortunes change and she has to find food for her parents. She is generous and unselfish. On two successive occasions she gives up her portion so that her parents can eat their fill. She is quick, intelligent, and has a good practical sense. She finds a simple way to end the disorganization and confusion at the alms-hall. When her adopted father Ghōṣaka is subjected to the king's wrath for refusing to give her over to the king's harem, she comes up with a solution that saves her adopted parents and gains for herself the status of chief queen.[7]

---

6. Obeyesekere, R. tr. *Jewels of the Doctrine: Stories from the Saddhammaratnāraliya*, Albany: State University of New York Press, 1991, p. 54.
7. There was clearly a status distinction implied between a woman who was taken into a king's harem and one who came with her own retinue and was given the status of a queen—even when there were more than one such "queen."

In the incident with Kujjuttarā [5c] when the maid confesses to having stolen money in the past, once again Sāmāvatī acts with restraint, does not scold her for past theft but instead asks to hear the Doctrine that had changed her life. When the maid demands a transference of roles, asks to be bathed in scented water, and have a seat prepared for her in order to preach to the queen and her retinue, Sāmāvatī in all humility renders her such service and pays obeisance to her servant, respecting her learning and knowledge of the Buddha's Doctrine.

Queen Māgandi's jealous attacks on Sāmāvatī and the falsehoods spread about her do not provoke Sāmāvatī. Instead she cultivates compassion toward both the king and Queen Māgandi and advises her friends to do the same. The power of her compassion is so strong that the arrow the king shoots is deflected. When overcome by her goodness the king abjectly kneels at her feet and asks for her protection, instead of making much of her power she humbly asks him to seek refuge in the Buddha who is also her refuge. When he insists again and again she continues to refuse him. The only boon she finally asks is permission to entertain the Buddha and listen to his sermons, which the king readily grants. At the very end when she and her retinue fall victim to Māgandi's plots and are trapped in a burning building from which there is no escape, she admonishes her friends to cultivate compassion, meditate on the element of pain, and so attain the Buddhist goal of *nirvāṇa*.

No wonder the monks find it hard to understand how so good a person should have had to suffer so cruel a death. The Buddha then relates the story of an Act of Demerit she committed in a past birth.

The fourth of the five stories in the cycle is the story of Vāsuladattā [4] but it is much more the story of King Udēnī. It relates his prowess and his adventures when captured. In the brief glimpse we have of Vāsuladattā she appears as an impulsive and quick-witted young woman who falls in love with King Udēnī (at first sight), cleverly tricks her father, and helps Udēnī escape. But just as in the story of Ghōṣaka the central character is not Ghōṣaka but his wife, so in the story of Vāsuladattā the important character is that of King Udēnī.

The story of Māgandi [5] is perhaps the most colorful and interesting of the cycle. It begins with an account of her vow of vengeance against the Buddha for his rejection of her as a bride. While her brahmin parents are converted by the Buddha's sermons and join the Order, Māgandi, angry at the insult, pursues unremittingly her vow of vengeance, even after she becomes King Udēnī's third queen.

The stories of King Udēnī's three queens are suspended when the cycle branches off into an unconnected story of the five hundred ascetics [5a] and the story of the Tree Diety (5b). The ascetics are supported by three wealthy merchants of Kosam̆bā of whom Ghōṣaka is one. They hear of the Buddha from the story of the Tree Deity they meet on their way to Kosam̆bā, and the ascetics in turn, tell the merchants about the Buddha. The merchants become devotees and each merchant builds a monastery for the Buddha to reside in. The Buddha thus becomes the link between the stories of the ascetics, the Tree Deity, and Ghōṣaka. These branch stories have little connection with the Māgandi story in which they appear. The only link is the Buddha who figures in the Māgandi story because of her vendetta against him.

The links between the marginal stories and the main stories may be slight but they do exist. The noble merchant Ghōṣaka builds the alms-hall to which Sāmāvatī's parents come when they are starving and homeless. The monasteries the noble merchants build is where the Buddha visits and preaches, where Kujjuttarā hears the Doctrine, and thereafter converts Sāmāvatī and her retinue. The kingdom of Kosaṁbā where most of this takes place is where King Udēnī rules.

Although a myriad substories are contained within the Udēnī and Ghōṣaka frame stories the central focus is clearly the conflict between Māgandi and Sāmāvatī, their actions, and the doctrinal points they illustrate. Just as the "cycle" begins with the marginal story of the two ascetics it ends with the extremely marginal story of the past births of Kujjuttarā. To continue the branch story image one might say—out on a limb!

The concluding sermon by the Buddha or narrator does provide a *kind* of overarching "unity." The events described can be read as the playing out of *karmic* consequences resulting from human actions performed by many characters through many births and rebirths in *saṃsāra*. But the sermons provide only a minimal unity. All of the moral issues raised are not answered nor are the various threads in the story neatly tied. For example, while we have a fairly complete account of Sāmāvatī's life and death and why she dies as she does, we are given no explanation why King Udēnī (who was also converted to the Buddha's Doctrine) did not extend the same compassion toward Māgandi, as Sāmāvatī did even as she burned to death. Instead he orders vicious, sadistic, reprisals against Māgandi and her entire clan. There is neither explicit nor implicit condemnation of that act in the text.

Nor is the issue of the "ethical morality" of the "means" employed by Udēnī's mother, or Ghōṣaka's wife, to ensure their own or their son's or husband's welfare, raised in the text. The latter virtually precipitates the death of Ghōṣaka's father but the moral implications of that particular act are not raised. Thus there is no overarching morality that neatly ties up all the moral issues raised in a story. Instead each story raises and illumines some *one or more specific* doctrinal issue arising out of a specific context. For the rest they seem to be spaces left for later monks and lay devotees to elaborate on in sermons on other, subsequent, occasions. The doctrinal position remains fixed but the issues of morality are left open for debate. Such open-endedness was probably necessitated by the pluralist context in which many moral and ethical issues governing everyday actions were a constant source of debate. The SR is itself a good example of that. It takes certain issues in certain stories (the stories themselves are often familiar to Buddhist audiences) and then makes a doctrinal point around one or more aspect of the story. The familiar story then becomes enriched in startling ways.[8]

WOMEN IN BUDDHISM: ISSUES OF SEXUALITY AND GENDER

The stories in this book deal with women from all stations in the medieval social world—queens, commoners, noblewomen, courtesans, servants, and peasants. All of them, without exception, are depicted as having the potential to achieve the highest goals of Buddhism and many do. We read of Viśākhā, whose intellect is "as sharp as a diamond," and whose organizational skills in our day and age would have put her at the head of a large corporation; of Sāmāvatī so firmly established in goodness that she can show compassion to her vengeful rival Māgandi even as she burns to death in a fire set by her rival; or the simple weaver's daughter whose faith in the Buddha gives her insights and an understanding of the Doctrine far superior to the rest of the august assembly at which the Buddha happens to be preaching. The Buddhist Doctrinal position is clear. It is what Alan Sponberg has described as one of "soteriological inclusiveness"[9] where being male or female was not a factor in the ability to attain to the highest goals of Buddhism. Such "inclusiveness" gave to women in Buddhist societies an enormous sense of freedom and self-worth, reflected in the poems of the early Buddhist nuns [The *Thērigāthā*][10] and also in our stories. That fundamental Buddhist doctrinal position is never questioned or qualified in the *content* of these stories.

Innumerable incidents reflect the status, intelligence, management, and organizational skills of women that were permitted full play in the social worlds to which they belonged. Their advice was sought and taken, not just in the dealings of the household but on larger social and political issues.

8. See Obeyesekere, Ranjini and Gananath, "The Tale of the Demoness Kāli: A Discourse on Evil," *Journal of the History of Religions* (May 1990): 319–344.

9. Sponberg, Alan, "Attitudes towards Women and the Feminine in Early Buddhism," in Jose Ignacio Cabezon ed. *Buddhism, Sexuality and Gender,* Albany: State University of New York Press, 1992, pp. 3–35.

10. These were the poetic expressions of nuns, who were believed to have lived in the time of the Buddha. The poems deal with their personal experiences as women and as nuns. They were included in the Buddhist canon and thereby have been preserved for posterity.

Viśākhā's grandfather chose to send her to escort the Buddha. It is she who is given the task of arranging suitable accommodations for the enormous royal entourage of kings, subkings, generals, and governors that accompanied the bridegroom. She sees to all the niceties of protocol and hospitality not forgetting the humble workers and elephant keepers who accompanied the nobles. Similarly Sāmāvatī advises her adopted father Ghōṣaka on how to organize the alms-hall and advises him on how to deal with King Udēnī's demands. Both men accept her advice without question.

Nor is education the sole preserve of men. Māgandi's mother is well versed in the Vēdas and the study of signs and omens, while her brahmanic husband is not. She berates him for his ignorance. The female ascetic Kuṇdalakēsī studies the thousand discourses and becomes so expert that she travels all over the land and none can defeat her in debate.

"Men living in those areas fled the moment they heard that the wandering female ascetic was approaching, afraid of her very name" [SR p. 417].

Yet this is not the complete story. The texts are sprinkled with antifeminine comments, sometimes authorial, sometimes put into the mouths of the characters, sometimes attributed to the Buddha. In the story of Māgandi, her mother makes what is perhaps the most devastatingly negative statement about sexuality and women. Bemoaning her husband's ignorance of the science of signs that led him to seek the Buddha as a bridegroom for his daughter, she adds,

> This is not the footprint of one who will ever pollute himself by laying his chest on that lump of flesh called a woman's breast. Nor is it the fooootprint of a lustful one who will bring his face to touch a woman's mouth, that toilet full of impurities such as spittle and her body with its thirty-two kinds of filth. [SR p. 161]

When the Buddha rejects Māgandi's hand the SR author has him say,

> Even when I saw the divine maidens in the sixth heaven, that ultimate place of desire, not one lustful thought was aroused in me. Therefore will I now desire your daughter, that container with its nine orifices filled with feces and urine? Quite apart from taking your daughter by the hand and kissing her I would be disgusted even to wipe my feet on her as I would on a door mat. [SR p. 161]

It is no wonder that Māgandi takes umbrage at the insult and vows vengeance. However, the Buddha's statement in the Pali text of which this is supposed to be a translation is as follows:

> Even after seeing Aratī (infatuation) Ratī (lust) and Rāgā[11] (passion) no passing thought of lust crossed my mind. What then of this container (the human body) full of feces and urine. I would not desire it to even wipe my feet.

The masochistic virulence of the SR is not found in the Pali text nor when the same incident is repeated in the Story of Mara's Daughters. In these the tone is very different and the statement is contextualized.

> Though your daughter's body seems to her and you to be beautiful it is filled with the thirty-two Impurities found in a human body. . . . It is like a pot of feces decorated on the outside. If there were some dirt on my foot and she were like the rag on which to clean it, I would not use her body even to clean the dirt on my foot. [SR p. 560]

The comment applies to the nature of all human beings and is in keeping with the Buddhist worldview on impermanence and the decay inherent in the human body. It is in the tradition of meditative texts on revulsion and a well-known trope in the commentarial literature. It is not specific to women's bodies nor to Māgandi. The SR author's translation of the verse however, does make such a specific connection and thus presents a significant shift from the original doctrinal position.

What then caused this mysogynist shift? Is it a reflection of changing attitudes toward women and sexuality in the thirteenth-century Sri Lankan world? Or does the distortion in the translation of the Pali text merely reflect the views of celibate monks threatened by female sexuality? If so, is it personal to the author or does it reflect the attitudes of the monastic order in general? These are not questions one can answer with any certainty given the paucity of socioeconomic data for the period. But we do have two versions here of a single text, written about eight centuries apart. Comparing them does give us a hint of shifts and changes that seem to have occurred.

Several of the negative comments on women do not exist in the DA but were introduced into the thirteenth-century text by the author, sometimes as parenthetical comments but at others, as an expanded interpolation or variation of the original. Such shifts could indicate changes in society's attitude toward women and their social roles, or they could be part of an ongoing debate on such issues.

For example in the story of Viśākhā, the introductory paragraph states,

---

11. They are the three daughters of Mara.

> Just as a Bōdhisatva may be born in a low caste but not lack goodness so with the story of Viśākhā we shall illustrate how, though born a woman (and women are of limited vision), and though forced to associate with people who were of the right caste but held wrong beliefs, yet she herself did not lack vision. [SR p. 268]

One can interpret the parenthetical remark and the paragraph as a whole as reflecting the translator's personal views on issues of caste and gender, or alternatively, as reflecting views prevalent in the society of his time. The fact that they are added as parenthetical remarks indicates a subtle attempt to incorporate certain attitudinal shifts with the accepted Buddhist position on caste and women that the story of Viśākhā so clearly illustrates. It is also significant that this introductory passage is not found in the DA. We can therefore assume that certain shifts in the attitude toward women and on the importance of the caste system had taken place in the periods between the DA and the SR texts. Were these the prevalent attitudes in the society of the time and so the inclusion of such qualifying comments were necessary when describing the extraordinary activites of a woman, or did the author-monk do so in order to influence the views of his audience and bring them in line with the mysogynist views that had developed among the *Sangha*? Was the earlier Sinhala version on which the DA was based, more firmly grounded in a doctrinal Buddhist worldview? We can only speculate that this was so. The existence of two (of the three) texts, eight or more centuries apart, does invite such speculation.

There is another passage in the same story that occurs in *both* the DA and the SR, which also gives insights into the position of women. Viśākhā refers to daughters as "saleable goods . . . [if] in some way damaged they cannot be sold . . . and will then be a burden to our parents" [SR p. 272]. The belief that women had to be "given away in marriage" in order not to be a burden on their parents was prevalent in Asian societies (Buddhist and brahmanic) both in the fifth centry C.E. as well as in the thirteenth century. The passage occurs in both texts. Men and women "allow" their parents to make the arrangement.[12] It is so even today in traditional South Asian cultures. Yet the image cannot be taken at face value. There were responsibilities and obligations on all sides and such responsibilities were underlined in Sri Lankan Buddhist society. Parents must ensure that the "arrangements" result in the child's happiness and several stories reflect the extent to which they go to do this. Viśākhā's father sends a band of "elders" to accompany

12. This is specially so in Sri Lanka in the case of strategic marriages among the upper and middle classes and less so at the village level where cross-cousin marriages are the norm.

her to her in-law's home and see that she is not unfairly treated. Thus when Viśākhā's angry father-in-law orders her to leave his house immediately she can answer with great dignity, "I did not come here like a serving girl picked up at a well . . . one who has parents does not walk out of the house merely because she is asked to go." The implication here is that a woman given in marriage by her parents has certain rights and cannot be thrown out of the home of her in-laws without due process. Once she has explained her actions and cleared herself of all blame however, Viśākhā says with equal dignity, "Have you not investigated the matter and know now that I am free from blame? It was not right to have left then. Now it is not right I should stay. Therefore I will leave," and she commands her retainers to prepare for her return to her parental home. It is her father-in-law who then begs her to stay.

Similarly, in the story of Uttarā when she is given in marriage to a man whose family are not followers of the Buddha, upset, she upbraids her father thus:

> On the grounds of making a marriage, why have you put me in this prison? If you intended to do so, instead of calling me your daughter, you should have branded me and sold me to any taker, because in a buyer one cannot check whether he is a man of faith. By coming to this family of non believers I cannot perform a single Act of Merit.

The passage highlights the complex system of rights and obligations that governed relationships—whether between parents and children or between masters and servants. While marriages were arranged by parents, and sons and daughters accepted such arrangements, it was the duty of parents to make the necessary inquiries about the family to which a daughter or son was married and to do everything in their power to see that their child's happiness and best interests were served. This is so even today in traditional Sri Lankan families where "arranged" marriages are the norm. The responsibility of investigating the "suitability" of the match rests squarely with the parents. Several social institutions such as that of the marriage broker or kinsmen known as *dänamuttā* (knowledgeable elders) exist to enable such investigations.

Parents have the same responsibility toward their children as children have to marry and to thereby perpetuate the lineage. Punnavaddhana (later to be Viśākhā's husband), at first is reluctant to get married. He then demands that his parents find an impossibly beautiful woman. They accept his request and send out emissaries in search of such a woman. This pattern occurs in several stories. Failure to make such a search, however impossible the request, would be a shortcoming on the part of the parents. Uttarā feels her father failed in his duty in marrying her to a family of nonbelievers. The father, equally upset that his daughter is unhappy, sends her money to hire a courtesan to serve her husband and relieve her for a time of her wifely obligations so she can engage in religious activities of her choice.

Here we get an insight into the role of courtesans in medieval South Asian society and their status as independent professionals earning a legitimate income. This is further emphasized in the story of Sirimā, the famous and wealthy courtesan of Rajagaha, sister of the royal physician Jīvaka, and later to become an ardent supporter of the Buddha and his monks. Again, in the story of the monk, Sunderasamudda, the daughter of a courtesan is encouraged by the monk's parents to seduce their son and bring him back into lay society. They promise to reward her if she succeeds, by making her his wife. She cleverly manages to entice the monk into her upper room and there tries to "arouse him by displaying her feminine charms." There is a long and erotic description of the "conventional" ways in which a woman tries to arouse a man—also no doubt a part of the standard literary conventions of the day.

> She twisted and turned and bent as if writhing with desire. She picked her nails as if cleaning the dirt that had got under them. She rubbed one foot against the other. She rubbed her calves against each other. . . . She fondled the children. She got them to fondle her. . . . She spoke in a loud voice. She spoke softly like someone off a sickbed. . . . She danced. She sang. She played the drums. She wept as if chillie powder had got in her eyes. She adorned herself in his presence. . . . She gazed at him. She shook her hips. She shook her private parts. She displayed her thigh. She turned and hid it. She took off her upper garment and exposed her breast and waist. She raised her arm and displayed her armpit. . . . She put out her tongue and licked her lips. She loosened her clothes, then tightened them. She let down her hair, then tied it up again. Thus as if performing a magic show suggesting the pleasures that could be had from such feminine graces she stood before the monk. . . . [SR p. 775]

For a celibate monk to indulge in such a detailed and erotic account of sexuality suggests that such descriptions were part of accepted literary conventions and that monks, who were the custodians of the literary tradition, were not only familiar with such descriptions but lingered lovingly over them.

It also suggests that in the period of the original text (probably pre-fifth century C.E.) and certainly also in the time of the Buddha, there was no social stigma attached to the profession of courtesan. They were very much a part of the society, women of independent means, engaged in a profession. Both men and women (as in the case of Uttarā) had recourse to their services. Monks, (even if they did not have firsthand experience) could include such erotic accounts in their religious works as a part of accepted literary conventions.

While the content of several of the stories do not present a negative view of courtesans a remark interpolated by the thirteenth-century translator in the Uttarā story suggests a shift. Uttarā, who had no hesitation in hiring the courtesan, Sirimā, for her husband, and is deeply grateful to her for providing her a chance to engage in religious duties, yet addresses her later as one "engaged in the lowly profession of a courtesan." The disparaging comment occurs only in the SR and seems slightly out of character in the context. It indicates again a monk's views on an ongoing debate (probably between monks and laity) on institutions like that of courtesans.

Another very common social convention referred to in many of the stories is that of young women being "confined to a room at the top of a seven-storied mansion" in order to preserve their virginity. Whether this was again a purely literary convention (it occurs in many Indian tales) or also a social convention is hard to say. Certainly many of the young women in our stories are confined in this way but find ways to circumvent the inconvenience. Kuṇḍalakēsī, from her tower, sees a thief being dragged to execution, falls in love with him, and successfully persuades her parents to obtain him as a husband. Patācārā was similarly confined "to prevent any misconduct. In spite of this she became intimate with a young man of her own household" and eloped with him. Another young woman falls in love with the hunter Kukkuttamitta (story not included here) disguises herself, and follows him when he leaves the city. When the hunter tells her "I do not know whose daughter you are and I do not want you to follow me," her reply is peremptory. "This is not something I do on your orders. I do it for my pleasure. So stop talking and drive your cart." Kukkuttamitta keeps protesting but finally gives up and takes her with him. She marries him and bears him seven sons!

The young woman who later became Ghōṣaka's bride was also confined to such a room but that did not prevent her from sneaking into the room of her young guest and reading the letter that was sewed to the lining of his coat!

These are but a few examples. There is clearly a certain ambivalence at play. The social (or literary) conventions call for the seclusion of young women of high birth to protect their virginity. In practice such conventions (if they ever existed) were constantly undermined. Nor is there any social (or authorial) opprobrium attached to such subversions. The convention is noted more in the breach than in the practice.

Similarly, the literary conventions that applied to descriptions of women's beauty and sexual allure are constantly used in both texts but in a such a way that the Buddhist context undermines the conventions. Thus Sirimā's beauty is extolled but only in order to emphasize the contrast with its present state—that of a putrifying corpse. The poetic conventions are consiously overturned in the text.

> Her hair which was like a black river flowing down a golden mountain was once described by poets as bees swarming around the stamens of her lotus blossom face. How does it look now? Where is that forehead that was like a half moon appearing from behind a blue-black cloud? Where are those brows considered by the ignorant to be a pair of heavenly bows? Where are those eyes described as the sapphire-blue windows of a gem-studded palace? People now wrinkle their noses at that nose once described as a golden hook. Where are those lips that were like a beaded ship sailing on the ocean of her face? Where are her teeth that apppeared from inside her mouth like the sixteenth part of a moon? Her ears once seen as traps to entice young men, now exude mountains of worms. Her neck compared to the neck of a golden pot is now so swollen that there is no top or bottom end to it. No one has any use for her except as an object on which to meditate. . . . [SR p. 512]

Poetic conventions are deliberately overturned to stress the Buddhist meditational theme of revulsion of the body and to illustrate the doctrine of impermanence and decay. This too developed into a literary convention in Buddhist texts.

How then do we read these texts? On the one hand, during the time of the Buddha and immediately thereafter, the texts suggest that Buddhism did introduce a considerable revolution especially in the position of women and persons of low caste. But such a revolution must be read in relative terms. Its impact was no doubt confined to Buddhist communities and even in such contexts waxed and waned during different periods.

Women in Indian brahmanic society, in the Buddha's time, did have a powerful position *within* the household—as mother. Buddhism and Jainism extended their role *outside* the family and that was revolutionary. The early poems of the nuns (included in the Buddhist canon) reveal the sense of freedom that came from being able to escape their traditional female roles. As nuns they could travel across the land, and did. As wealthy women belonging to the growing mercantile class they could use their wealth in religious and public works, donate buildings to the monks, supervise arrangements of large-scale monastic complexes, and have a public social role as Viśākhā seems to have done. Some of these freedoms filtered into later Theravāda Buddhist societies of South and Southeast Asia and still exist in spite of strong brahmanic influences in the intervening centuries. They account for some of the seeming contradictions in the position of women in these societies today. For example, in Sri Lanka, marriages are still "arranged" for many middle-class and lower middle-class women but even after marriage, women are free to follow their careers whether as professionals or at other levels in the workforce. Again, husbands, even nonearning husbands are given a certain status within the home but women often control the purse strings and are the decision makers in many a household.

In the graffiti scribbled on the wall of the rock fortress of Sigiriya in Sri Lanka between the eighth and twelfth centuries C.E. there are several poems by women. These are some of the few secular writings that have survived the centuries. They suggest that even in early Sri Lankan society, education was not confined to men. The readiness with which women in Sri Lanka today, both rural and urban, enter the education system and move into positions of power and responsibility in the workplace, is perhaps a reflection of that tradition. The ease with which women from all levels of society and in large numbers, are accepted by their male counterparts in the workforce, is a further reflection of this tradition of openness. Many women in Sri Lanka, even in rural areas, travel freely, manage their money, and handle business transactions. The enormous courage and resilience of rural women who today go abroad alone, for employment, often with little or no knowledge of the language or culture of the worlds into which they go, is a further measure of the confidence and sense of independence generated by the culture. Recent studies have shown this to be true for other Theravāda Buddhist societies such as those of Burma, Thailand, and Cambodia.

The right of women to divorce their husbands, return to their parental homes, and on their return reassert their rights to a share in the parental estate was recognized under traditional Sinhala law. Nor were there restrictions on widow or divorcee remarriage. Thus the traditional Buddhist countries of South Asia reflected far greater flexibility on such issues which is perhaps why, unlike in India, bride burning and widow immolation did not exist.

However, one cannot ignore the impact of brahmanic Hinduism as a cultural, religious, and political force in many Buddhist societies both on the subcontinent and in South Asia. This was particularly so during the tenth to fifteenth centuries C.E., the result sometimes of conquest, sometimes of cultural interaction. In spite of the Buddhist doctrinal position of soteriological inclusiveness the Hindu idea of male superiority also became a powerfully imprinted concept in medieval South Asian society and surfaces again and again in the stories.

In the Story of Soreyya there is a long authorial account of men who commit adultery being reborn as women (as a punishment) and women who perform Acts of Merit being reborn as men (as a reward). Such a value judgment was no doubt reinforced by the day-to-day realities of life in what came to be Hindu-Buddhist societies.

The impact of colonialism and Western value systems during the seventeenth, eighteenth, and nineteenth centuries especially in countries like Sri Lanka was equally profound. Victorian values, readily absorbed by the elites of colonial times spread to the fast-growing, urban, middle, and lower middle classes during the course of the twentieth century. In Sri Lanka, it has resulted in what scholars have come to term a form of *Protestant Buddhism.* Victorian puritan values, tying in with brahmanic Hindu values resurfaced as "traditional Sinhala-Buddhist values" and had a "negative" impact on the position especially of middle- and upper-class women in twentieth-century Sri Lankan society. This is illustrated by the fact that women in middle-class society have a greater degree of restrictions on their personal and sexual freedom than do their counterparts in the villages of Sri Lanka.

Our text (especially when compared to the DA) provides us with glimpses of changes that may have occurred in the position of women during the two periods, while also establishing the consistencies and continuities. One must not forget, however, that even such glimpses are refracted through the personal lenses of individual monks situated over a period of many centuries and perhaps engaged in their own debates. They do not necessarily add up to a complete or rounded portrait of what it meant to be a "Buddhist Woman" in either period. What we have are insights into particular situations within specific contexts that form a kind of collage from which we can draw perhaps some tentative conclusions.

There is the added complication of working with translations from several languages—Pāli, Sinhala, and English. Translators are fallible creatures and each translator often chooses to emphasize what happens to be significant for him or her and for the society of that time. My decision to select and translate these particular stories reflect both my own, and current feminist interests. Such selectivity must necessarily produce its own distortions, often unwittingly, sometimes consciously, as in the case of the parenthetical comments and additional sermons of the author of the SR. These are the hazards of translations and of the reworking of texts. One must however be grateful that translations and translators have existed over the centuries and, however flawed, have given us access to works that might otherwise have been lost.

1

The Udēnī Cycle

THE STORY OF UDĒNĪ

To illustrate the positive and negative consequences of both Acts of Merit and Demerit[1] and therefore to relate the story of Sāmāvatī and her five hundred women and Māgandī and her five hundred kinsmen, at this point we shall first relate the story of Udeni.[2]

1. Throughout these texts I have capitalized certain Buddhist concepts for which I've had to invent English phrases—for instance; Act of Merit for the Sinhala concept of *piṇ* and Act of Demerit for the concept of *pau*. Where the concept is commonly known in English as with terms like *karma, saṃsāra,* and *nirvāṇā*, I have kept the familiar usage as they are the same in Sinhala and Pali. There are however some doctrinal terms that are slightly different in Sinhala from the Pali. In such situations I have consciously used the Sinhala term—for instance; *sōvān* for the Pali *sōtāpaṇṇa,* or in the case of place-names such as Kosol for Kōsala and Baranäs for Varanāsi because the Sinhala text makes the distinction.
2. This is a typical link passage and it appears in both the DA and the SR. In the Sinhala text it is placed at the end of the previous story while the DA (in the Burlingame translation) begins with it. The DA and SR passages are not identical. While both authors can see the central focus of the stories as being Sāmāvatī and Māgandī the SR makes a specific reference to the structure by stating that the story of King Udēnī is a sort of background for the other two. The DA by contrast makes no reference to the Udēnī story but goes on to relate it.

1a

Long ago King Allakappa ruled in the country of Allakappa and King Veṭhadīpa ruled in the kingdom of Veṭhadīpa. They were friends from their youth and studied under the same teacher. At the deaths of their parents they each became king to a land ten thousand leagues in extent. Even after they became kings they would meet from time to time, talk, and spend their days in laughter and friendship. As they lived thus they became aware of the births and deaths taking place around them and among their people. They realized that life was impermanent, that not a single possession followed one from this world to the next, that not even one's own body that one considers a part of one from birth and that one has come to think of as one's very own, follows one into the hereafter. Therefore [they decided] one should leave everything and go away.

"What use are royal comforts if we are bound thus in *saṃsāra*[3]? We will abandon the life of householders and become ascetics," they said. They handed their kingdoms to their wives and children, joined the order of ascetics, and lived together in the Himalayan mountains.

One day they met and talked thus:

"We gave up royal comforts and became ascetics not because we had no other means of livelihood but in order to find a way to escape from *saṃsāra*. That was why we became ascetics. But when we two live in the same place, if we happen to engage in the least bit of frivolous talk, then in spite of having become ascetics we will not be acting like ascetics at all. Let us therefore each live alone, you on one rocky mountain and I on another and let us meet every fortnight on fast days."

They decided thus. Then again they added, "Such a meeting every fortnight can also result in an addiction to company. Therefore let us not meet. Instead you light a fire on your rocky mountain and I'll light a fire on mine and by that sign we will know that the other is alive and well."

They lived thus indicating that each was well and free of dangers. After some time the ascetic Veṭhadīpa died and was reborn as a Mahēśākya god.[4] When the fast day arrived and there was no fire on the mountain Allakappa knew that his friend had died.

---

3. The continuous cycle of rebirths in which beings are trapped. For Buddhists the way to break this cycle is to follow the Eightfold Path and achieve *nirvāṇa*.
4. There are two categories of gods; the one is *Mahēśākya* or the "greater gods" and the other is *Alpēśākya*' or the "lesser gods."

The moment Veṭhadīpa was born in heaven he surveyed his undeserved heavenly luxuries and pondered how or for what Act of Merit[5] he had obtained all this. He realized that it was a result of the disciplined life he had led ever since he left the life of a householder. He then thought he would like to visit his friend who had taken on the ascetic life with him. He transformed his heavenly body into that of a wandering traveler, and went to his friend. Allakappa greeted him and stood on a side.[6]

"Where have you come from my good man?" inquired the ascetic.

"Your Reverence, I'm a traveler from a distant land," replied the deity.

"But is there no one else with you? Do you perform your ascetic observances alone here?"

"I have one other ascetic friend," he replied.

"Where is he now?" asked the deity.

"We had decided to each light a fire on our mountain every fifteen days to indicate that all was well. This full moon day there was no fire on his mountain so I know that he is dead."

"Is that so?" said the deity. Then he added, "Your Reverence, I am none other than that ascetic, your friend."

"Where have you been reborn?"

"By the power of the disciplined life I led I have been born in heaven as a Mahēśākya god-king. I came just now to see you. Do you have any problems living here?"

"I am not troubled by much but I do have a problem with elephants."

"Your Reverence, what do the elephants do?"

"They scatter their dung on the ground I have swept. They kick up dust with their feet. I'm exhausted just with cleaning elephant dung and making the ground smooth."

"Do you want them to stop coming?"

"Yes," he replied.

'If that be so I will do something to make them go away without having to kill them'[7] thought the deity and gave him a *vīna*[8] and taught him a

---

5. An Acts of Merit s. *pin* or *puṇya karma* refers to a volitional act that has good *karmic* consequences in this life and in following rebirths. Acts of Demerit s. *pau* or *pāpa karma* are the reverse and bring about bad consequences.
6. [s.*ekatpassa*] means literally (one step behind). This is a posture of respect. To stand directly in front and address a person would be impolite.
7. I frame thoughts or internal speeches within single quotes to differentiate from speech.
8. A stringed musical instrument sometimes translated as "lute."

magic formula to charm elephants. The *vīna* had three strings and he taught him three *mantras*[9] saying, "Your Reverence, when you strike this string and recite this first *mantra* the elephants will turn and flee out of sight. If you play this string and recite this second *mantra* they will retreat glancing ever backward. When you play this string and recite this third *mantra* the chief of the elephant herd will bend down before you, kneel, and offer you his back to climb on. You can do what you wish with this." The deity then departed.

From that point the ascetic recited the relevant *mantra* and kept playing the string to chase the elephants away. He thus rid himself of the elephants, achieved mental and physical serenity, and lived happily in his hermitage.

1b

At that time a king named Parantapa ruled in the land of Kosaṁbā. One day he sat on the upper balcony with his pregnant wife enjoying the morning sun. The queen had covered herself in a red fur shawl belonging to the king, worth a hundred thousand, and had on her finger the king's ring worth another hundred thousand.[10] She sat beside him engaged in pleasant conversation.

Just then a creature known as the elephant-bird happened to be flying overhead, saw the queen wrapped in the fur shawl and believing her to be a piece of meat, spread its wings and descended to snatch her up. The king heard the sound of it descending and fled into the inner chamber. Being heavy with child and by nature timid, the queen was unable to rise quickly and leave. The bird snatched the queen in its talons and flew away. That bird had the strength of five elephants. He could fly off with any creature, take it wherever he wished, and then devour it.

The queen was terrified, fearing for her life as she was being carried away by the bird. But being intelligent she thought, 'If I were to cry out now I will be dropped because all creatures are scared of the human voice. I will fall to earth and both I and the child in my womb will die. When he sets me down in someplace in order to eat me, at that point I will raise a huge clamor and chase him off.' This elephant-bird was in the habit of flying to a wide-spreading banyan [ficus] tree growing halfway up in the Himalayas, perching there and then devouring the pigs, deer, or other prey it had brought. The bird now carried the queen to that banyan tree, placed her on its canopy of branches, and surveyed the area. When birds alight with their prey they are in the habit

---

9. Magical formulas.
10. The unit of currency is often not specified. The intention is to convey a suggestion of magnitude, not a precise value.

of looking back over the region from which they have come. The moment this bird looked back surveying the path it had taken, the queen thought, 'now I shall chase it' and she clapped, shouted loudly, and drove it away.

That very day as the sun was about to set the queen went into labor and at the same time a great storm arose thundering from all directions. This queen, raised in the lap of luxury, with no one now to offer even a word of comfort or say "Don't be afraid," underwent unheard-of suffering and did not sleep a wink all night. As the night ended, the storm clouds dispersed, dawn broke, and the child was born, all at the same time. Taking into account the stormy weather, the rocky promontory, the dawn breaking, all at the moment the child was born, the queen named him Prince Udēnī.[11]

The hermitage of the ascetic Allakappa was not far from this banyan tree. On rainy days he was in the habit of not going into the forest for fear of the cold but instead going to this tree to collect the bones dropped by the birds. He would smash them and boil them into a soup. That day he thought, 'I will pick up some bones' and was looking under the tree for them when he heard the sound of the child crying above. He looked up and saw the queen.

"Who are you?" he asked.

"I am a woman, a human being," she replied.

"How did you get here?" he asked.

She told him how the bird had brought her there.

"In that case I will help you down."

"I am afraid of caste pollution, Your Reverence," she replied.

"To what caste do you belong?" he asked and when she replied that she belonged to the *kśatriya*[12] [warrior] caste he said, "I too belong to the *kśatriya* caste."

"If that be so tell me the *kśatriya* code," she said and he did so.

"In that case climb the tree and take my son down," she said.

The ascetic found a way to get up the tree, climbed to the top, and first brought the child down and then helped the queen and took them to his hermitage.[13] Without in any way breaking his vows as an ascetic he took

---

11. One could translate it as "Prince Dawn" since the word *udaya* in Sinhala means "dawn" or "morning."
12. There are four major categories in the Hindu caste hierachy. The brahmins or priestly caste, the *kśatriyas* or "warrior caste," the *vaiśya* or "merchant caste," and the *śudras* or "low castes."
13. There is an interesting difference in the way the two texts handle the question of caste pollution. The DA, directed to an Indian audience where caste was an important social factor, says, "Obeying the queen's behest not to touch her with his hand he set the boy down; then the queen herself came down" (DA p. 250). In the SR by contrast, once the *kśatriya* issue is settled no further questions are raised.

compassion on them brought them honeycombs free of larva[14] and wild rice[15] that he cleaned and made into gruel and gave the queen.

While he looked after them in this manner the queen thought, 'Because I was carried here by the bird I don't know how I got here nor do I know the way back to human habitation. There is no bond of trust between me and this ascetic. If he were to leave us now and go elsewhere my son and I will both die. Therefore I must make him break his celibate vows and bind him to us with the bonds of sexual passion so that he will not leave us.

> muṭṭhassa cittaṃ bandanti pekkhite mihitena ca
> atho'pi dunnivatthena mudunā bhaṇitena ca
>
> [With smiles and states of undress and soft
> speech (women) captivate the unmindful (men)
> when they are observed by them.][16]

which is to say that because it is in a woman's nature and because it came naturally also to this ascetic born to the pleasures of royalty, she made him break his vows of celibacy by removing her clothing and exposing beautiful passion-arousing parts of her body. From then on the two lived together happily.

One day the ascetic with his powers saw certain astrological signs that indicated that the life of King Parantapa of Kosaṁbā had ended. He said to the queen, "Dear One, King Parantapa, ruler of Kosaṁbā, has died."

"Your Reverence, why do you say that? Do you have some old enmity against him?" she asked.

The ascetic replied, "Do not say that, Dear One. I have no cause for enmity. I said so only because it is astrologically indicated that harm has befallen that king."

On hearing that the queen was overcome with great grief and began to weep. When the ascetic asked her why she wept she told him that she was the queen of King Parantapa of Kosaṁbā.

---

14. Honeycombs with larva are often eaten by villagers. Here the point is that the ascetic is consciously avoiding harming any living thing.
15. [s.*sayanjāta hāl*] that literally means "spontaneously arisen rice." It is a term used in folklore and myth to describe forms of rice that grow unmediated through human labor. I translate it simply as "wild rice."
16. Few readers-listeners of the SR knew Pali. The SR author quotes the Pali verse and follows it with his paraphrased version. I have added an exact translation of the Pali stanza after the text in order to indicate the shifts and changes that often occur in the SR author's paraphrase.

"Dear One, do not weep. All creatures who are born must die," said the ascetic.

"I know that all creatures born must die."

"Then why do you weep?" he asked.

"I weep because my son is not fortunate enough to obtain the royal heritage of his father."

"If that be all, do not grieve. I know a way to obtain the kingdom for your son," said the ascetic and called the young prince to him.

He gave him the magic *vīna* to charm elephants and taught him the *mantra*. On the day when a great many elephants were about to gather under the banyan tree he said to the prince, "O prince, before the elephants arrive you must climb the banyan tree and sit in its branches. When the elephant herd arrives recite this *mantra* and play this string. All the elephants will turn from you and flee without looking back. When the elephants leave get down from the tree and come to me."

The prince did as he was told and informed the ascetic that he had done so. Then on the second day the ascetic said, "Today you must climb the tree and when the elephants come play this string and recite this *mantra*. Then the elephants will keep looking back at you while they run away."

The young prince did as he was told and reported back to the ascetic that he had done so. On the third day the ascetic said to the queen, "Your son will now take over his father's kingdom. Give him instructions and send him forth."

Then the queen called her son and said, "Son, you are the child of King Parantapa of Kosaṁbā̄. Tell the people that when I was with child I was carried away by a giant bird. Tell them also that these were the names and identities of the ministers and nobles of that country. If any of them are still alive today, show them this ring that was on your father's finger and this fur cape." She gave him the ring and cape and told him the names and other identifying marks.

The young prince then went to the ascetic and asked, "What should I do now?"

"Today you must climb the banyan tree and sit on the lowest branch, recite this mantra, and play this string. At that moment the chief elephant of the herd will come to you and offer you his back to climb. Climb on him and go claim your father's kingdom."

The young prince then worshiped[17] his mother and the ascetic and took leave of them, climbed the banyan tree, sat on the lower branch, recited the *mantra,* and played the third string of the *vīna*. At that moment the great

---

17. The gesture of folded hands in worship does not necessarily indicate devotion as to a deity. It is often used as a gesture of greeting and respect. I also translate it as to "pay obeisance."

elephant-king, chief of the herd came, bent low, and offered his back. The prince climbed on his back and whispered in the elephant's ear, "I am the son of King Parantapa of Kosaṁbā̄. Obtain for me my father's kingdom."

The elephant-king heard him and gave a thunderous roar that could call up thousands of elephants. A large herd of thousands of elephants of all sizes heard him and gathered round him. Then the elephant roared in such a manner as to ask all the old elephants and the very young ones to leave. When they heard that roar the very old and very young elephants left. Thus the prince rode to a nearby village accompanied by thousands of enormous elephants.

"I am the son of King Parantapa. Those who wish to obtain favors come with me," said the prince. He gathered together many villagers, entertained all who came, surrounded the city, and sent a message saying, "Either fight me or give me the kingdom."

The royal ministers responded, "We will not give you the kingdom nor will we fight with you. The queen of our king was carried off by a bird when she was with child. We do not know if she is alive or dead. Until we know something definite about that we will neither give you the kingdom nor fight with you."

When he heard those words the prince said, "If that be so, I am that queen's son." He mentioned the names and identities of the ministers as the queen had told him to do. But the people of the city did not accept him. He then displayed the king's personal ring and his fur cape. The ministers recognized the ring and cape decided that what he said was true. They opened the city gates, conducted the prince in a great procession into the inner city, crowned him king, and established him in his kingdom.

This is the story of King Udeni's birth.

2

2a

In a land named Ajita that was wracked by drought there lived a man named Kotuhala with his wife Kāli and their child Kāliya. Unable to survive the famine the man decided to take his family and go to the city of Kosaṁbā̄. Taking whatever was necessary for the journey they left. People [in their city] were dying of diarrhea and had been advised to level their homes and leave.[18]

18. Literally the phrase is "to break down the walls and leave." The idiomatic equivalent in English is perhaps to "pull up one's stakes and leave." The phrase occurs often enough in these stories to suggest that one method of coping with the epidemics and rampant infections that medieval societies faced was to order people to level their homes and leave.

When the provisions they had taken for the journey were exhausted, weakened by hunger the man was unable to carry his child any further. The man then said to his wife, "Dear One, if we live we can beget another child. Let us leave this child here on the road."

Since a mother's heart is softer than a father's the mother said, "As long as I have life I will not abandon my son."

"What then should we do?" he asked.

"You take a turn carrying him and then I will take a turn carrying him," she said and took the child and carried him like a garland worn around her neck.[19]

Then the father took his turn. But when he carried him the young child's body slipped lower and lower and as he held him against his stomach the pangs of hunger grew strong. Unable to bear the pain he said again and again to his wife, "Dear One, if we stay alive we can have more sons. If we continue to carry this child we and he will all die. Let us leave him here and go on."

Again and again the mother stopped him from doing that. Then, too tired to argue she spoke no further. The young child, transferred back and forth between the mother's arms and the father's, exhausted, fell asleep. Realizing the child was asleep the father sent the mother on ahead and leaving the child on a quilt of leaves under a tree, ran off.

The mother walked some distance and looked back. Not seeing her son she asked, "Husband where did you abandon my son?"

"Dear One, I could no longer carry him so I placed him on a quilt of leaves beneath a tree and left."

"Don't kill me my husband. I will not live without my son. Go immediately and bring him back," she said and beat her breasts and wept. Since her sobs and laments were searing he went back and picked up the child again.

For that Act of Demerit, this man who abandoned his son at this point, for this length of time, was himself abandoned seven times during his (subsequent) journey through *saṃsara*. Thus do not imagine any Act of Demerit to be a trifle.

As they proceeded they came to a village of cattle herders. One of the cattle herders happened to be performing a ritual for [the welfare of] his cows. A certain *Pasē* Buddha[20] was wont to visit this cattle herder's home for his daily food. On that particular day the cattle herder made his offerings of

---

19. The contrasting attitudes of the two parents to the child are emphasized in the image.
20. The term refers to Buddhas who achieve Enlightenment but do not preach the Doctrine to others. They have been referred to in the literature as "silent Buddhas." The Pali word is *paccēka*.

food to the *Pasē* Buddha and held his celebration. A great deal of milk-rice had been prepared for the feast.

Seeing the travelers approach the cattle herder inquired where they came from. Hearing their story this soft-hearted man, filled with compassion for their plight, gave them great servings of milk-rice and clarified butter. The wife took the milk-rice and said, "Husband, if you live I will live too. You have gone hungry for a long time. Here, eat your fill."[21] She poured the clarified butter for him keeping only a small amount of it and a little portion of the milk-rice for herself.

The husband ate great portions of milk-rice but since he had been without food for seven or eight days his greed was not easily satisfied. The cattle herder gave him more rice and ate some remaining milk-rice himself.

The traveler could not take his eyes off the cattle herder as he gave a fistful of milk-rice to the dog who sat under his table. 'A bitch who daily receives such food must have performed great Merit in the past,' he thought. That very night, unable to digest the quantity of milk-rice he had eaten the man died and was conceived in the womb of the bitch.

The wife cremated her husband and continued to work in that household. She was given a measure[22] of rice [as payment] which she cooked and served as an offering to the *Pasē* Buddha saying, "Your Reverence, may the merit from this deed accrue to my dead kinsfolk." Then she thought, 'I should continue to live here. My master invites the *Pasē* Buddha often to this house. If I have something to offer I will offer it to him and if I don't have anything to offer then I can at least see him often, worship him, perform the necessary services and rituals, cultivate a serene mind, and gain great merit.' Thus she decided to live and work in that household.[23]

2b

In the seventh or eight month[24] the bitch gave birth to a single pup. The cattle herder regularly gave the pup milk from one of his cows. The pup was fed

21. It is a practice in traditional South Asian societies for a wife to first serve her husband before she eats—a practice seen even today in the more traditional Sri Lankan households.
22. A measure was equal to about four cups.
23. The woman makes a conscious decision to live and work in the house because of the opportunity she sees of doing Acts of Merit. By contrast the husband Kotuhala dies of greed and overeating and is born as a dog.
24. The author seems to have no knowledge of the gestation period for a dog. He assumes that it is a little less than for humans for whom the gestation period was considered to be ten months—perhaps lunar months.

well so it grew big and strong in a very short time. Whenever the *Pasē* Buddha took his meal [at the cattle herder's house] he invariably left a fistful[25] for the dog. As a result the dog became very attached to the *Pasē* Buddha.

Every morning and evening the cattle herder would go to attend on the *Pasē* Buddha. When walking along the forest paths he would beat the ground and the bushes with a stick and make a loud noise in order to drive away any fierce wild creatures.[26] The dog would accompany him. One day the cattle herder informed the *Pasē* Buddha, "Your Reverence, when I'm not free to fetch you I will send this dog. Let that be the signal to come visit us." From then on, when he had no time he would say to the dog, "Go son, accompany my *Pasē* Buddha here."

The dog would leave at a bound and when he reached the place where his master used to beat the underbrush to drive away wild creatures he too would bark furiously and drive away bears, leopards, and other wild beasts.

The dog would go to the *Pasē* Buddha (who had got up early, worn his robes and was waiting inside the temple for him), stand in front of the temple door and bark three times to indicate that he had arrived. He would then enter the temple. The *Pasē* Buddha, realizing it was time for his midday meal would follow. The dog would race ahead barking and barking to drive away wild animals. Sometimes the *Pasē* Buddha would hurry along another path that he knew. Then the dog would block his path, stand in front barking, and force the *Pasē* Buddha back on to the track that led to his own house. One day the *Pasē* Buddha took another road. Though the dog blocked his path the *Pasē* Buddha pushed him aside with his foot and proceeded. Seeing the *Pasē* Buddha leave without heeding him the dog ran behind, grabbed a corner of his robe, and dragged him back onto the usual path. In this way the dog developed a great attachment to the *Pasē* Buddha.

After some time the *Pasē* Buddha's robes became badly torn and ragged. The cattle herder offered him new cloth for a robe. The *Pasē* Buddha took the cloth and said, "Lay devotee, I cannot sew these robes myself. I would like to go to a comfortable place where I can get the help of companion monks to cut and sew the robe.[27]

---

25. It is customary for monks and ascetics, when they receive offerings of food, first to leave aside a fistful for birds or animals.
26. This is still done by villagers as they cross forest areas. As Buddhists they do not wish to have to attack or kill wild creatures they may chance to encounter, so working on the principle that wild animals retreat into the forests away from noise and disturbances they try to drive them out of their path by shouting and beating the bushes.
27. The procedure for cutting, sewing, and dyeing monks' robes is stipulated in the *vinaya* (Rules of Discipline). It is a communal ritual among monks.

"Your Reverence, can you not stay here and sew your robe?" asked the cattle herder.

"I cannot do that here, lay disciple," the *Pasē* Buddha answered.

"If so Your Reverence, do not spend too much time away. Have the robes cut and sewn and return soon," he said.

The dog listened to the conversation between the two. The *Pasē* Buddha then said, "Wait here for me, cattle herder," and leaped into the air and flew toward the Gandhabba mountain.[28]

Dogs (unlike humans who say one thing but think another) do not have a deceitful devious intelligence but only a single line of reasoning, so when this dog saw the *Pasē* Buddha depart in that manner, he barked and barked and gazed at him and barked again and as the *Pasē* Buddha disappeared from his range of vision his heart burst with grief and he died. Though he had done no other Act of Merit yet because of his great affection for the *Pasē* Buddha he was reborn in the Tavtisā[29] heaven as a Mahēśākya deity attended by thousands of divine maidens and enjoyed great heavenly pleasures.

Thus good men even if they do no other Act of Merit should develop love, however infinitesimal, for the Three Jewels[30] and enjoy heavenly blessings beyond description or deserving.

2c

The deity thus born in heaven, could be heard for a distance of over twelve leagues when he so much as whispered something to someone. When he talked in a normal tone the sound would carry for ten thousand leagues throughout all of the Tavtisā heaven. This was the result of nothing more than that as a dog he had barked to protect the *Pasē* Buddha. Thus he acquired the name of the deity Ghōṣaka [Resounding Noise]. After he had enjoyed great heavenly blessings for a period, sometime later that deity died.

Gods who live in heavens die for one of these four reasons: when their life span is completed, when the Merit they have accumulated is used up, when they indulge in too much food, and when they are angry. Of these four, "Termination of Years" occurs when one has done a great deal of Merit, is born in heaven, enjoys its blessings, and thereafter is reborn in other heavens. That is known as the Termination of Years.

---

28. *Arahats* were believed to be able to fly through the air.
29. Pali—Tāvatimsa. One of many heavens in Buddhist cosmology.
30. The Buddha, the Dhamma or his Doctrine, and the Sangha or his Order of monks, are referred to by Buddhists as the Three Jewels or Triple Gems *(tri-ratna)*.

If one has done only a small Act of Merit then it is as if one has sowed four measures of rice in an enormous field. When that Merit is used up that deity will die. This is known as the Termination of Merit.

When a deity overindulges in the five sensory pleasures, is intoxicated, and does not eat, his body shrivels, he faints, and dies. That is called "Termination of Food."

If a certain deity envies the blessings of another deity and unable to obtain it becomes jealous and angry, he dies. That is called "Termination by Anger."

The god Ghōṣaka was so intoxicated by overindulgence in heavenly pleasures that he did not realize the need for food and so died as a result of the "Termination of Food."

Ghōṣaka was then conceived in the womb of a courtesan in the city of Kosam̆bā̆. On the day the courtesan gave birth she called her maid and asked, "Is it a daughter or a son?"

When she heard it was a son she said, "Girl, wrap him in a basket and go dump him on a rubbish heap," and it was done as instructed. Courtesans bring up their female children but bury their male children at birth. They perpetuate their lineage through their daughters. Crows and dogs flocked around the infant. But as a result of the Merit he had gained when he was born as a dog and had protected a *Pasē* Buddha with his bark, not one of the thousands of crows and dogs that surrounded him dared to take one bite off his body. [They were scared away by his loud cries.]

As he was lying on the garbage dump a passing stranger saw the dogs and crows surrounding some object and decided to investigate. He walked up to the garbage dump, saw the child, and was overcome with paternal feelings. Saying "I have now got a child" he took him into his house.

At about the same time a noble merchant in the city of Kosam̆bā̆ saw a brahmin astrologer hurrying in and out of the palace and asked, "Reverend Sir, have you studied the astrological constellations today?"

"Yes I have examined them. What other work do we have to do?"

"What is going to happen to this land?" he asked.

"Nothing much, other than that a child born today in this city will gain high honor and wealth."

The noble merchant who knew that his wife was about to give birth sent messages to his home inquiring whether her child had been born. When he heard that she had not yet given birth he went to the palace, paid his obeisance to the king, and returned quickly home. He then called his servant Kāli,[31] gave her a thousand gold coins, and said, "Take these thousand coins,

31. Almost all servants in these stories seem to have the generic name Kāli—a far cry from the powerful goddess Kāli of the Hindu pantheon. It can be read as a conscious parodic reversal.

check out the whole town and if you see a child who was born today bring him to me." So saying he sent her off.

She searched the entire city and seeing the man carrying a child from the garbage dump into his house she asked, "When was this child born?"

He replied, "Today."

She then said, "Give this child to me."

When he refused she promised him one gold coin, then another and another and finally increased it to a thousand gold coins.

The maid brought the child to the rich nobleman. The nobleman thought, 'If my wife gives birth to a girl I will give her in marriage to this boy. If she gives birth to a son however, then I will dispose of this boy.' He decided to [temporarily] care for the boy. Sometime thereafter his wife bore a son. Then the noble merchant thought, 'If this [other] boy lives my son will be deprived of the status and wealth of a noble merchant. I must get rid of him.' He called his servant Kāli and said, "Look here girl,[32] take this child and at the time when the cattle herders let out their flock place him across the gateway where the herds come out. Then they will trample him. Tell me if he is dead or not."

She agreed, took the child, and when the cattle herder opened the door she hid and stealthily placed the child across the doorway. That day an old bull who generally went out after all the other cattle now pushed his way ahead of the rest and stood over the child protecting him beneath his four legs. Hundreds of cattle passed by brushing against the sides of this old bull. The cattle herder saw the bull and thought, 'This bull normally comes out after all the other cattle. Today he was the first to leave but stands in the middle blocking the doorway. He went up to investigate, saw the child lying between the bull's feet, felt affection for the child, and saying, "Today, I have obtained a child of great Merit," he carried it to his home.

The servant Kāli reported the matter to the noble merchant.

The merchant then sent the same girl with [yet another] thousand gold coins to buy the child back. Thereafter, he said to her, "Mother,[33] today at dawn the merchants of this city will leave with five hundred caravans. Take this child and throw him across the path of the five hundred wagons. He will be trampled by the oxen or he will be squashed by the wagon wheels. Bring me news of what happens." The girl agreed and took the child and threw him in the path of the five hundred wagons. The oldest of the caravans led the way. The bulls in this wagon would come up to where the child lay, throw

32. Younger maidservants were sometimes called "girl" by older employers. But the more respectful kin terms such as *mother* were generally used for older employees.

33. Here the same servant is addressed by the more generally used kin terms. Wet nurses especially were treated as servants *and* mothers.

off their yokes, and walk back. Although again and again they yoked them to the wagons the animals would not take a single step forward. While they were thus trying to yoke the animals, dawn broke. Then the leader of the caravans thought, 'These bulls are normally obedient but today they will not go forward even on smooth ground. I must investigate why they turn around. He saw the child thrown in the middle of the road and thought, 'This is indeed a very noble being' and pleased that he had obtained an extremely blessed child carried him to his home.

[There is a repetition of three further similar attempts to kill the child that fail.[34] They are as follows:

The child is abandoned in a cemetery to be devoured by dogs and ravens or devils. He is saved by a goat-herd because of his loud cries. Again the nobleman finds him and buys him back. He is then thrown off a steep rock but he lodges safely on a clump of bamboos intertwined with vines. He is rescued by a flutist.[35] The nobleman buys him back. He then bribes a potter to kill the boy who will come to him with a message. He is to chop him into pieces and burn him in his kiln. On his way to the potter, young Ghōṣaka is accosted by the nobleman's son who is playing with his friends and losing a game. He begs his older brother to play and win the game for him and offers to run his father's errand for him. The boy takes the message and is killed. Ghōṣaka thus survives and the nobleman's child is killed instead. The nobleman is grief-stricken when he learns what happened.]

The story continues:

Although the child's good fortune was made evident in this manner the nobleman could not stand to look upon his face and kept thinking of ways to kill him. 'I will send him to the headman who is in charge of a hundred of my villages and have him kill him' he thought and sent a letter saying, "Bearer is my ugly and unlucky son. Kill him and bury him stealthily. As soon as the task is complete I will know how to recompense you." He wrote this letter, called young Ghōṣaka, and said, "Son, deliver this letter to the headman of our hundred villages," and sewed it to a corner of his cloak. Now this young merchant-prince Ghōṣaka could not read. That was certainly the case. For how would the nobleman who had been trying to kill him from the day he was born and who was disconsolate that he had not succeeded be likely to teach him his letters? The young man departed,

34. I have decided to summarize rather than translate these incidents as they follow a similar pattern and so are repetitive.

35. Flutes were made of bamboo, hence the rationale for being found in a bamboo clump by a flutist.

himself bearing the letter sewn to a corner of his cloak, which authorized his own death.

"Dear Father, is there no provision for the journey?" he asked.

Then, as if with genuine affection, the nobleman said, "Why my dear son, why would you need to carry food for the journey? At a certain village along the way there is a noble merchant-friend of mine. Go to his house, eat a meal, and proceed on your way."

Young Ghōṣaka paid his respects and took leave of his father.

He came to the merchant's village along the way, inquired where his house was and went there. He met the wife of the merchant. When he said that he came from the capital city she asked, "Whose child are you?"

"I am the son of the friend of this noble merchant," he replied.

"Are you young Ghōṣaka?" she asked.

"Yes Mother," he replied.

The moment she set eyes on him motherly feelings arose in her.

Now this noble merchant had an extremely beautiful, sixteen-year-old, only daughter. The young woman was kept guarded in a bedchamber on the top floor of a seven-storied building with a single servant to cook for her and attend on her. At the time she had sent her servant on an errand to the street of the merchants. While the servant was on her way there the merchant's wife called out to her and asked where she was going.

"I am on an errand for Your Excellency's daughter," she replied.

"Leave your errand and come here. Get some water and wash the feet of my son who has just arrived. Prepare a bed for him, oil his feet, and let him sleep. Then you can go on your errand," she ordered. The servant did as the merchant's wife ordered and later returned to her mistress.

"What were you doing sauntering around in the streets all this long while?" asked the merchant's daughter since her servant had taken a long time.

"Mistress, do not blame me. A noble merchant-prince called Ghōṣaka has turned up. I had to perform tasks for him that your mother ordered and only then went into the street on your errand. I have but just now returned."

At the mere mention of the name Ghōṣaka love arose in the young woman's heart. It suffused her whole being, every vein and bone in her body. There was none other like him. She had been his wife in a former life when he had been born as Kotuhala before his birth as a dog. Later, from her Act of Merit of offering to the *Pasē* Buddha the measure of rice that she had earned as a servant she had now been born in this noble merchant family. This former love continuing through the chain of births now took possession of the young woman's entire being. That is how it is. Flowers such as the lotus that grow in water are born of a mixture of mud and water so know that love that arises between creatures is the result of having lived together in the past, or because of some mutual help rendered in the present.[36] Thus the Buddha has said,

> pubbeva sannivāsena pachuppannahitena vā
> evaṃ taṃ jāyate pemaṃ uppalaṃ va yathodake

> [Through previous association or present help rendered
> love grows like a lotus out of the water.]

The young woman then asked, "Mother, where is that man?"

"He is stretched out on his bed asleep."

"Is he carrying anything?"

When she was told that apart from a letter sewed in the edge of his cloak he had nothing else the young woman was curious to know what was in it. Waiting for a time when the parents were not around, stealthily, she slipped down from the upper story, went to the young man's room while he was still asleep, untied the letter, and took it back to her room. There she locked her door, opened a window, and since she could read, she read the letter.[37]

"Oh what a half-witted simpleton this man is! He carries the order for his own murder! Now if I hadn't seen this he would soon be dead."

She felt sorry for him, tore up the letter, and wrote a new one as if coming from the noble merchant.

"To our chief of a hundred villages.

I write to introduce to you our son, young Ghōṣaka. Please arrange a marriage for him with the daughter of our friend the noble merchant who lives in your neighboring city and draws revenue from a hundred villages. After the marriage, construct a two-storied house for them with walls and guards to protect them and set them up in residence there. When you have done so write to me that you have done such and such and I shall reward you for it." She folded the letter and sewed it back in the corner of his cloak.

The young man got up after his rest, ate a meal of rice, and slept there that night. The next day he set out very early for the next village and met the village headman.

---

36. Love at first sight was attributed to *karmic* causes and therefore accepted. Although the general pattern was for marriages to be arranged by the parents who chose partners of similar status and caste for their children, the phenomenon of young people (most often a woman) falling in love (very often outside the caste or kin group) occurs again and again in the stories and is treated with a degree of permissiveness. It is even given sanction here by a quotation attributed to the Buddha.

37. The comparison between the man who could not read and the woman who could, suggests that it was not unusual for women to be literate.

"Friend, what brings you here?" asked the chief when he saw young Ghōṣaka.

"My father has sent you a letter," he answered.

"Give it to me, friend; what does it say?"

The headman read the letter and was very pleased.

"See young man, what love and regard my noble chief has for me! His Excellency has asked me to arrange the marriage of his oldest son." He ordered his farmers, "Go immediately and gather wood and skins and other goods." He further instructed the farmers from the hundred villages to gather timber and materials without delay and to construct a great two-storied house and to bring all manner of gifts from the hundred villages. Thereafter, he invited the daughter of the merchant who lived in the adjacent area, escorted her in a great procession, and gave her in marriage to young Ghōṣaka. He then informed the noble merchant [Ghōṣaka's father] of all that he had done.

The noble merchant received the news. 'Alas, nothing I do works out right. What disaster is this?' he thought and was greatly depressed. Then, his earlier grief at the loss of his son together with his present disappointment caused a burning in his stomach and the noble merchant was stricken ill with a bad case of diarrhea.[38]

Ghōṣaka's wife then gave orders. "Do not give the young master any letters that come from the noble merchant his father. Show them first to me."

The noble merchant [Ghōṣaka's father] in turn decided, 'I will not let that wicked son inherit my wealth.' So he called his assistant and said, "Brother, I wish to see my young son Ghōṣaka. Send a messenger and bring my son to me immediately." The assistant wrote a letter and sent a messenger to bring young Ghōṣaka back.

The noblewoman, [Ghōṣaka's wife] saw the man standing in the entrance doorway and asked, "Nephew,[39] why have you come?"

"My lady, His Excellency the nobleman is sick. He would like to see his son and has sent me to conduct him back."

"How serious is the illness?" she asked.

"He can still eat and drink," replied the man.

At that, without telling Ghōṣaka anything she arranged for the man to have comfortable lodgings, gave him food to eat and betel nut [to chew], oil for his head and for the lamps, and in addition some payment so he could live comfortably till told to return. A second messenger sent by the noble merchant [Ghōṣaka's father] was kept in the same manner.

---

38. The connection between mental depression or anxiety and physical sickness manifest as diarrhea must have been an accepted part of medical lore at the time. It is referred to in several stories.

39. This is again a use of a kin term for a subordinate. It is also a way of conferring status, in this case intentional, in order to win the goodwill of the messenger.

Meanwhile the noble merchant's diarrhea became much worse. Before one bedpan could be removed another had to be placed beneath him. Then the noble merchant called his assistant and said, "What is it Brother? Didn't you send messengers to fetch my son?"

"I did, Your Excellency. I sent two messengers but both have not returned."

"If so, send yet another immediately," he ordered.

"Very well," answered the assistant and sent a messenger for the third time.

The young noblewoman saw the third messenger arrive and again inquired how serious the illness was.

"He is very serious indeed. They have barely time to replace one bedpan with another," he replied.

'Now is the best time to go,' she thought, and that day she said to Ghōṣaka, "My Lord, I hear your father is very ill."

"What should we do?" he asked.

"Let us gather the tribute from the hundred villages and go see him," she said.

Ghōṣaka agreed, gathered the revenue from all the villages, loaded them into carts, and set off for the city. The noblewoman then said, "My Lord, your father is very weak. It would take too long to travel with all these goods. Let us leave them here and go ourselves." She ordered that all the goods be deposited in her family home. She then said to the prince, "My Lord, when you go into the room, greet your father and stand at his feet. I will stand by his head." Thus she instructed him and as she arrived she set up her guards throughout the house. She went into the room, greeted the nobleman, and stood by his head. Ghōṣaka stood at his feet. At the time the nobleman was lying on his back looking up. His assistant who was massaging his feet said, "My Lord, your son, young Ghōṣaka is here."

"Where is he now?" he asked.

"He stands by your feet," he answered.

The noble merchant saw his son, then called his treasurer and asked how much treasure there was in the house.

"The total wealth is 40 crores.[40] Other goods, produce, treasure, property, rice-fields, houses, cattle, elephants, horses, palanquins, and the like, as of now amount to so much," he replied.

The nobleman began to say, "I won't give all this wealth to my son Ghōṣaka" but the young man's merit was so great that it was uttered as "I want to give." The noblewoman standing by his head heard those words and fearing that if he were to say more it might bode ill instantly began to weep

40. One crore is equal to 10 million or 100 lakhs. It comes from the Indian word *karor*.

and tear her hair as one demented with grief. She cried, "My Lord, what are you saying? Are we so unfortunate that such words should strike our ears?"

She then fell upon his breast weeping loudly, hitting her head again and again on his chest so he could not utter another word. That very instant the nobleman died.

King Udēnī heard the news of the noble merchant's death, arranged for the funeral, and inquired if he had any heirs. The king was told there was a child called Ghōṣaka and that while yet alive the noble merchant had gifted all his wealth to this son.

The king then sent a message asking Ghōṣaka to visit him.

There were heavy rains at the time and the kingdom was flooded. On his way to see the king Ghōṣaka came to a stream and instead of wading through it jumped over it. He then went to have audience with the king, worshiped him in greeting, and stood respectfully on one side.

"Are you Ghōṣaka?" the king asked.

"Yes Your Majesty."

"Do not grieve that the noble merchant your father is dead. All his wealth and honors I now bestow on you." Thus he comforted him and said, "Child, return now to your home."

The noble merchant-prince bowed to the king and took his leave. On the way back he waded through the stream that he had jumped over before. From his balcony the king saw young Ghōṣaka who had first jumped across the stream now wade though it on his return. He sent for the young man again and asked, "Son, why did you jump over the stream on your way here, and then wade through it on your return? I saw you do that."

"Your Majesty, I jumped over the stream on my way here because then I was like a little boy with no responsibilities. Now, Your Highness has given me honors and I must act with dignity. Therefore I waded the stream."

'This is an exceedingly perceptive and energetic young man. I will give him a nobleman's title immediately,' thought the king.

He then bestowed on him all the land and properties that belonged to his father and in addition gifted him a hundred each from every one of his own different treasures. He then placed the bands of office on him, sat him in a chariot, made him circumambulate the city, and sent him home. Thereafter everything Ghōṣaka happened to look at seemed to whirl around dizzingly.[41]

Ghōṣaka's wife, the noblewoman was in the palace talking to the servant Kāli.

---

41. The casual remark produces a vision of Ghōṣaka dizzied by his new status and by being literally whirled round the city. The DA version has "Then Ghōṣaka mounted his chariot and drove around the city clockwise. Every place he looked at quaked and trembled" (vol. 1, p. 265). The SR version seems much more apt and in character.

"Mother Kāli," she said, "your son obtained all his wealth and honors because of me."

The servant Kāli asked how that could be.

"This nobleman came to my father's house carrying a letter sewn to his cloak that had instructions to kill him. I tore up that letter and replaced another with instructions that he be given in marriage to me. From that time to this I have protected him."

"Mistress, is that all you know? Ever since he was a child this nobleman's father tried to kill him but failed. He spent a lot of money on that task."

"Mother, that was a very wrong thing to do."

While they were talking thus she saw her husband Ghōṣaka return after circumambulating the city.

'This man obtained all this wealth because of me,' she thought and smiling to herself she kissed him.

"Why do you smile?" asked the prince but she said nothing.

"If you don't tell me why you smiled I will this instant behead you," he said and lifted his sword.

"My noble husband has obtained so much wealth and honor because of me I thought and so I smiled as I kissed you," she said.

Unaware of his father's efforts to kill him the merchant-prince said, "My father gave me all this wealth. What did you give me?"

The noblewoman said, "Your father sent a letter instructing that you be killed." She then related all the ways in which she had helped him but Ghōṣaka could not believe her.

The noblewoman realized that and said, "You don't believe me. Ask your wet nurse Kāli and allay your doubts."

He called the servant Kāli and asked, "Is it true that my father sent a letter with instructions to have me killed?"

"Yes my son. From the time you were a child your father tried to kill you and spent a great deal of his wealth on the task. Seven times you escaped death and now you have obtained the rank of a noble merchant and a hundred each of every kind of wealth. What this young noblewoman said is not false. It is true."

On hearing her story the nobleman Ghōṣaka said, "Good deeds are indeed wonderful! I escaped death in these several ways only because of Acts of Merit I performed in a past life.[42] I must therefore not be neglectful in doing good deeds. I must hasten to do good." So thinking he ordered that

42. In the SR version Ghōṣaka seems to ignore the point just made about his wife's role in saving his life and helping him to achieve his present status. The author seems to hastily conclude the story in order to get to the "moral" of the tale. In the DA version Ghōṣaka says, "How great was my presumption! But since I have escaped from so terrible a death I must no longer live the life of Heedlessness." He then goes on to establish the alms-hall.

each day a thousand [gold coins] be spent to feed sixteen blind and deaf beggars. He appointed his friend the nobleman Mitta to organize the giving.

This is the birth-story of young Ghōṣaka.

3

At the time when the noble merchant Ghōṣaka was living in Kosaṁbā a noble merchant named Bhadravatī lived in the city of Bhadravatī.[43] He established a friendship with the noble merchant Ghōṣaka though they had not met. They inquired from merchants traveling between their respective lands about each other's ages and wealth and sent each other gifts to confirm their friendship.

About this time, a severe epidemic of the plague broke out in the merchant Bhadravatī's home town. First the flies in the houses died then progressively the gheckos [house lizards], the rats, the chickens, the cats, the dogs, the cattle, the buffalo, the servants, and other workers all died. Last of all the owners of the homes died. Only if they demolished their homes and left did anyone survive.

When everyone including his slaves and servants had died the noble merchant demolished his home, took his wife and daughter and left thinking, 'We will go to our friend the noble merchant Ghōṣaka and live with his help.' The provisions they carried for their journey were soon consumed while they were yet on their way. Greatly weakened by sun and wind, faint from hunger and thirst, and having suffered great hardship they finally arrived at the city of Kosaṁbā. There they stopped at a watering place, washed their hair, bathed, and came to a resting hall close to the city gate.

The noble merchant then said to his wife, "Dear One, if we were to arrive in this weak and destitute state not even the mothers who bore us would look kindly on us. How then can we go like this to see our friend? I have heard that our friend spends a thousand a day in alms to the indigent. Let us send our daughter to the alms-hall, get some food and drink, rest here a few days, and when our bodies are somewhat strengthened go to visit our friend the noble merchant."

The nobleman's wife agreed that it was a good idea. They stayed that night in the resting hall and next day sent their daughter to the alms-hall.

---

43. This is a typical link passage that ties the stories together however tenuously. It is customary in Sri Lanka for people to be named after the city or village from which they come. The practice is still common today.

This young noblewoman who had grown up in the lap of luxury, now deprived of the considerations of modesty her status required,[44] though suffering greatly, humbly took her place, plate in hand, and stood among the beggars waiting for food.

"How many portions do you want?" she was asked.

"Three if you please," she replied.

She returned with the three portions and sat down to eat with her parents.

The mother said to her husband, "Suffering is something that can hit even the greatest. But if *you* stay alive we too can live happily. Therefore do not bother about us. You eat this food," and she fed him to his heart's content. Since the noble merchant had not eaten for many days, now, eating a great amount of food he was unable to digest it and died at dawn the very next day.

The mother and daughter wept and mourned for him and then cremated the body. On the second day the daughter left the mother in the resting hall and went again to beg for food. When asked, "How many portions do you need?" that day she answered, "I would like two."

She brought the food to her mother and pleaded with her to eat, and fed her. The mother too could not digest her food and died that very night. Now alone, suffering great grief at the loss of her parents, suffering too from the lack of food, unable to bear the pangs of hunger, weeping, the young noblewoman went the next day and stood with the beggars for food.

"How many portions do you need today?" she was asked.

"One" she replied.

The official who was administering the distribution of food who knew that earlier she had asked for several portions and was now asking for one, said, "The day before you took three portions; yesterday you took two; today why do you take but one? Have you only just realized how much your stomach can hold?"

As if struck with a weapon at a vulnerable spot or as if acid was poured on an open wound, mortified by those words and unable to bear the shame the young woman said, "Sir, they were not portions I took for myself. When my mother and father were still alive I took three portions for them and me. Today I am alone and so I took one portion."

She then related the story of her parents and herself and everything as it had happened.

The official distributing the food heard her story and was moved to tears. He called the young woman to him, kissed her, and comforted her and said, "If you were the daughter of the noble merchant Bhadravatī then from now

44. Women of rank would not go unescorted to a public place like an alms-hall.

on you shall be my own daughter. Though your parents are dead, do not grieve anymore." He consoled her thus, took her to his home, and established her in the position of a daughter.

One day, hearing the loud commotion coming from the alms-hall the young woman inquired, "Can't you distribute alms without all this conflict and confusion?"

She was told that it could not be avoided.

"I will make a suggestion," she said. "Have two doors to the alms-hall through which one at a time can pass and ask them to enter through one door to obtain their food and leave through the other one. If you do that there will be no more fighting."

The official in charge of distributing alms agreed it was a good idea, ordered two doors to be made, and following the advice of the young woman distributed alms without further commotion. The young woman's name had been Sāmā. After her advice for ending the conflicts by adding a fence with doors to the alms-hall she was called "Sāmāvatī" [Peaceful One].[45] From that time on the confusion in the alms-hall subsided.

The noble merchant Ghōṣaka had been gladdened by the noise and confusion of the beggars in the alms-hall for he had thought, 'There's a great deal of activity in my alms-hall.' Now, not hearing any noise for the past two or three days he called Mitta the official in charge and inquired, "Is my alms-hall so quiet now because you have no more alms to distribute?"

"Alms are distributed every day and the beggars get their alms," Mitta replied.

"Then why has it been so quiet these past two or three days?" he asked.

"I discovered a way to have them obtain their alms quietly," Mitta replied.

"Why did you not do so at the beginning?" asked Ghōṣaka.

Mitta said he had not known of it then.

"From whom then did you learn how to do it now?" he was asked.

"My daughter advised me what to do," Mitta replied.

---

45. The DA has a long passage here about how she asks that a fence should be constructed round the alms-hall and hung with two doors and then goes on to say that because the word for fence is *väṭa,* henceforth she was called Sāmā-vatī (i.e., she who built the fence). In Sinhala, *vatī* is often used simply as a feminine suffix and is commonly used with proper names as a form of respect. The Pali translator of the original Sinhala not knowing the usage perhaps introduced the section about the fence in order to make sense of what he thought was the meaning of the word *vatī.* The temptation to ascribe etymologies and the mistranslations that result are not the domain just of modern translators and philologists. Here is possibly a fiifth-century example of a wrong etymology.

"How is it you have a daughter that I do not know of?" asked Ghōṣaka. The official then told Ghōṣaka of the nobleman Bhadravatī and related the entire story from the point where their house was affected by the plague epidemic to where he had taken their daughter as his own.

The noble merchant Ghōṣaka asked, "Why did you not inform me of this? The daughter of my friend the nobleman is my daughter."

He called Sāmāvatī to him and asked, "Child, are you the daughter of the noble merchant Bhadravatī?"

"I am Your Excellency," she replied.

"If that is so have no fear. You will be like my very own daughter," he said and drew her to him, kissed and consoled her, and ordered that she be given a retinue of five hundred women and given the status of his daughter.[46]

One day festivities termed *Astrological Celebrations* were held in that town. During those festivities, even high-status women who usually do not descend from their upper-story rooms or so much as step out into the street, would leave on foot, attended by their retinues, and go to rivers and streams. There they would sport to their hearts' content, wash their hair, bathe, adorn themselves in garlands of flowers and perfumes, and walk about lightheartedly. Thus, on that day, the young noblewoman Sāmāvatī too, attended by her retinue of five hundred women, crossed the royal compound to go to the river to bathe and wash her hair in preparation for the festivities. King Udēnī who was standing at the main window of his palace saw her and inquired, "Whose courtesan is this woman?"

"Nobody's," they answered.

"In that case whose daughter is she?"

"She is Sāmāvatī the daughter of the rich merchant Ghōṣaka," they replied.

On hearing that the king, who had fallen in love with her at first sight, sent a message to the merchant saying, "Send your daughter to our harem."

"I will not give our daughter in bondage," replied the merchant, "According to the customs of our farmer caste we are reluctant to expose our female children to peoples' disparaging remarks. Therefore, fearing the scornful words of others I will not give my daughter," he said.[47]

---

46. The ties between fathers and daughters (parents and children) are close and given overt public expression in gestures of affection considered acceptable in the culture. By contrast men and women in most other relationships do not kiss in public.
47. The nobleman Ghōṣaka belongs to the *govi kula* or "farmer caste" that is considered a high caste in Sri Lanka because of the absence of a brahmin caste group. Only kings who belong to the *kśatriya* caste are higher than the farmer caste. Ghōṣaka's refusal to give his daughter into the low-status position of a member of the king's harem is a mark both of his status and of his affection for his adopted daughter.

The king heard this and was enraged. He ordered the nobleman's house to be sealed and had the noble merchant and his wife expelled. When Sāmāvatī returned home after bathing and washing her hair she was not allowed to enter. She inquired what had happened and was told, "My child,[48] the king has asked that you be sent to join his harem. I told him we do not give our daughters in bondage. The king has therefore thrown us out of our house."

Then Sāmāvatī said, "It was wrong not to obey the king's order. You should have said, 'If you will take my daughter together with her retinue of five hundred women,[49] then I will give her to you.' "

"If that is your wish my daughter I will do so," said the nobleman and sent a message to the king in the terms Sāmāvatī had requested. The king agreed and conducted Sāmāvatī and her retinue of five hundred women to the palace, anointed Sāmāvatī, and appointed her his chief queen with the five hundred women as her retinue.

Thus good men who have heard this story of how those who have done Merit in a past birth, even when bereft of parents and all kinsmen, obtained wealth and happiness by the power of such deeds, should know that Acts of Merit alone are their only refuge. As long as they live in *saṃsāra* they should strive to perform as many Acts of Merit as their strength permits and try to win all blessings that are available to gods and men.

This is the birth-story of Sāmāvatī.

4

Sāmāvatī's husband, King Udēnī, had another queen named Vāsuladattā. She, however, was the daughter of King Caṇḍapajjota of Ujjeni. How did she become a chief queen to King Udēnī?

One day returning to the city from his pleasure gardens King Caṇḍapajjota of Ujjeni surveyed his vast possessions and asked, "Is there any other human being in this world who enjoys such wealth?"

---

48. Here the Sinhala term used is *putā* that literally means "son." The term for "daughter" is *duwa*. But in homes in the central highlands of Sri Lanka the distinction is not that emphasized and the term *putā* is still used for both sons and daughters. I have therefore translated it as "child."

49. Not being a woman of the *kśatriya* (warrior) caste, if she went to the king without her retinue she would merely be a member of his harem and have no status. But if she is accepted with a retinue of ladies-in-waiting then her status would be that of a consort of the king. Sāmāvatī with her characteristic practical good sense tells her father he should not have refused and angered the king but rather ensured her status and protection by offering to send her to the palace with her retinue.

"What wealth is this?" said his ministers. "King Udēnī of the kingdom of Kosaṁbā has a hundred thousand times as much!"

"In that case I will capture him," said the king.

"Your Highness, that king cannot be easily captured."

"I will use whatever stratagem is necessary to capture him," said the king. The ministers reiterated that it was impossible.

"Why so?" asked the king again.

"Oh Great Monarch, that king knows a magic *mantra* called the *Hastikānta mantra* [the charm that subdues elephants]. Once he recites his *mantra* and plays his *vīna* he can drive away any hostile elephant and capture any elephant he wishes to own. There is no other king who has elephant mounts like his."

"I will capture this king by some means or other," vowed the king.

The ministers hearing the king's violent words said, "Oh Great King, if you wish to capture King Udēnī construct a wooden elephant and place it somewhere just beyond his city. When he hears of an elephant or horse this king will go to any lengths to capture it. Once the king has left his city and come far enough we can capture him."

King Caṇḍapajjota agreed that it was a good scheme. He had a wooden elephant constructed with a hollow in its belly sufficient to hide sixty men inside and make it move. He had embroidered cloths pasted on it. He invited artists to paint it to look like a live [caparisoned] elephant and placed it beside a lake close to that king's territory with piles of elephant dung scattered here and there around it.[50]

A Vedda [hunter] saw the elephant and thought, 'This elephant is fit for our King Udēnī.' He ran to the city, described the great beauties of the animal, and said to the king, "Great King, I saw a beautiful elephant with a body as white as a silver rock."

The king asked the man to lead the way, mounted his royal elephant, and left accompanied by his retinue.

King Caṇḍapajjota heard from his spies that King Udēnī had left the city. He too went to that place and emptying out the middle of the road placed his men in hiding on either side. Unaware that King Caṇḍapajjota was in hiding waiting for him, King Udēnī saw the wooden elephant and thinking it to be real went in pursuit of the animal. The men inside the elephant activated the mechanism to make it run. King Udēnī recited his *mantra* as usual and began to play

---

50. A close parallel to the story of the Trojan horse. The one was a stratagem to get inside a city; this is a scheme to drag the king out of the city. But the stories so closely resemble each other that one wonders whether, as with Aesop's fables and the Jātaka stories, some kind of cross-connection existed.

his *vīna*. The more the king played the faster that wooden elephant ran as if he had not even heard the sound of the *vīna*. Unable to capture the animal while riding on his own elephant the king mounted a horse and rode in pursuit.

Just as in the story of the *Ummagga Jātaka,* when the king reined in his horse to stop, the animal was bridled in such a way that instead of stopping it ran all the way to the city of Uttara Pancāla taking King Brahmadatta with him, so did the wooden elephant run without stopping. As the king rode faster and faster in pursuit, his retinue was left behind. Meanwhile the forces of King Caṇḍapajjota who were on either side of the road encircled King Udēnī, captured him, and gave him to their king. Realizing that the king had been captured by enemies, King Udēnī's armies decided to remain where they were and set up camp there.

King Caṇḍapajjota having taken King Udēnī's life in his hands put him in a prison under guards and for three days drank in celebration of his victory. On the third day King Udēnī asked his guards, "What does your king do?"

"He is so overjoyed at having captured an enemy that he is drinking in celebration," the guards answered.

"Your king does what even women would not do. When one has captured an enemy one must either kill him or if not release him. Instead he makes him suffer by locking him in a prison. What is there to celebrate in that?"

King Caṇḍapajjota heard of this from the guards, came to where King Udēnī was imprisoned, and asked if what he had heard was true.

"It is true, King," he answered.

"In that case I will let you go. But teach us the magic formula that you know."

"Good I will teach you the *mantra* if you will learn it in the proper manner, which is that you should first pay obeisance to me. Will you do that?" asked King Udēnī.

"What? Must I pay obeisance to you for the sake of a *mantra*? I certainly will not," said King Caṇḍapajjota.

"In that case I will not teach you the *mantra*," said King Udēnī.

"If you do not teach me the *mantra* I will punish you," said King Caṇḍapajjota.

"Good. Command me to be killed. Your royal command can affect my body but can it control my mind? However much you may punish me I will not teach the *mantra* to one who does not pay obeisance to me."

King Caṇḍapajjota heard King Udēnī's bold unyielding words and thought, 'How can I learn this *mantra*? It is not safe to permit any other person to learn this *mantra* either. I will get my daughter Vāsuladattā to learn it and I will learn it from her later.' So he said to Udēnī, "Great King, will you truly teach the *mantra* to one who pays obeisance to you?"

"Yes, I certainly will do that."

"In that case, there is a hunchback in our palace. I will place her behind a curtain and you can teach her the *mantra*."

"It matters not who it is. I will teach it to whoever pays obeisance to me," replied King Udēnī. "I do not say this as one who, not having people to pay him obeisance is desirous of such worship. It is simply as a gesture of respect that one shows to a teacher. Knowledge that one acquires after paying one's respects to a teacher always bears fruit. That is the only reason for my request."

The king then went to his daughter Vāsuladattā and said, "My child, there is a man who suffers from such a bad skin disease that one cannot bear to look on him. But he does know a very powerful *mantra*. I cannot have anyone else learn it from him and he will not teach it to one who will not pay obeisance to him. You stay behind this curtain, pay obeisance to him, and learn the magic *mantra*. I will later learn it from you."

Thus afraid that the two people might develop an attraction for each other the king hid them from each other making out that his daughter was a hunchback and that King Udēnī was suffering from a skin disease.

Thereafter, King Udēnī sat behind a curtain and taught the *mantra*. Vāsuladattā sat on the other side of the curtain and learned it. One day though he recited the formula again and again Vāsuladattā kept repeating it wrong. King Udēnī became impatient and shouted, "You good-for-nothing hunch-back! Have you lost the use of your tongue or lips? You have repeated this *mantra* daily and you still get it wrong! Can't you say it like this?"

At that, the princess equally angry said, "You leper! What was that you said? Do you dare label someone like me a hunchback?" and she pulled aside the curtain. The two stared at each other and realized the truth of the situation. They knew that the king had deceived them because he was afraid they would be attracted to each other. They were powerfully attracted and instantly made love behind that very curtain. From that point on the lessons ended.

Unaware of what his daughter was being taught let alone her not learning the *mantra*, King Caṇḍapajjota constantly asked his daughter, "Child, have you learned the *mantra*?"

"I'm still learning it," she would reply. So he believed she was learning it and had no suspicions.

One day King Udēnī called Vāsuladattā to him and said, "Dear One, what a husband does for a woman neither one's parents nor one's kinsmen can do for her. If you save my life I will place you at the head of five hundred women in my royal household and make you my chief queen."

On hearing that Vāsuladattā said, "O King, remember well your promise."

She then went to her father, paid obeisance, stood respectfully on a side, and when he asked, "Have you learned the *mantra*?" she replied, "Yes, I have learned it. But there is one necessary medicinal ingredient that must only be obtained by starlight. In order to collect it we need a conveyance. Besides, since we are going for a special purpose we must leave from whatever gate we choose. Therefore order your guards not to stop us."

Obsessed with a desire for the *mantra* and not aware of the danger the king agreed. The princess then kept open whatever door she wished to take.

The king had five kinds of conveyances. What were they? A she-elephant called Bhaddavatī who could travel fifty leagues a day, a slave named Kāka[51] who could travel sixty leagues, two horses named Telakaṇṭhi and Muñjakesī who could travel a hundred leagues, and an elephant named Nalāgiri who could travel one hundred and twenty leagues a day.

4a

In a past life this king had rendered services to an important personage. One day, that important person bathed and washed his hair outside the city, and was on his way back when he met a certain *Pasē* Buddha who had gone to the city to beg for food. But because Māra,[52] the god of death had taken possession of all the inhabitants of the city the *Pasē* Buddha had not got even a spoonful of rice. He was on his way back and his bowl was still in its washed [empty] state. When the *Pasē* Buddha reached the city gate, Māra in the guise of a man came up to the *Pasē* Buddha and said, "Your Reverence, did you not obtain anything at all?"

"What is it Māra? Have you arranged to provide food?"

"Then please return to the city. I will see that you obtain rice."

The *Pasē* Buddha heard his words and thought, 'If I were to return to the city this Māra will once more take possession of the bodies of these citizens and he will get a chance to clap his hands and mock me.' So he ignored Māra's words and left.

Now the important person happened to see the *Pasē* Buddha returning with his begging bowl still in its washed state and said, "Your Reverence, have you obtained any food?"

"I have walked the city and am returning," the *Pasē* Buddha responded.

---

51. It is possible that the term *kāka* that in Sinhala means "crow," here was used to refer to the bird. Crows were released by early mariners for the speed and flawless sense of direction with which they flew toward land. Since all the other conveyances described here refer to animals, it is likely that *kāka* in this context refers to a bird-messenger. Somewhere in the process of translation and changing contexts this meaning was perhaps lost.

52. In Buddhist literature Māra is the god of death and also the personification of evil.

The man thought, 'For some reason instead of directly answering my question the *Pasē* Buddha has put it another way. I think he has not got any food.' He saw the empty begging bowl but he was not sure whether there was or was not rice in his house and so could not offer to take his bowl.[53] He said instead, "Your Reverence, please be seated a moment."

He ran to his house and inquired if they had rice ready and cooked. "Yes, the rice is ready," they answered.

He then called one of the servants and said, "Child, there is none other than you who can run fast at this moment. Go this instant, pay your respects to the *Pasē* Buddha, ask for his begging bowl, and bring it to me." At the very first word the man ran out and returned with the begging bowl.

That important person filled the bowl with the rice prepared for him and said, "Take this bowl and without delay and offer it to the *Pasē* Buddha. I will give you the Merit so acquired."

The messenger agreed, ran quickly, offered the bowl to the *Pasē* Buddha, worshiped him making the five-pointed gesture of reverence,[54] and standing respectfully on a side, said, "Your Reverence, since it was late and I was afraid your eating hour would be past I ran quickly taking your begging bowl. When I was returning with the bowl full of food I ran just as fast. For having run in this manner to perform this Act of Merit, may I, in another life, be blessed with four conveyances that can carry me, one at fifty leagues a day, another at sixty leagues a day, a third at a hundred leagues a day, and another at a hundred and twenty leagues a day. While I was running back and forth my body was wracked by the heat of the sun. Since I suffered that too in the cause of obtaining Merit, by the Merit so acquired may I have power and status like the noonday sun? Moreover, because the donor transferred the Merit from the gift of food to me and I accepted with a serene mind, may I obtain the bliss of *nirvāṇa* that you have attained."

The *Pasē* Buddha said, "May all your wishes and desires be realized," and recited the following stanza:

Icchitaṃ patthitaṃ tuyhaṃ khippamēva samijjhatu
pūrentu sabba saṃkappā cando paṇṇarasi yathā.
Icchitaṃ patthitaṃ tuyhaṃ sabbameva samijjhatu
pūrentu sabba saṃkappā maṇijōtirasū yathā' yi

53. It is a custom that if one wishes to make an offering of food to a monk one asks for his begging bowl, fills it with food, and gives it back.

54. An extremely reverential form of worship where one touches the earth at five points, with one's hands, elbows, knees, feet, and forehead.

[May all your wishes and desires be realized forthwith
May all your aspirations be fulfilled
May all your wishes and desires be realized
May your aspirations be fulfilled as with a wish-conferring gem]

He then gave the Sermon of Merit Transference[55] and left. This is the story of his past. Then his name was Cullupasthayakaya. In this life he was King Candapajjota. Because he had run fast and presented that begging bowl full of rice to that *Pasē* Buddha in a past life, in this life he had the five conveyances.

One day King Caṇḍapajjota went to his pleasure gardens. King Udēnī heard about it and thought, 'Today we will take the opportunity to flee.' He thus filled large leather bags with gold, placed Vāsuladattā on the she elephant named Bhaddavatī, then he too climbed on and left together with her.

King Caṇḍapajjota heard of it from his city guards.

"You fellows, give chase immediately," he ordered and sent his forces in pursuit. King Udēnī saw the armies in pursuit and opening the bag of gold he was carrying on the elephant's back he scattered the coins as he fled. The soldiers stopped to pick up the gold and only thereafter, followed in pursuit. In the delay caused by the soldiers' greed as they stopped to get the scattered gold, King Udēnī was able to flee to where his own forces were camped. His forces saw the king approaching from afar and went to meet him, surrounded him, and led him with great celebration to the city. When the king arrived in the city the first thing he did was to anoint Vāsuladattā and appoint her a chief queen as he had promised.

This is the story of Vāsuladattā.

5

Another woman named Māgandī also obtained the status of chief queen to that king [Udēnī.][56] How did that happen?

She was the daughter of the Brahmin Māgandi of the province of Kuru. Her mother's name also was Māgandī. Her uncle too was named Māgandi. This young woman Māgandī was exceedingly beautiful, as lovely as a divine

---

55. [s. *anumevan bana* or *anumōdana bana*]. It is customary for monks after they receive food and other offerings to preach a sermon transfering Merit to the donor(s) for their generosity. I have translated it as the "Sermon of Merit Transference."
56. Here King Udēnī becomes the link in the stories of the three women.

maiden. Her father could not find a husband good enough for his daughter. Whenever requests for her hand came from rich men of noble lineage with great retinues, he would humiliate them saying, "You are not good enough for my daughter," and send them away.

One day, the Buddha rose at dawn from a *Trance State of Great Compassion,*[57] looked on the world, and saw that the brahmin Māgandi and his wife were in a state of readiness to become *Anāgāmins*[58] [Non-Returners]. So, carrying his robe and bowl himself he went to a place just outside the village where fire worship was being performed. The brahmin saw the Buddha endowed with the thirty-two major marks of a Great Being[59] and the eighty minor characteristics of one foremost in perfection and he thought, 'There is no one in this world that compares with this jewel of a man. He alone is fit to marry my daughter. I will give my daughter in marriage to him.'

He went up to the Buddha and said, "Look here monk, I have a daughter. Till now I have kept her safely protected in my house as I have not seen a man good enough to marry her. Now, seeing your perfect form I think she is fit for you and you are fit for her. I will give her to you as your wife. Wait here till I fetch her."

The Buddha neither assented nor refused.

The brahmin ran home, called his wife, and said, "Good woman, what are you doing wasting time? I have just seen a monk who is a suitable match for your daughter and I left him waiting on the road. Adorn your daughter and come with her without delay." He had his daughter beautifully adorned and together with his wife led her to that place.

As when the heavens were invaded by the Asura demons the people of the entire town became excited seeing the brahmin go forth in this way. "What an amazing thing! Formerly, when the noble men of Anga, Magadha, Kāsi, Kōsala, Vajja, Malla, and others came to ask for his daughter in marriage, in spite of their fabulous wealth and retinues he would say, 'You are no match for my daughter's beauty' and refuse their offers of marriage. Today, this same man says he has seen a monk fit for his daughter and

57. [s.*Maha karuna samāpatti*] (Trance State of Great Compassion). It is but one of the many different States of Trance to which *arahats* can attain and that provides them with Supernormal Powers.

58. An *Anāgāmin* or Non-Returner is one who has reached the third stage in the Four stages on the Path to *nirvāṇa*. They are called Non-Returners because they will not be reborn in *saṃsāra*.

59. [s.*mahā puruśa*] (great being) was the title given to a Buddha who possessed the thirty-two major beauty marks and the eighty minor marks of an auspicious Being.

hurriedly takes her along to him. We must see what kind of a man this is." The crowd followed behind in wonderment.

When the brahmin arrived with his daughter the Buddha however was not at the place where the brahmin had left him. He had left his footprint there for all to see and was seated a little further away. Now unless the Buddha wills that his footprint be seen wherever it is placed it is not to be seen. If he wills that it be seen only by certain people then they alone and no one else can see it. If he wills that it should remain for a certain period, then even if it pours down rain on all the four continents of the earth and creates a vast flood, and however many elephants, horses, cattle, and buffalo stomp over it, not a hair's breadth of it will be damaged. Even if someone with magical powers wishes to remove it and creates a great storm or cyclone, that footprint will not move one infinitesimal lice-egg's distance or one dust particle's distance away from that spot. No one can cause that footprint to be erased.

Then the brahmin's wife looked at the brahmin and asked, "Where is this man you saw?"

"I left him sitting here. Let me see where he has gone," replied the brahmin. Looking around he saw the footprint where the Buddha had sat before and pointed to it. The brahmin's wife saw the footprint and since she was well learned in the threc *vēdas*[60] and the science of signs, she recognized the markings on the footprint and said, "Brahmin, what are you saying? This is not the footprint of one who will ever pollute himself by laying his chest on that lump of flesh called a "woman's breast." Nor is it the footprint of a lustful one who will bring his face to touch a woman's mouth, that toilet full of impurities such as spittle and her body with its thirty-two kinds of filth.[61] What is the use of saying more? This is definitely not the footprint of one who seeks the pleasures of the five senses. This is surely the footprint of one

---

60. *Vēdas* are the sacred books of the brahmins. The wife was clearly better versed than the husband in the *vēdas*.

61. The DA version merely has the following:

> "Now the brahman's wife was familiar with the three Vēdas, including the verses relating to signs. So she repeated the verses relating to signs, considering carefully the signs borne by the footprint before her. Finally she said, 'Brahman this is no footprint of one who follows the Five Lusts.' So saying she pronounced the following stanza" (Burlingame, vol. 1, pp. 275–276).

The misogynist diatribe seems to have been an addition made by the author of the SR. The impurities of the human body were to be regarded by Buddhists as part of the human condition. The SR author describes them as specifically female impurities. What is more he has a woman state it.

who has distanced himself from lust, who is a powerful antidote to anger, is like an unguent to dispel delusion, is a noble being who has attained Omniscience and rid himself of all Defilements. Further expounding on the marks on the footprint she recited the following verse:

rattassa hi ukkuṭikaṃ padaṃ bhave
duṭṭhassa hoti sahasānu piḷitaṃ
muḷhassa hoti avakaḍḍhitaṃ padaṃ
vivaṭṭacchadassida midisaṃ padaṃ

[The footprint of a lustful person is not straight
that of an angry person would be too firmly indented,
that of a deluded man tends to slide
This kind of footprint can only belong to an Omniscient One]

Then the brahmin said to her, "Look here woman, you are the kind of person who sees crocodiles in a saucer of water. Do you now see thieves inside our house? Say no more. Be quiet."

At that the brahmin woman said, "Look here brahmin, you have been born into the brahmin caste and yet without the smallest iota of knowledge of the sciences you insist on saying only what you wish.[62] Whatever you may say, I say that this is not the footprint of one who seeks to indulge in the pleasures of the five senses."

Then the brahmin looked this way and that and saw the Buddha seated like a fistful of ambrosia. "Perhaps there sits the person I spoke of," he said and went up to the Buddha and said, "Look here monk, I have brought my daughter to give her in marriage to you. Take her as your wife."

Without saying, "I do" or "I do not need your daughter" the Buddha said, "Brahmin I have one thing to say to you."

When asked to continue, he began to recount his past, beginning with the Great Renunciation.[63]

"O Brahmin! In fear of *saṃsāra* I left the heavenlike kingdom of Kimbulvat [Kapilavastu], a chief queen like Yasodhara, a gem of a son like Rahul and with no desire to be a universal monarch, a position that was

62. The brahmin's wife pours scorn on her husband for his ignorance and for his refusal to accept his own limitations. The DA does not press the point about the wife's superior learning. The SR does.

63. The Buddha's final act of renunciation when he left his wife and son, family, and kingdom in his quest for Enlightenment is referred to as the Great Renunciation [s.*mahābhinikmaṇa*].

already in my hand, as a man runs away from an anthill infested with she-snakes, I left the palace with its forty thousand goddesslike courtesans and ran away at midnight not once looking back. For six long years even Māra who followed me like a shadow could not find a single strand of lust in me. Like a fox who stares at the *kāla* flowers imagining them to be meat and finally, tired, slinks away, so Māra left. For six years I performed great penances and thereafter at the foot of the Bodhi tree I attained Insight, defeated Māra, sent tremors through the universe from earth to the Aknitā heaven, and became an Awakened One, a Buddha. Then, when the three daughters of Māra, Aratī [Infatuation], Ratī [Lust], and Rāga [Passion], wishing to avenge the defeat of their father came hurling harsh words I met their three faces with the three basic Truths, *anicca* [transience], *dukkha* [suffering], and *anatta* [soullessness], not with lust. Even when I saw the divine maidens in the sixth heaven that ultimate place of desire not one lustful thought was aroused in me. Therefore, will I now desire your daughter, that container with its nine openings filled with feces and urine? Quite apart from taking your daughter by the hand and kissing her I would be disgusted even to wipe my feet on her as I would on a doormat." He said this in a verse.[64]

> disvāna tanhaṃ arathiṃ ragañca
> nāhosi chando api methunasmiṃ
> kimmevidaṃ muttakarīsapuṇṇaṃ
> pādāpi naṃ samphusituṃ na icche

> [Even after seeing Arati (infatuation), Rati (Lust), and Raga
> (passion) no passing thought of lust crossed my mind.
> What then of this container (the human body) full of feces and urine,
> I would not desire it even to wipe my feet.]

On hearing the stanza the brahmin and his wife achieved the Stage of *Anāgāmin.*

The brahmin's daughter however, vowed vengeance. She thought to herself, 'If he didn't like me, instead of saying "I do not like her" does he have to insult someone like me by calling me a container of feces? No matter. Someday, when I have found a husband suited to me in age, birth, and wealth, then I will wreak vengeance on this mendicant-Gōtama who abused me in this way.' In this manner she cultivated a hatred for the Buddha.

---

64. This is the SR author's version of the Pali stanza. What is stated as a general comment on the impurities of the human body is paraphrased as essentially female impurities and couched in a strongly worded rejection of women. In making them the words of the Buddha the SR author gives them further authority.

How was it? Did the Buddha know she would vow vengeance against him or did he not? Certainly he did. If he did, why then did he recite that stanza? He did so because he knew the parents would benefit from it. That is how it is. Even though there are those who are unfortunate enough not to be able to attain the Fruits of the Path[65] in this life, who vow vengeance on the Buddhas and end up in hell yet, the All-Knowing Ones will ignore them and still preach the Doctrine to those who are ready to attain the Fruits of the Path.[66]

Thereafter, the parents led their daughter away and gave her in the charge of their younger brother, her uncle. The two of them joined the Order of the Buddha as disciples and shortly thereafter became *arahats* or Enlightened.

The uncle thought, 'My daughter is not to be given in marriage to any old weakling. She is fit only for a king.' He took her to the city of Kosaṃbā, adorned her in rings, toe-rings, and other ornaments so that she looked like a divine maiden and said to King Udēnī, "This jewel of a woman is fit only for you."

He then presented her to the king. Entranced by her great beauty the king fell in love with her, gave her a retinue of five hundred handmaidens, and appointed her a chief queen.[67] Thus the king had three chief queens each with five hundred handmaidens.

5a

At the time there also lived in that city three wealthy noble merchants named Ghōṣaka, Pāvāriya, and Kukkuta. During the rainy season five hundred ascetics would come down from the Himalayas and go from house to house

65. [s. *mārga phala*] The four stages and four "fruits" of Spiritual Attainments that lead to *nirvāṇa* are: *sōvān* (Stream Enterer) the first stage, that is, one who enters the Path; *sakadāgāmin* (Once-Returner) one who is well established in the Path but will be born one more time in the human world; *anāgāmin* (Non-Returner) one who will not be born ever again in *saṃsāra*; *arahat* (the Enlightened One) and the "fruits" that accompany each stage.
66. While Magandi takes the Buddha's verse literally and as a personal insult to her, her parents understand it as a rejection of the impurities associated with the human condition. They develop understanding and become *anāgāmins*. The point being made is that the Buddha is willing to suffer personal injury or hostility in the interests of preaching to those who have the possibility of becoming enlightened.
67. Implicit is the suggestion that as with the case of Samavati, only if a woman joins the king's harem accompanied by a large retinue of women can she have the status of a queen and not be just another woman of the harem. Here the king gives Māgandi a retinue.

begging in the city. The merchants were pleased, invited them into their homes, seated them, gave them tasty food offerings, saw to all their needs during the four months of the rainy season, and when the period was over sent them off with promises to do the same the following year. The ascetics thus spent eight months in the Himalayas and four months with them.

[On one occasion] during this latter period, while on their way down from the Himalayas they slept at the foot of a large banyan [ficus] tree in a forest grove. The oldest among them thought, 'The deity who dwells in this tree must have great power. I wish he were good enough to provide us with some water to drink.' The deity residing in the tree read their thoughts and provided them with water to drink. They then wished for water to bathe. The deity provided water for them to bathe. Thereafter they wished for food and again the deity produced food too. The ascetics then thought, 'This deity has given us all we wished. Would that we could see him too.' At that the deity ripped apart the tree trunk and appeared before them in his divine form.

The ascetics saw the deity and addressed him. "You possess great powers. What Acts of Merit did you perform to obtain them?

"What use is that to you, Your Reverences? It is better you should not ask it," he replied.

"Divine King, we are indeed greatly moved by the beauty of your form and your power. We would like to hear what Acts of Merit you performed in previous births."

"It is better it remain unsaid," he replied.

Since the Act of Merit he had performed was but a trifling thing the deity was shy to talk about it. The ascetics however pressed him again and again so he said, "Well then, listen," and narrated the story of the Act of Merit he had performed.

5b

In a previous birth, poverty-stricken and looking for work this deity came to the noble merchant Anēpidu [Anātapiṇḍika], told him his situation, and began to work for him. One full moon fast day not long after, the noble merchant Anēpidu returned home from the temple and said, "What? Has no one informed the servant of this house that today is the Full Moon fast day?"[68]

68. Lay Buddhists use the Full Moon day as a time for keeping the Eight Precepts that are more rigorous than the Five Precepts observed in their daily life. The three additional Precepts are to abstain from sexual intercourse, from eating after midday, and from sitting on high seats.

"No," they replied.

"In that case cook rice just for him tonight," he ordered and had a measure of rice cooked for the servant.

The man worked in the fields all day and at evening when they served him his rice, though hungry, he did not immediately sit down to eat.

'All these past days there is a great commotion at this time. People shout, Bring rice; bring lentils; bring curries." Today everyone sits silent. I'm the only person being served rice. I wonder what the reason for this is,' he mused.

"Have the others in this household eaten?" he asked.

"No," they replied.

"Why have they not eaten?" he asked.

"In this house we do not eat an evening meal on full moon days," they replied. "We practice the religious observances and keep the Eight Precepts. Everyone, even down to nursing infants have their mouths washed, have a sweetened paste made of four ingredients placed on their tongues, and perform the religious observances. When scented oil lamps are lit children of all ages big and small get on to their beds and meditate on the impurities of the body. We forgot to tell you it was the day of the full moon observances so we have cooked just for you. Eat now."

The man then said, "If it is not too late and I too can keep the observances even at this stage, I will do so too."

"The noble merchant is the one who will know if that is possible or not; we don't," they said.

"In that case go ask him," he said and sent them off. They went to the noble merchant and inquired.

The merchant said, "If he does not take his meal and washes his mouth, and keeps the observances then he will have the benefit of having kept the observances for half a day."

On hearing that the man immediately washed his mouth and began the observances. However, as he had worked all day and eaten nothing he was troubled by hunger and suddenly developed stomach pains. Unable to bear the pain he tied a rope [to a post], held onto one end of it, and began to roll about.

Hearing of this, the noble merchant Anēpidu went to him carrying a lamp with a jeweled handle and bringing some paste with the four kinds of sweets. He asked, "What is the matter, child?"

"My Lord, my body aches."

"If so eat this medicinal preparation."

"My Lord, have you eaten that tonight?" the man asked again.

"Our bodies are not in pain. Don't ask about what we do. You must take this medicine," he said.

"My Lord, I should have kept the observances for a full day but did not do so. If I must die let me die but I will do nothing to undermine the half day of observances I have kept."

Though the merchant repeatedly asked him to take it the man refused to consume the medicinal preparation fearing it would impede the observances. Like a fading garland he died at dawn the following day and was reborn as the deity of the banyan tree.

The deity related this incident and added, "The noble merchant Anēpidu who helped me at the time was committed to the Three Jewels, the Buddha, the Dhamma, and the Sangha. I obtained these blessings because of the half day of observances I performed under his guidance."

When they heard the name Buddha the five hundred ascetics were suffused with love and devotion for the Three Jewels. They stood up and with hands folded in obeisance bowed to the deity saying, "Did you mention the name Buddha?"

He said he had. Three times they asked the question and three times he answered "Yes, The Buddha has been born on earth." Then they gave a cry of joy, saying three times,

ghoso'pi so dullabho lokasmiṃ
ghoso'pi so dullabho lokasmiṃ

[Even the sound of the name Buddha is not easily heard in this world, even the sound of the name Buddha is not easily heard in the world.]

"Even the sound of the name Buddha is not easily heard in this world. It is still more rare to hear of someone who has heard the words of such a Buddha. Therefore O Deity, because of you we have heard the wonderful sound of the Three Jewels, a sound not heard for a period of over ten thousand years."[69]

Then the junior ascetics said to the senior among them, "Now that we have heard of the existence in the world of the Three Jewels so hard to come by, we must not delay. Let us go immediately to see the Buddha."

At that the senior ascetic said, "O children, there are three merchant princes in the city of Kosaṁbā who have helped us greatly. Let us have our

---

69. A Buddha appears on earth only after several aeons and the Doctrine he preaches also lasts only for five thousand years. The Buddha, his Doctrine, and the Order of Monks he establishes are the Three Jewels. The combination comes into existence only during the lifetime of a Buddha. Therefore to be alive during the lifetime of a Buddha is considered a great blessing.

meal there tomorrow and inform them too that the Three Jewels are now in existence in the world. Then we can go on. Be patient till then." He got the junior ascetics to agree and to stay on for that day.

The next day, aware that the ascetics were due, the three noble merchants prepared rice-gruel, arranged seating, and went forward to meet them. When they saw them they worshiped them in greeting, escorted them to their homes, sat them down in the seating prepared for them, and offered them food. The ascetics ate the meal and said to the noble merchants, "Now we must leave."

The noble merchants said, "Did we not get a promise from you that you would spend the four months of the rainy season with us? Where are you going now?"

The ascetics answered, "The Three Jewels, the Buddha, Dhamma, and Sangha, are now in existence in the world. We go to see the Buddha."

At that the noble merchants said, "If Your Reverences are going to see the Buddha we too will go with you to see that Buddha."

"O lay devotees, you will take time to make preparations for the journey. We will therefore go on ahead. You follow after," they said.

They went to the Buddha and full of joy gave thanks. As if offering red lotus buds for a lotus seat they placed their joined palms to their foreheads in worship and stood on one side.

The Buddha then read their thoughts and as was his wont he preached to them in consecutive order on the themes of Generosity, Discipline, and so forth. At the end of the sermon all of them became *arahats* with Fourfold Analytic Powers.[70] They wished to remain near the Buddha as monks and when the Buddha raised his right hand and said, "Monks, come here" they became monks and obtained through their psychic powers all the accoutrements [for a monk] and brought glory to the Buddha's dispensation.

Thereafter the three noble merchants of Kosam̆bā arrived with five hundred pack mules loaded with ghee, honey, rice, textiles, and other items needed for offerings. They came to the city of Sävät, saw the Buddha, heard him preach, and all three attained to the stage of *sōvān* [Stream-Enterers]. They made offerings of the items they had brought with them, stayed there with the Buddha for almost half a month, and then invited the Buddha to visit the city of Kosam̆bā.

The Buddha said, "O householders, empty places attract the mind of the Enlightened One."

"Your Reverence, we understand your request. When we send you a message inviting you to come, please do," they said and returned to the city of Kosam̆bā.

---

70. [s. *sivpilisimbiyāpat*] has been translated as the "Fourfold Analytic Powers" or special analytic capabilities that *arahats* attain.

There the noble merchant Ghōṣaka built the Ghōṣaka monastery, the noble merchant Kukkuta the Kukkuta monastery, and the noble merchant Pāvāriya the Pāvāriya monastery. Thus the three noble merchants built three great monasteries and sent messages inviting the Buddha. Out of compassion for them the Buddha came to the city of Kosam̆bā. Hearing the Buddha had arrived the three noble merchants went ahead to greet him, conducted him to the temples with great ceremony and worship, and set up a roster for each of them to take turns to make offerings and to wait on the Buddha. In compassion for them the Buddha spent one day in each monastery. When he resided in a particular monastery he would go begging to that particular nobleman's house.

5c

A garland maker named Sumana, who served the three noble merchants came to them and said, "My Lords, I have served all three of you for many years now. Do not give me anything in return except only the chance to make a food offering to the Buddha for just one day. There can be no greater reward than that."

The noble merchants replied, "If that is so we give you permission to make the offering tomorrow. Make your offering."

The garland maker was delighted. Like a universal monarch who receives a great treasure of seven precious jewels, overcome with joy he invited the Buddha and prepared the offerings.[71]

At the time King Udēnī used to give eight gold coins to purchase flowers daily for Sāmāvatī. A servant of Sāmāvatī's called Khujjuttarā would take the gold coins to the garland maker Sumana and purchase flowers daily to present to Sāmāvatī. On that particular day the garland maker saw Khujjuttarā, Sāmāvatī's servant, and said, "Today I have invited the Buddha. After the food offering I will make offerings of scented flowers. You can help with the food preparation, hear him preach, and then take whatever flowers are left." She agreed.

Sumana the garland maker made offerings of food to the Buddha and his monks and stood holding the bowl waiting for the preaching of the Sermon of Merit Transference. At that very moment the Buddha in a melodious voice

71. In certain versions of the text the Māgandī story ends here. The next section is titled "The Story of Sāmāvatī's Death by Burning." However, in the most recent edition of the text (1985) edited by the Sinhala Department of Colombo University based on eleven extant *ōla* (palm leaf) manuscripts and six published versions, the Māgandī story extends to include that of the death of Sāmāvatī.

began the sermon. Khujjuttarā heard the Buddha's sermon and as she did so achieved the state of *sōvān* adorned in a thousand ways.

Formerly Khujjuttarā was in the habit of hiding away four of the eight gold coins [given to her to purchase flowers] and paying the garland maker only four. On that occasion since all thoughts of deception had been rooted out she purchased flowers for the entire eight gold coins.

Sāmāvatī saw the unusually large quantity of flowers and said, "Mother, did the king give you a lot of money today to buy flowers?"

Khujjuttarā replied,"No, my lady."

"Then how is it there are so many flowers today?" asked Sāmāvatī.

"My lady, on all those past occasions I stole four of the eight gold coins and bought flowers only with four. That is why up to now there were fewer flowers."

"Why then didn't you take the coins today?"

"When I went to the garland maker's house to get flowers today I saw the Buddha, All-Knowing, with a body shining as of solid gold, accompanied by five hundred monks, receiving offerings of food. I stood before him and heard words sweeter than I have ever heard. I shed the three evils of belief in self, doubts, and erroneous beliefs and practices, and since I was free of all Demerit and have become a *sōvān* today I bought flowers with the full eight coins. Hearing her words Sāmāvatī too was filled with joy and instead of saying, 'Woman, return to me this instant all the money you stole from me over so long a time,' said, "Mother, can we too drink of that doctrinal nectar that you have tasted?[72]

"Yes, you can," said Khujjuttarā. "But you must first wash my hair and bathe me."[73]

Sāmāvatī then washed Khujjuttarā's hair with sixteen pots of scented water, bathed her, and offered her two white garments to wear. Khujjuttarā wore one white garment and draped the other piece of white cloth over her shoulder.[74] She then climbed onto the beautifully decorated seat for preaching, asked for a finely ornamented fan and holding it in her hand, called Sāmāvatī and her five hundred women, and preached a sermon exactly as the Buddha had done.

---

72. The contrasting terms of address, *woman* and *mother* in this context underline the difference between a derogatory term of address to a servant and a respectful one.
73. A reversal of status has occurred. Kujjuttarā is now a *sōvān* and therefore in a sense of higher status than the queen to whom till now she had been a servant.
74. Buddhists in Sri Lanka even today dress in this manner, with one white lower garment and another over their shoulders, when they take *sil,* that is, observe the Eight Precepts on Full Moon days.

Hearing that sermon Sāmāvatī and her five hundred attendants all became *sōvān* even as they sat there. They worshiped Khujjuttarā and said, "You who have given us a taste of this divine *nirvaṇā* shall henceforth be our mother. From now on you will not have to perform any menial service. As our mother, go daily to the Buddha, listen to all his sermons, bear them in mind, and preach them to us. In that manner, Khujjuttarā went daily to the Buddha and heard him preach, conveyed it back, and became conversant in the doctrinal texts of the *Tripiṭaka.*[75] The Buddha declared in Pali:

> 'etadaggaṃ bhikkhave mama sāvikānaṃ upāsikānaṃ bahussutānaṃ dhammakathikānaṃ yadidaṃ Khujjuttarā-yi'
>
> [O monks, of all my female disciples, learned devotees and preachers of the Doctrine I proclaim this Khujjuttarā to be pre-eminent.]

meaning "Khujjuttarā is preeminent among my female disciples, who are well learned in the doctrine and can best expound it," and placed her in that status.

Those five hundred women then said to Khujjuttarā, "Mother, we would all like to see the Buddha. Can you show him to us by some means or other? We would like to make him offerings of scented flowers and other things.

"Noble ladies," said Khujjuttarā, "Life in the palace is very difficult. I cannot conduct you all outside the palace."

Then Sāmāvatī and her five hundred women said, "Mother, do not make our lives useless and destroy us by not showing us the Buddha."

"In that case," said Khujjuttarā, "Make a hole in the walls of your chamber so small that two persons cannot look out. Purchase flowers, perfumes, incense, and other such things and when the Buddha walks by to visit the homes of the three noble merchants you can see him and make your offerings. They did so, saw the Buddha as he went to the homes of the noble merchants, and as he returned from there and made their offerings and worship.

5d

Then one day Māgandī went from her apartment to Sāmāvatī's, saw the apertures in each of the bedrooms, and inquired what they were. Not knowing

---

75. Tripitaka are the three caskets that were said to contain (metaphorically) the Buddhist texts. They were the *sutta pitaka* or the "casket of texts or sayings," the *vinaya pitaka* or the "casket of disciplinary rules of conduct for monks," and the *abhidhamma pitaka*, "the casket containing the more abstract philosophical doctrine."

that she had vowed vengeance on the Buddha they said, "The Buddha has come to this city. We have made these apertures so we can worship him from within here." Then Māgandī thought, 'I know what to do to my enemy that monk, Gōtama, when he comes here and to those five hundred women who worship him.'

She went to the king and said, "Your Majesty, Sāmāvatī and her five hundred attendants engage in unseemly conduct with strangers. In two or three days they will kill you."

"They will do no such thing," said the king, ignoring her remarks.

"Your Majesty, go yourself and examine their bedrooms," Māgandī insisted.

The king went to the bedrooms, saw the apertures, and inquired what they were. When he was told exactly what they were used for he was not angry with them, said nothing, had the apertures closed up, and ordered that netted windows be constructed instead. From then began the practice of having upper windows in the bedchambers.

Then Māgandī unable to do anything to hurt them thought, 'I may not be able to do any harm to these women but I will do something to harm this Gōtama-monk.' She bribed the citizens and said, "When this Gōtama-monk comes begging to the city, all of you gather your young people, stand by, and hurl insults and abuse at him and drive him away. Thus when those of false views unhappy with the Three Refuges[76] saw the Buddha enter the inner city they chased behind him saying, "You are a thief, an ignorant fellow, a fool, a camel, a bull, a donkey, a useless beast. There is no heaven for you. Misfortune will be your lot." Thus they insulted and abused him with the ten different forms of insults.

Hearing of this the Elder Ānanda came to the Buddha and said, "Your Reverence, the people of this city are not at all well disposed toward the Three Refuges. They insult and abuse you. Let us leave this city and go elsewhere."

"Ānanda, when we go to the next city, if the people of that city also abuse and insult us where then should we go?" asked the Buddha.

"Your Reverence, the land of Daṁbadiva is by no means small. If that happens we will go to yet another city."

"If those citizens also abuse us in the same manner where then do we go, Ānanda?"

"Your Reverence if they too abuse and insult us we can go somewhere else."

---

76. Buddhists seek "refuge" in the Buddha, the Dhamma, and the Sangha. Hence the term *Three Refuges* [s.*tuṇ saraṇa*].

The Buddha replied, "O Ānanda, it is not right that we should go elsewhere. If a dispute occurs it is proper to leave only after that dispute is settled. Once it is settled we can go to another place." He then asked, "Ānanda, who are they who insult and abuse us?"

"From the servants and workers on up everyone insults and abuses you." Ānanda replied.

"O Ānanda, I am like an elephant who has entered the battlefield. Just as the elephant who has set foot on the battlefield patiently bears the arrows hurled, likewise it is fitting that I bear all these insults and forgive them." Thus taking himself as the subject he preached these three stanzas from the Elephant text [of the Dhammapada].

ahaṃ nāgova saṃgāme cāpato patitaṃ saraṃ
ativākyaṃ titikkhissaṃ dussilohi bahujjano.

dantaṃ nayanti samitiṃ dantaṃ rājābhirūhati
danto seṭṭho manssesu, yotivākyaṃ titikkhtī.

varamassatarā dantā ājaniyā ca sindhavā
kuñarā ca mahānāga attadanto tatho varaṃ.

[Just as the elephant in battle withstands arrows discharged from bows, so will I bear all abuse. The multitude is generally not virtuous.

Only the disciplined elephant is taken to gatherings. The king mounts only the tamed elephant. So among men the disciplined one who bears insults is noblest.

Among horses the thoroughbred are the best. Of elephants the disciplined Kujjara elephants are the best. Better than all these is the self-disciplined one.]

The meaning is given later in the first story of the Elephant. I will not give it here.[77] The Doctrine preached in these three stanzas proved of great use to those who were there. The Buddha then said, "Ānanda, don't think about all

77. This is unusual for the author. He generally explains the meaning of a verse or gives his interpretation of it for the benefit of his Sinhala lay listeners who generally do not know Pali. The comment suggests that though the tone and style of these stories is that of a sermon directed to listeners, they were also intended to be read.

this. They will abuse us for about seven days. On the eighth day they will be silent as if dumb. If a dispute arises concerning the Buddha it will not last beyond seven days.

Then Māgandī, unable to drive the Buddha out of the city with insults and abuse pondered on what she should do next. She decided she would do something to harm the five hundred women who attended on the Buddha.

One day when the king was drinking palm wine and she was in attendance on him she sent a message to her uncle. What did it say? Bring eight live chickens and eight dead chickens. When you arrive stand at the top of the staircase and inform the king that you have come. Even if the king asks you to enter, do not go in but first send the eight live chickens and then the dead ones. She bribed a servant to also do her bidding. The brahmin did exactly as he had been instructed. He stood at the top of the stairs and sent a message to the king. When the king invited him in he said, "I will not enter where the king is drinking," and remained outside.

Māgandī then called the servant she had bribed and said, "Go to my uncle."

That servant took the eight live chickens given by the brahmin and brought them to the king saying, "Your Majesty, here is a present sent by your chief minister."

"That will make a fine dish," said the king. "Whom shall we ask to cook it for us?"

"Your Majesty, Sāmāvatī and her five hundred women sit around and do nothing. Let us ask them to cook it," said Māgandi.

The king said to the servant, "Go, take these to them. Tell them not to depute anyone else for the task but to kill and prepare the birds themselves and to send it to us."

"Yes Your Majesty," said the servant, who took the eight chickens and conveyed the king's message to Sāmāvatī and her women.

"We do not kill. If you send us dead chickens we will prepare them as instructed," they said refusing the king's request. The messenger reported this back to the king.

Then Māgandī said, "Great King, you should investigate whether they do or do not kill. They did not cook the chicken for you but if you order them to cook it for the monk, Gōtama, they will kill the chickens themselves and cook them in an instant."

"In that case send a messaage to that effect," said the king. Then the servant who had been bribed earlier pretended to take those chickens but having gone a little distance he gave the live chickens to the king's advisor and took the dead chickens to Sāmāvatī.

"The king has ordered you to cut up these chickens and cook them for the Buddha," he said. Not knowing the ruse and thinking that it was done out of reverence for the Buddha and because the chickens were already dead, they said it was a fitting task and accepted the chickens. The servant returned to the king and when asked "What happened friend?" answered, "The moment I said it should be cooked as alms for the Buddha they immediately took them from me."

Māgandī added, "When it was said that it was for you they piously said they did not kill but when they were told it was for that Gotama-monk you saw for yourself how they accepted it. I, knowing their true nature, told your majesty several times about their unbecoming behavior but you did not believe me. Do you even now realize the truth of what I said?" Though she spoke thus the king said nothing, intending to check things out further. Thereafter, Māgandī, whose devious plans had up to now not succeeded in causing harm now sat thinking of a further plan to kill them all.

In those days the king used to visit Sāmāvatī, Vāsuladattā, and Māgandī in turn, spending seven days in each one's apartments. Māgandī, figuring that the king was due to visit Sāmāvatī the next day or the day after, asked her uncle to bring her a cobra that had a medicinal preparation rubbed on its fangs to neutralize the poison. She kept the snake with her. The king was in the habit of taking his musical instrument, the *vīna,* wherever he went because of its magic power. There was a tiny aperture in the body of the *vīna.* Māgandī slipped the snake in though this hole, covered it with a bunch of flowers, and kept the snake hungry for two or three days.

Knowing the king was to leave [her quarters] she went to him and asked, "Your Majesty, to whose apartments do you go tonight?"

"To Sāmāvatī's apartments," replied the king.

"My Lord, last night I had a very bad dream. Do not go there today," she said. Three times she tried to stop him but when she realized the king could not be stopped, she said, "In that case I will accompany Your Majesty to see what happens." The king tried to stop her but she insisted on accompanying him.

The king adorned himself with the garlands and ornaments Sāmāvatī presented, perfumed his body, changed his clothes, partook of flavorful royal food, placed his *vīna* with its magical power by the bed, and went to sleep.

Pretending to walk up and down Māgandī removed the bunch of flowers that had been stuffed over the aperture of the *vīna*. Instantly, the snake that had not eaten for two or three days fell onto the bed with his head puffed up and hissing loudly. Māgandī seeing the snake and pretending to know nothing about it screamed, "Your Majesty, a snake!" She shook him awake. "This foolish king refused to listen to my warnings," she said, scolding him. "Oh you useless, disobedient, wicked women. What benefits have you not had from this king? Did you imagine that once the king was dead you could all live happily? Don't for one moment think so." In this manner she shouted and scolded Sāmāvatī and her retinue.

"I told you I had seen a bad dream and asked you not to go to Sāmāvatī's quarters tonight. I, your loyal queen begged and pleaded with you but ignoring my words, enamored of these wicked women, you speedily rushed there; didn't you? Have you even now seen the consequences of that haste?" Thus she said all manner of things to provoke the king's anger.

The king saw the snake and fearing for his life, was consumed with rage. 'Can there be women who do such things?' he thought. 'These women are indeed wicked. I did not heed my queen Māgandī's words regarding their foolish ideas. First they all had openings in their chambers and went out and did as they pleased. Then when I asked them to cook the chickens they returned them. Today they have put a snake in my bed and have planned to kill me.'

Seeing that the king was angry Sāmāvatī summoned her retinue of five hundred women and said, "Sisters, the king is angry with us for no fault of ours. We have no other refuge. Our Buddha has said that compassion for those who harm us is a divine medicine that can counter all harm. Therefore, let us extend compassion equally toward this king, to Māgandī who tries to harm us with her lies, as well as to ourselves. Let us not harbor ill will toward anyone." She advised them thus.

The enraged king drew the bow that usually requires a thousand people to handle, placed a poisoned arrow against his fingernail, straightened it, pulled the back of the arrow against the string, lined Sāmāvatī and her retinue of five hundred one behind the other, drew it to the full length of his shoulder, and released it. However, because of the power of Sāmāvatī's compassion that arrow stopped in front of Sāmāvatī and turned around as if it had only just now come through her breast. At that the king thought, 'Up to now any arrow I shot from this bow would pierce even a huge rock, not stop midway. Today, this arrow travels through empty space, has nothing serious to stop it but it has turned around, and is now pointed at me. Even this mindless arrow knows of Sāmāvatī's goodness. I, though born a man, seem to be the only one who does not understand her goodness.' He flung his bow aside, placed both hands to his forehead, and bending down at Sāmāvatī's feet said, "Sāmāvatī, I have gone out of my mind. I do not know what should or should not be done. Please protect me who am so foolish. You alone can help me. I will take refuge in you." He then recited the following stanza:

sammuyhāmi pamuyhāmi sabbā muyhanti me dasā
sāmāvatī maṃ tāyassu tvañca me saranaṃ bhava yi.

[I am confused and have lost my mind. Every direction I turn is confusing. Sāmāvatī please protect me. May you be my only refuge.]

Sāmāvatī heard what the king said. But instead of saying, "Good, Your Majesty, I will be your refuge" said, "Your Majesty, why must you take me for your refuge? Even the arrow you shot at me turned around and was directed at Your Majesty because I had taken refuge in that noble personage of great goodness and power, namely the Buddha, whose goodness cannot be compared with any other in this world. Therefore take refuge in that Buddha and you will continue to be my protector forever more. She recited these two stanzas:

idaṃ vatvā sāmāvatī sammāsambuddha sāvikā
mā maṃ tvaṃ saraṇaṃ gacchā yamahaṃ saraṇaṃ gatā.

esa buddho mahārāja esa buddho anuttaro
saraṇaṃ gacchā taṃ buddhaṃ tvaṃ ca me saraṇaṃ bhavā yi.

[Samavati devotee of the perfectly Awakened One said, "Do not take refuge in me. It is the incomparable Buddha who is my refuge. Take refuge in that Buddha and in turn, be my protector."]

The king heard Sāmāvatī's words, "Now I am even more afraid." He said in verse,

esa bhiyyo pamuyhāmi sabbā muyhanti me disā
sāmāvatī maṃ tāyussu tvañca me saraṇaṃ bhavā

[I am even more confused and have completely lost my mind. Sāmāvatī protect me and from now be my refuge.]

Sāmāvatī refused the honor as before. Then the king said, "In that case I take you as my refuge and I take the Buddha you speak of also as my refuge. I will grant whatever request you make."

"I accept that which you grant," Sāmāvatī replied.

The king went to the Buddha, established himself in the Three Refuges, and invited the Buddha with due formality. For seven days he conducted a great offering of alms. Thereafter, calling Sāmāvatī he said, "I have obtained these great benefits because of you. Rise up immediately and ask whatever you wish."

"Great King, I have no use for beaten or unbeaten gold," Sāmāvatī replied. "If you want to grant me a wish then invite the Buddha with his five hundred monks to my house to partake of an offering of alms and to preach the Doctrine to us."

The king went to the Buddha, worshiped him and said, "Your Reverence, please come regularly to this house accompanied by your five hundred monks. Sāmāvatī and her five hundred women desire to hear a sermon from you."

"O King," responded the Buddha, "The All-Awakened One has compassion for all. The populace too longs to see the Omniscient One. Thus if he were to go exclusively to one house what chance have they to acquire Merit?"

"In that case Your Reverence, assign one of your monks to preach to Sāmāvatī and her women."

The Buddha called the Great Elder Ānanda and said, "Ānanda, from now on preach to the women of King Udēnī's harem,"[78] and arranged for him to preach to them.

The Great Elder Ānanda, accompanied by five hundred monks went to the palace regularly and preached a sermon. The five hundred women in turn would regularly make offerings of food to those five hundred monks and listen to a sermon from the Great Elder Ānanda. One day the five hundred women heard the sermon preached by him and were so delighted that they donated their five hundred shawls. Each shawl was worth five hundred.

The following day the king saw the women without their shawls and inquired, "Where are your shawls?"

"Your Majesty, we heard a sermon from the Elder Ānanda and made a gift-offering of them to him."

"Did the Elder Ānanda accept all the five hundred shawls?" asked the king.

"Yes he accepted all five hundred shawls," they replied.

The king went to the Elder Ānanda, performed the five point gesture of worship, stood at one side and asked, "Your Reverence, do our queens listen to sermons only from you? Do they also make offerings for sermons preached?"

"It is so Your Majesty. They listen to sermons and yesterday they made offerings of five hundred of their shawls."

"Your Reverence, that is a lot of cloth. What will you do with so much cloth?"

"Great King, we take only what we need and give the rest to those monks whose robes are worn-out."

"What do they do with their old and worn-out robes?

"They give them to those who have even more worn-out robes."

"What do they do with their very worn-out robes?"

"They use them as bedspreads."

"What do they do with their old bedspreads?"

78. [s.*antapuraya*] literally meant "inner chamber." It referred to the special quarters in the palace occupied by the queens and their retinues of women. In the context of that time the word had little derogatory connotation.

"They use them as bedsheets."

"What do they do with their old bedsheets?"

"They use them as floor-rugs."

"What do they do with their old floor-rugs?"

"They use them to wipe their feet."

"What do they do with them when they are old?"

"'Let not what is given by the devoted be discarded as useless,' they say and tear it into small pieces and beat it to a pulp and use it to plaster walls."[79]

"Your Reverence, offerings given to the Noble Ones are then passed down in this manner and not wasted?"

"Yes, Your Majesty," replied the Elder. "Goods given as offerings to the *sāsana*[80] do not go to waste."

The king was greatly pleased and ordered five hundred more shawls brought and offered them at the feet of the Elder Ānanda. In this manner the Elder Ānanda received offerings of a thousand shawls each worth five hundred, on a hundred thousand different occasions. In the same way he received a thousand shawls worth a thousand each, on a thousand different occasions. He also received a thousand shawls each worth a hundred thousand, on a hundred different occasions. Apart from these, the shawls received in ones, two, threes, fours, fives, tens, and so forth, could not be counted. After the Buddha's death the Elder Ānanda walked all over the land of Daṃbadiva, himself making offerings of robes to monks living in all the monasteries.

Māgandī now thought, 'Everything I do turns out different to what was planned. What shall I do next?' She then devised yet another plan.

One day she left for the pleasure gardens with the king. [Before leaving] she sent a message to her uncle saying, "Go to Sāmāvatī's apartments, open the doors of all the storerooms containing cloths and oil, dip the cloths in the drums of oil, soak them, and wrap the cloth on the woodwork everywhere. Get Sāmāvatī and her five hundred women inside their quarters, close the doors, lock them from the outside. Get a lighted flare and torch the apartments from the top down and then make your escape." Her uncle agreed to do so.

He went to Sāmāvatī's quarters, opened the doors of the storerooms, took out the cloths, dipped them in drums of oil, soaked them, and began to wrap them around the woodwork. Sāmāvatī and her five hundred women saw him do this and coming up to him inquired, "What are you doing Uncle?"

---

79. Recycling, that is, not being careless or wasteful was considered a virtue. Monks especially were supposed to practice that virtue.

80. The term refers to the Buddha, his Doctrine, and the monastic order as a single entity. The nearest equivalent is the idea of a Buddhist church. I chose to keep the Sinhala word.

"Children, the king has ordered me to spread oil-soaked cloths on the timbers to prevent decay," he said. "It is hard to locate the good and bad spots. So do not stand near me children." With that he sent those who came up to him back to their chambers, closed the doors, locked them from outside, and starting from the top story he lit fires here and there. Climbing down he left the palace.

Then Sāmāvatī advised the other queens thus: "If we consider all those times in past births as we traversed this endless cycle of *saṃsāra* when we died in similar fires, even the Buddhas would not be able to keep count of all of them. Therefore cultivate compassion toward this brahmin engaged in such a heinous act and toward Māgandi who ordered this torture. Be vigilant in doing so." Thus she advised them. The queens then concentrated on the pain and made it the focus of their meditation as the palace burned around them. Some of them achieved the state of *sakadāgāmins* [Once Returners]; others achieved the state of *anāgāmins* [Non-Returners].

Monks who came to the city to beg, ate their meal and in the evening came to the Buddha, worshiped him, sat on a side and informed him of what had happened. "Your Reverence, while King Udēnī was in his pleasure garden the palace caught fire and Sāmāvatī and her retinue of five hundred queens burned to death. Of the five kinds of fate that befall the dead such as going to hell what fate befell them? What will happen to them in their next birth?"

The Buddha replied, "Oh monks, some of them were *sōvān* [Stream-Enterers]; some were *sakadāgāmins* [Once-Returners]; some were *anāgāmins* [Non-Returners]. Therefore those female devotees did not die with their purpose unfulfilled. They died fulfilled. The Buddha then made this joyful utterance: "Monks, creatures wandering in *saṃsāra* are not always vigilant about doing Acts of Merit. Sometimes they are heedless and do Acts of Demerit too. Therefore as wanderers in *saṃsāra* they partake of both happiness and sorrow.

When King Udēnī heard that Sāmāvatī's quarters had caught fire he ran there instantly but could not get there before it had burned down. When he arrived he put out the flames and consumed by grief sat amid his ministers recalling Sāmāvatī's acts of goodness. He pondered on who could have done this act and realized that it could have been done only by Māgandī. 'If I frighten her and question her she will not admit it. I shall therefore employ subtle ways to inquire into it,' he thought.

He called his ministers and said to them, "Listen good men. Formerly I lived in fear not knowing whether she who was my first queen would do me some harm. She kept looking for an opportunity to do so. Now my mind is at rest. From now on I shall live happily."

"Your Majesty, who did this for you?" asked the ministers.

"Whoever it was it was done out of love for me," he replied.

Māgandī who happened to be nearby heard the king's words and said, "Your Majesty, is there anyone else intelligent enough to do something like this? I instructed my uncle and got him to burn the palace quarters."

"There is no one but you who loves me," said the king. "I am very pleased with you. You have put my mind at ease. I will grant any request you wish to make. Ask your relatives to come immediately."[81] She agreed and sent a message to her relatives saying, "The king is well pleased with me and has promised me gifts. All of you come here without delay."

Māgandī's relatives who arrived in answer to her message were treated with great largesse. Hearing news of that [largesse] some who were not her kinsmen also bribed their way in. The king then rounded them all up, cut pits in the courtyard, stood them in the pits and filled them with earth up to their navels, spread straw on top, and set them on fire. When just their skins had burned he ploughed them down, shredding them into pieces and so killed them. Māgandī's body was cut with a sharp knife, the flesh prized from the fleshy parts, put in a pan of hot oil, cooked as if it was a food, and fed back to her.[82]

Now the monks who were gathered in assembly began to talk among themselves. "It is not fitting that a lay devotee of such goodness should have met such a death." The Buddha arrived and asked, "Monks, what were you discussing before I came?" When informed of it he said, "Monks, Sāmāvatī and her women did not do anything to deserve this death in this life. The death that overtook them is fitting only in the context of the Acts of Demerit performed in an earlier life."

"Your Reverence, what was it that all of them did in the past to cause such a death? Relate it to us in detail," asked the monks. The Buddha thus invited narrated the following story of their past.

5e

"Long ago when King Brahmadatta ruled in the city of Baranäs [Varanasi] he invited eight *Pasē* Buddhas to the palace regularly to eat their meal. The

81. The invitation to the relatives is perhaps because it was Māgandi's uncle who, at her bidding, had burned down Sāmāvatī's quarters. Relatives of a queen had power and influence at court so long as their kinswoman was in the king's favor. The reverse was true when she fell out of favor.

82. In this gory description of punishment there is no critique of the excessive brutality of the king, especially in his killing of Māgandi's innocent kinsmen who had nothing to do with her crime. It is in sharp contrast to Sāmāvatī's compassion toward her killers. The excessive violence indulged in by king in the execution of justice seems to pass without comment perhaps because Sāmāvatī is the center of focus in the story.

king's five hundred women attended on them. Of the eight *Pasē* Buddhas seven went back to the Himalayas. One of them retired to a grassy grove beside the river. There he engaged in meditation and arrived at a Trance State.

One day the king made an offering of food to the *Pasē* Buddha and then left for the river for water sports with his five hundred women. The women spent the better part of the day sporting in the water and thereafter feeling cold and wishing to warm themselves looked for a place to build a fire. They came upon the grassy grove and thinking it was just a heap of grass set fire to it from all sides. As the grass burned and shriveled they saw the *Pasē* Buddha [seated there]. They thought, 'Alas, what have we done! If the king were to see this he will surely punish us. Let us allow it to burn completely so that the king will know nothing of it.' All the women together gathered firewood from the surrounding area, covered the *Pasē* Buddha in a huge pile of wood, set it on fire, and left without a doubt that not even his bones would be left. These five hundred women who at first unknowingly and without intending to cause suffering set fire to the grass, subsequently devised a plan intended to cause suffering.[83] They were then caught in an Act of Demerit.

When *Pasē* Buddhas go into a trancelike concentration even if one were to haul a thousand caravans of firewood and set the place ablaze, quite apart from burning his body the fire cannot singe even a single hair. Thus on the seventh day that *Pasē* Buddha, completely unharmed, rose from his Trance State and comfortably left. But as a result of that Act of Demerit those five hundred women burned in hell for several hundred thousand years. Thereafter, as a further consequence of that Act of Demerit during a hundred lives in *saṃsāra* they died in this same manner when their houses burned down. This was the Act of Demerit they committed in a past life.

5f

When the Buddha told this story the monks asked again, "Your Reverence, for what Act of Demerit was Khujjuttarā born a hunchback? For what Act of Merit did she become ordained? As a consequence of what act has she become a *sōvān*? For what Act of Demerit did she become a servant and have to serve others?"

The Buddha replied, "Monks, during the time that the same king was ruling in Baranas, one of the *Pasē* Buddhas among the lot of eight had a

83. This is an important distinction in Buddhism. Acts of volition have *karmic* consequences. Acts unwittingly done, do not.

slightly hunched back. A woman who was attending on him, covered herself in a gold-colored cloak, took a gold plate in her hand and saying, 'Our *Pasē* Buddha walks like this,' mimicked him walking with a bent back just as he did. For that Act of Demerit she was born a hunchback.

One day the king invited that *Pasē* Buddha to the palace, called for the monk's bowl, served some hot milk-rice into it, and offered it to the Buddha. The bowl of milk-rice was very hot and burned his hands so when he took it he shifted it from hand to hand. A woman noticing the *Pasē* Buddha shifting the bowl from hand to hand took eight cloth rings made as pot stands and gave it to him saying, "Place the bowl on these." The *Pasē* Buddha did so and looked at the woman to see whether she desired to have them back. "Your Reverence, what use are these to us? Take them with you," she said.

The *Pasē* Buddha then left for the Nandamūla rock. Those cloth rings can still be seen there today, well preserved. As a result of that Act she is today a woman of great wisdom and expert in the *Tripitaka*. Because she attended those *Pasē* Buddhas in the past she has now attained to the state of a *sōvān*. These are the Acts of Merit and Demerit she has done in the dispensation of a former Buddha.

Then, in the time of the Buddha Kassapa, there was a certain noble merchant in the city of Baranas who had a daughter. One afternoon she took a mirror in her hand and began to adorn herself. A trusted companion, who was an *arahat* nun went to visit her. Nuns, though they are *arahats,* in the evenings, like to visit the families of those who attend on them. On that day, the nobleman's daughter had no one to send for something she wished to get. She happened to see the nun and said, "Your Reverence, will you bring me that casket over there in which I keep my ornaments?" The nun thought, 'If I do not fetch the casket of ornaments this noble merchant's daughter will be angry with me and burn in hell as a consequence of that anger. If I bring it to her she will be born as a servant in the service of others. It is better to be born a servant than to suffer in hell.' Therefore, out of compassion for her she brought the casket of ornaments and gave it to the nobleman's daughter. For that Act of Demerit of getting such service from that nun, she was born a servant and had to serve others."[84]

On another occasion the monks gathered in council and talked among themselves saying, "Sāmāvatī and her five hundred women were burned to death in their own quarters. Māgandī's five hundred kinsmen were set on fire with straw heaped on their heads and their bodies were mowed down with

84. The Acts of Merit and Demerit were done over different time periods resulting in several separate stories even though the consequences of those acts came together in a single lifetime.

iron ploughs and so died. Māgandī herself was fried in oil as in a sauce of molten lead and killed. Of these which can be said to have lived and which to have died?"

The Buddha arrived there and said, "Monks, if one is slow to do Acts of Merit even if one were to live a hundred years one is as good as dead. But if one is not negligent in performing Acts of Merit even though dead one is alive. Thus even if Māgandī had been alive she would be as good as dead. Though Sāmāvatī and her five hundred women died, they are not dead. Monks, those who are not slow to do Merit do not die." The Buddha thereafter preached the following sermon.[85]

"Oh monks, to be constantly vigilant and to engage in Acts of Merit is the way to *nirvāṇa*. If one is confused, lacks mental control, is addicted to pleasure, and thus slow to do Acts of Merit then that is the way to death. Why so? Those noble ones who do good and achieve *nirvāṇa* are not born again and so cannot die. Those foolish ones who do not do Acts of Merit and instead engage in Acts of Demerit are not released from *saṃsāra*, are born again and again, and so must die again and again. Wise ones who hasten to do good do not die, unlike those foolish ones who engage in Acts of Demerit. Those who are slow to do good see no end to their sufferings in *saṃsāra*. Those who hasten to perform Acts of Merit see an end to their *saṃsāric* sufferings. Those who delay in doing good are not released from the bonds of birth and though alive are as good as dead. Those who do not delay in doing Acts of Merit and whose Acts are come to fruition instantly achieve the Path and the Fruits. In their second and third incarnations they are not subject to rebirth; though they die they are not dead. Those who are heedless and do not do Acts of Merit are like the dead. They cannot help themselves in any way, so though not dead, are as good as dead.

The wise understand this well and take delight in these things that are the province of Buddhas, *Pasē* Buddhas, and *arahats:* namely the nine Spiritual Attainments[86] and the Thirty Seven Doctrines [Conditions] conducive to Enlightenment. These in turn have divisions such as the Four States of Mindfulness. Those wise ones who are not negligent attain the following twofold Trance States of Concentration; namely the eight states of Meditative

---

85. What follows is a rather tedious sermon very much in the style of village monks who wish to fill out their time by saying the same thing in many different ways.
86. [s. *nava lovuturā dahaṃ*] also translated in Buddhist literature as the "Nine Transcendental or Supramundane States." They consist of the Attainments of the Four Stages of the Path (*mārga*) the Four Fruits (*phala*), and "Enlightenment" or *nirvāṇa*—a total of nine. I translate the term simply as "Spiritual Attainments."

Concentration focusing on Objects, and the path of Insightful Meditation concentrating on Characteristics.[87]

From the time he leaves the state of a householder up to the point of achieving the state of an *arahat* he constantly maintains his physical and mental effort and never flags until he achieves the desired goal that can only be attained by intense human effort. Thus with constant effort he realizes *nirvāṇa* going through the four stages that are called the Noble Stages of Achievement." So these wise ones who go through this process realize the noble state of *nirvāṇa* free from fear that arises from the Fourfold Associations such as Lust."

At the end of this sermon many attained the Four Stages of the Path and the Fruits such as *sōvān*. Therefore virtuous beings should develop faith, not be slow to do good, and strive to attain *nirvāṇa* that is free from decay and death and can never satiate.

---

87. Such categories taken from the Abhidhamma were interspersed in sermons to illustrate a monk's erudition and familiarity with the more abstruse parts of the Doctrine. This entire section is added by the thirteenth-century translator and does not appear in the DA.

2

Viśākhā

Moreover, just as a Bōdhisattva may be born in a low caste but not lack goodness so with the story of Viśākhā we shall illustrate how, though born a woman (and women are of limited vision)[1] and though forced to associate with people who were of the right caste but held wrong beliefs, yet she herself did not lack vision. She performed many Acts of Merit and just as one cuts short something that is too long so she shortened her long journey in *saṃsāra*. This *saṃsāra* is considered long as its beginnings are imperceptible. Many who are blessed may realize its end. We shall relate this story so that others too may shorten their long journey in *saṃsāra*.

How does it go?

In the time of the Buddha Piyumatura,[2] seeing how a certain female lay attendant who had obtained eight Fervent Wishes[3] attended on that Buddha and wishing to do likewise, Viśākhā made a Fervent Wish to become a chief female lay attendant. She maintained this wish over a period of four uncountables and one hundred thousand aeons.[4] She was then born in Daṁbadiva in the city of

1. The literal translation of the text is "though born as a woman with limited ideas." The phrase "with limited ideas" is used to describe the word *woman* as a generic category. The point being made is that Viśākhā, though born a woman, was different.
2. One of the many Buddhas who preceded, by several aeons, the Buddha Gōtama.
3. Buddhists when they perform an Act of Merit make a "Fervent Wish" or *prārthanā* for a better rebirth. It is the nearest thing to a prayer in Buddhism.
4. The common phrase in Buddhist cosmology is [s. *sārā saṅkya kalpa lakśayak*] literally, four uncountables and one hundred thousand aeons. Time is counted in vast periods of cycles or *kalpa*s (translated as aeons for lack of a better term). But even "infinite" or "uncountable time," *asaṅkya,* is also measured and counted which somehow seems to extend the concept of infinity.

Bhaddiya in the Angu territory to Dhananjaya, the son of the great noble merchant Manda. She was conceived in the womb of his wife the noblewoman Sumanā and was born at the end of ten months. When she was seven years old the Buddha came to the city of Bhaddiya to preach to the Brahmin Sela and to others who were waiting, like lotus buds wait for the sun's rays, to attain to the full bloom of *nirvāṇa*. The Buddha, accompanied by many monks, arrived at the city of Bhaddiya after having traversed the three regions of the Inner Circle, the Central Circle, and the Peripheral Circle. He did so because there were fortunate[5] people in that city.

At the time, the great noble merchant Manda was the head of a household of five, all people who had done much Merit. The household consisted of the great noble merchant Manda, his chief wife a noblewoman named Sandapiyuṃ, her son the noble merchant Dhananjaya and his wife Sumanādēvi, and a servant named Puṇṇa who belonged to all of them. In addition there were four other noble merchants of great wealth named Jōtiya, Jatila, Pūrṇaka, and Kākavalliya, all in the territory under the rule of King Bimsara [Bimbisāra]. Together with the great noble merchant Manda there were thus five noble merchants of great wealth.

When he heard that the Buddha had come to the city of Bhaddiya where he lived, the great noble merchant Manda called his granddaughter, his son's child, Viśākha, and said, "Granddaughter there is a task of great benefit for you and for us. Gather your retinue of five hundred young women, ask them to bring you offerings, climb into five hundred carriages, and conduct the Buddha to this city."[6]

She agreed and left. Just as a piece of diamond though small cuts sharply and as a gemstone though tiny is vastly valued, so though young she was very intelligent and knew well to distinguish between what was good and bad. She went in the carriage to where the Buddha could see her, then dismounted, and going up to him worshiped him and stood on one side.

The Buddha studied her abilities and preached to her as if giving a child, yet young, a gift for coming to see him. Just as a sick person recovers the moment a medicine for that particular illness is administered, so by listening to a sermon and becoming a *sōvān* she recovered from three serious diseases[7] and was rid of the fear of *saṃsāra*. The five hundred young

5. People are considered "fortunate" to be born during the period of a Buddha's dispensation. They must have done Acts of Merit in the past to hear the Doctrine from a Buddha.

6. It is significant that the grandfather chooses her, a young woman, to go with her retinue to invite the Buddha.

7. They are *lobha* (attachment), *dosa* (ill will), and *moha* (illusion) which characterize the human condition and that are overcome when one becomes a *sōvān*.

girls who accompanied her also became *sōvān* and together they arrived at the city of *nirvāṇa*.

The great noble merchant Manda also went to the Buddha, heard him preach, and became a *sōvān*. On the second day he invited the Buddha to his home and made offerings of tasty foods to him and to his retinue of monks. In this manner for the duration of a fortnight he made great Offerings of alms. The Buddha remained in the city of Bhaddiya until all those who were fit to achieve *nirvāṇa* had done so. He then went on to another city.

At that time the sister of King Bimsara was married to the king of Kosol [Kōsala] and King Kosol's sister was the wife of King Bimsara. The two were thus brothers-in-law. One day the king of Kosol thought, 'King Bimsara has five very wealthy noble merchants, Jōtiya, Jatila, Mendaka,[8] Pūrṇaka, and Kākavalliya. I have none like them in my country. It would be a good idea to ask King Bimsara for one of them.'

He then went to the city of Rajagaha and there enjoyed King Bimsara's pleasant hospitality. When asked the reason for his visit he said, "You have five noble merchants in the land under your command. My country is like a temple that has no gods, like a pond that has no water, a tree that bears no fruit, a monastery without monks, a kingdom without a king. It lacks noble merchants. I came hoping to take one back with me. I would appreciate it if you send one of them with me."

"These are established families with large extended kin groups of children and grandchildren. They come of nobility rooted here over generations. They are firmly established and it would be impossible to move them," he [King Bimsara] replied.

"If you can't uproot any of the great nobles and if I don't get even one, then I too won't leave," said King Kosol.

'He is insistent so what shall I do?' thought [King Bimsara] and consulted his ministers. He realized that it would be as impossible to move the five noble merchants Jōtiya and others as it would be to move the earth, so he thought of the noble merchant named Dhananjaya, the son of the noble merchant Mendaka.

"I will talk to him and let you know," he [King Bimsara] said. Then he called him [Dhananjaya] and said, "Son, the king of Kosol has come to take back with him someone who can hold office as a noble merchant in his kingdom. Will you go with him?"

"However rich we may be we are but the subjects of our kings so how can we refuse? We have to go,"[9] he [Dhananjaya] replied.

---

8. Mendaka is the Pali form from which the Sinhala Manda is derived. Manda is how he is referred to earlier in this story.

9. The DA version merely states, "Your Majesty if you send me I will go." The SR version is a more nuanced response.

"Since you are not a small household can you agree to go just like that? Then make preparations to leave," said the king.

Dhananjaya made his preparations. The king treated him with great largesse because he was going at his personal request.

Then, handing him over to the king of Kosol, King Bimsara said, "If not for the fact that you so earnestly request it this is not someone I would easily part with. Take him with you."

[The king] led him away. As the king had been away [from his kingdom] for many days he did not wish to delay any further so they traveled rapidly not spending more than one night in one place. One evening they stopped at a comfortable resting place to take a break. The noble merchant Dhananjaya inquired; "To whom does this land belong?" King Kosol replied that the region belonged to him.

"How far is the city of Sävät?"[10] he asked again.

"About twenty-eight leagues," he was told.

Then he thought, 'We are a large company of people so it would be inconvenient to live too close to the city. It is easier to live a fair distance away.'

He said to the king, "If Your Highness has no objections we would like to remain right here."

The king agreed, built a city there, and then continued on.

They named the city Sāketa because they had stopped there to rest in the evening.

There was [already] a noble merchant named Migāra in the city of Sävät. If one asks why the king went searching for noble merchants when there was one already [in his kingdom] it was because though he [Migāra] was a merchant in name he was not rich like Jōtiya and the other four noble merchants. When the king said his kingdom was empty of noble merchants it was because there were no wealthy merchants there.

The noble merchant Migāra had a seventeen-year-old son named Pūrṇavardhana. His parents said to him, "Son we will bring a young noble woman for you [as a bride] from any family you wish."

"I have no desire for such complications in my life," he said refusing [their offer].[11]

---

10. p. Sāvatti was the capital city of the kingdom of Kōsala.

11. In several of these stories, when parents try to arrange a marriage their sons usually refuse "to complicate their lives." Then when pressed they make unreasonable demands for a perfect female who they hope can never be found. Marriage in traditional South Asian societies—especially among wealthy upper-class families—was considered a duty and an obligation for both men and women, not a matter of romantic love or infatuation, though such exceptions were also not uncommon.

"Don't say that, son. If you have no children your lineage will end. Choose someone from a suitable family and send for her."

His parents made the request again and again and he knew he would have no peace if he were to refuse so he said, "In that case, if you find a woman whose hair is like a black cascading river flowing down a golden mountain, blue-black like a swarm of bees attracted to a beautiful lotuslike face, hair that when untied falls down to the ankles yet curls up without touching the ground. One whose lips are like a pair of pearly boats sailing on the ocean of her beauty, whose teeth are lovely like a row of diamonds set on a sheath of coral, whose face, lit up by a set of pure teeth is like the sixteenth phase of the moon of sixteen phases. Moreover, if she be dark her complexion should be like a blue lotus. If she be fair, her skin must be unblemished and soft as a *kinihiri* petal. She should look like a sixteen-year-old even after she has given birth to ten children. If you can find someone like that I will consent to marry."

The parents invited a hundred and eight brahmins to their house, fed them milk-rice and inquired if a woman such as the one described could be found on earth. The brahmins had never seen anyone like that but they consulted their *vēdic* texts and said that such a one did exist. In that case, they were told to find such a woman and bring her. The parents chose eight of the one hundred and eight brahmins, gave them great wealth, and said, "If you find such a person and bring her you shall be entertained even more richly on your return."

Then giving a golden necklace worth one hundred thousand they said, "When you see such a woman adorn her with this so she can meet her expenses for rice and betel."[12]

They [the brahmins] went to all the main cities and made inquiries but did not find anyone like that. On their way back they stopped at the city of Sāketa. It was a day of festivities when everyone came outdoors. 'Today our search may be successful,' they thought.

This festival was an annual event in that city. On the festive day, even those who [normally] do not set eyes on the sun or moon,[13] step out into the open with their retinues and walk on foot to the riverbank, in full view of everyone and free of restrictions. [During the festivities] the sons of distinguished persons from among princes, brahmins, merchants, and farmers, stand along the road and choose mates from among those of their corresponding

12. In offering the gift as "pin money" for rice and betel—an initial gift of a trifle—the value of the necklace is ironically emphasized!

13. The reference is to young women of rich families and of high caste who were kept in seclusion in their households.

social groups by garlanding them.[14] The eight brahmins also waited in a certain hall by the riverbank.

Just then, the sixteen-year-old Viśākhā, like the full moon in its sixteenth phase, decked in the shining rays of her ornaments and accompanied by a starlike galaxy of five hundred young women went to the river, bathed, and stood on the riverbank. At that moment there was a sudden shower of rain. The five hundred young women instantly ran for shelter to the hall. The brahmins in the hall looked them over and decided that not one of them had the requirements stipulated by the noble prince. They waited to see who else would turn up. Shortly thereafter, Viśākhā walked slowly into the hall. Although eager to hasten her journey in *saṃsāra* she was in no particular hurry for ordinary journeys. As she had not hurried she came in all wet. The brahmins seeing her remarked, "Alas, this girl is surely lazy. With someone like her a husband will not get even the dregs [of gruel]."

"What did you say?" Viśākhā inquired and when they told her she asked again, "Why did you say that?" The brahmins answered, "Your retinue all ran in without getting wet. You did not run and came in wet. That was why we made that remark."

"Do not rush to conclusions. Though the others came running in I am stronger than them. I did not run for a reason," Viśākhā replied. They asked what that was.

"There are four categories of beings who are unattractive when they run and there is another, further reason.

"Who are they who are unattractive when they run?" asked the brahmins.

"Since you don't seem to know, I had better tell you.[15] If a king adorned with his crown jewels were to tuck up his clothes and run it would be very unattractive. Those who see him will ridicule him saying, 'This king runs like a peasant.' He should walk slowly as befits a king. If the king's elephant, decked in all its ornaments were to run, it would be ungainly. He should walk with slow elephant grace. A monk should not forget his normal even pace and run. Those who see him will say, 'He has forgotten how a monk should walk; he runs like a layman.' He will be ridiculed. It befits him to walk slowly. Above all women who run are most unattractive. People will say, 'What, she runs like a man and has no feminine grace' and laugh at her. She should walk

---

14. The DA only refers to this as a practice engaged in by the warrior caste or princes. The SR makes it a practice common to all social classes. Each however, is expected to choose a mate from his\her particular social group.

15. Note the confident, even ironic tone with which Viśākhā addresses the brahmin strangers.

slowly. I did not run because I thought, 'Why should I act in a manner not fit for a woman.'[16]

The brahmins heard her and asked, "My child, we now understand your reasons. But what was the other reason?

Just as one may intend to listen only to one short sermon but if the manner of preaching is very good one ends up listening to many, the brahmins engaged her in further talk in order to see her teeth. She explained the other reason too.

"When parents give birth to daughters they do not abandon them after they are born, as pigs do [their young]. They massage and mould their arms and limbs and hope to get some profit from it. We are salable goods. Saleable goods if covered and protected can be sold. If they are in someway damaged they cannot be sold. If, afraid of getting wet, we run and fall and break an arm or a leg then when the time for getting married comes there will be none to take us and we will be a burden to our parents.[17] What can happen if one gets wet? One goes home, changes one's wet clothes, dries oneself, and unhurriedly takes off one's ornaments. I thought of all this and came in unhurriedly," she said.

As she talked the brahmins noticed the two rows of her beautiful teeth like a pure white set of conch shells and said, "Such physical beauty is indeed fit for this" and garlanded her with the golden necklace. When she was garlanded [Viśākhā] knew that she was selected by a particular person and so inquired from what town they had come. They said they were from the city of Sävät. She then asked the name of the noble merchant who was the father of the young man who had sent them. It was the noble merchant Migāra, they said. She asked the name of the son and was told that it was young Pūrṇavardhana. She knew then that the caste was right and accepted it.[18] She [next] sent a message to her father saying, "When I came here I walked but send a carriage now for my return." Why did she have to return by carriage? Because she had been garlanded and was now betrothed. From the time one is garlanded one cannot go on foot [uncovered]. The children of the rich go

---

16. A very clear statement of what the culture thought of as feminine grace. A woman could walk to the riverbank in full view of the public and free of restrictions but she should not "run like a man."

17. These were the traditional cultural norms of the time prevalent among the wealthier social groups in many Asian societies. It was the responsibility of parents to see their children married. Unmarried girls were considered a burden.

18. There are reservations implicit in the questions. Caste and background were important factors in the acceptance, not the man himself. It is Viśākhā, not her parents who conducts the inquiry.

in palanquins and other such carriages and conveyances. Others would carry an umbrella or even a palm leaf to cover their heads. If even that was not available they would cover their shoulders with a corner of the cloth they were wearing. Viśākhā's father sent five hundred carriages for her.[19] She and her retinue climbed into the carriages and left. They took the eight brahmins with them.

The noble merchant saw the garland on his daughter and inquired of the brahmins from where they had come. When they said they were from the city of Sävät he asked the names of the nobleman and his son. He learned that the name was Migāra and the son's name was Pūrnavardana. He then inquired what wealth they had. They answered that it was four hundred million.[20]

'That is very little when compared with our wealth. It is like a mustard seed placed beside Mount Mēru. However, since they are from a family of noble merchants and since they have already garlanded her what use are such considerations?' he thought and accepted.

The noble merchant Dhananjaya entertained the messenger brahmins for one or two days and sent them back. They returned to the city of Sävät and said to Migāra, "You sent us to find a certain person and we have done so."

The noble merchant Migāra inquired whose daughter she was and when told she was the daughter of the noble merchant Dhananjaya he said, "Even if his daughters are not as beautiful [as stipulated] they are of great Merit. We must bring her soon" and informed King Kosol that he was going there to fetch the bride. The king then said, "I was the one who obtained him [the noble merchant Dhananjaya] from King Bimsara and brought him to that place so I will come too."

"Good," said Migāra and sent a message to the noble merchant Dhananjaya saying, "When we come to visit you the king will accompany us too. The royal retinue is large. Let us know if you can feed such a great number."

The noble merchant Dhananjaya's pride was even greater than his wealth. He responded saying, "Not just one king but even if ten additional kings were to come and stay here it would not matter. Bring them with you."

On hearing that the noble merchant Migāra, leaving behind only those who had to look after the houses in the city, gathered together all the rest, about seven million people and went to the city of Sāketa. He stopped within two leagues of the city and sent a message saying that the king and he had arrived. The noble merchant Dhananjaya sent gifts to the king and to the

---

19. There is an immediate change of status once a garland is accepted and the woman is "engaged to be married." A covering, however meager is a mark of her new dignity.
20. The term is forty *kela*. One *kela* was equal to ten million.

noble merchant Migāra. He then said to his daughter Viśākhā, "My child, your father-in-law has come accompanied by the king of Kosol. Where shall we lodge him and what residence shall we allot the king? Where shall we accommodate the subkings, the generals, the governor of Lanka,[21] the governor of the Tamils, the minister of Finance and other such personages?"

The nobleman's daughter whose mind was sharp as a diamond and who had made Rebirth Wishes over one hundred thousand aeons, commanded that this particular residence be given to her father-in-law, this palace for the king, and these residences for the viceroys and the generals. Thus she allotted residences for all. She then called up the workers and assigned a certain number to attend on the king and a certain number to attend on the viceroys, ministers, and others. She also ordered some of her own workers to take over the care of the elephants and the horses of the guests for the duration of their stay lest the elephant keepers and the horse keepers should say that they came for Viśākhā's wedding but had no pleasure from it as they had to look after their animals.[22]

That very day Viśākhā's father summoned five hundred of the most skilled goldsmiths to make the bridal ornament for Viśākhā. He gave them twenty-five thousand [coins] of the purest gold and for the thread work that had to be done in silver he gave silver together with forty *näli* measures full of precious gems,[23] twenty-four measures of pearls, twelve measures of coral beads, and four measures of diamonds. The goldsmiths began their work.

The king stayed several days and sent a message to the noble merchant saying, "When so many of us stay for so long a period it becomes very hard

---

21. Here is an illustration of the interpolation of the translator's thirteenth-century context into the fifth-century text. The governor of Sri Lanka and the governor of the Tamils were nonexistent categories in the time of the Buddha or of Viśākhā. They were a part of the thirteenth-century translator-author's world. The Tamil presence too would be very much a factor in the Sri Lankan consciousness during this period as Sri Lanka at the time was recovering from the devastating attacks of the South Indian ruler Māgha of Kālinga who conquered Sri Lanka in the twelfth century C.E.. The DA version merely states, "Your father-in-law has arrived and with him the king of Kōsala. Which house shall be made ready for him and which for the king and which houses for the viceroys?" (DA vol. 2, p. 68).
22. Viśākhā's organizational skills and the authority with which she handles the vast concourse of people who descended on her father have been replicated in generations of Theravada Buddhist women who see her as the Buddhist ideal of feminine competency and caring. The special attention paid to the humblest servant of a guest is even today regarded as an important duty for a hostess.
23. Gemstones and pearls are measured here not by their carat weight but by the quart, suggesting the immense wealth involved.

on you. Give your daughter in marriage to this nobleman's son quickly and help to speed our departure.

The noble merchant sent a message back to the king saying, "It is now the rainy season so it will be impossible to travel for the next four months. Your retinue consists of about seven crores. I will be responsible to see to all their needs. You can leave when it is time to do so." In this way he indicated to the king his wealth and power.

From that day on the city of Sāketa was decorated as for continuous wedding festivities. Food was served individually so that each one felt he or she was the recipient of special hospitality. Three months passed in this manner. The work on the [jeweled] ornament was not completed. Just as Viśākhā's Merit was very great so there was a great deal of work to be done on her ornament and it took time to complete.

Those who were preparing the meals told the noble merchant, "There is no dearth of rice and other things but there is no more firewood to cook the meals."

"Just because we lack that can we stop providing them meals? Break down the old elephant stables and the dilapidated horse stables and old houses and use them for firewood," the merchant commanded.

They did this for two weeks and then again said they were out of firewood.

"It is impossible to go far to look for wood because of the heavy rains. It is equally impossible not to provide them meals. Open the linen cupboards and take all the coarse cloth, make them into wicks, soak them in pots of oil, and use them as firewood for cooking," he ordered.

They did so and another two weeks passed and the four months were over. The work on the ornament was also complete. That ornament was not woven with thread. What had to be done with thread was done in silver thread. When the ornament was worn it fell from her head to her ankles. There were rings at different points in order to keep it in place. The hooks were of gold. The clasps were of silver. There was a chain with a hook for the headpiece. There were two hooks for over the ears, one for the neck, two for the shoulders, two for the two elbows, and two for the hips. From that point as there was no further need of them for the lower part, there were none. On the very top of the ornament was a dancing peacock. On its right wing were five hundred bronze feathers overlaid in gold. On the left wing were similar five hundred bronze feathers overlaid in gold. Its beak was of coral beads. Its eyes were blue sapphires. Its body and feathers were also of blue gems. The bronze wings were overlaid in silver. Its feet were similarly of silver. When the ornament was worn the peacock on Viśākhā's head looked like a live peacock dancing on a golden rock. The sound of the thousand bronze feathers was like a heavenly song or an orchestra of five kinds of instruments. Only if one stood close could one know it was not a real peacock. The ornament was worth nine crores in gold. The workmen were paid a hundred thousand for their labor.

What merit had Viśākhā done to obtain such an ornament?

In the time of the Buddha Kassapa she had made an offering to twenty thousand *arahats* of cloth for robes and thread and needles with which to sew them. When the sewing was completed, with her own income she provided all the necessities for dyeing them. The bridal ornament that she obtained was a result of this Act of Merit. If a woman makes an offering of robes, bowl, or any of the eightfold requisites for monks[24] she will acquire worldly blessings in the form of such superb bridal ornaments. If men make such an offering the result will be that in the time of a Buddha they will hear the words, "Monks, come hither" and instantly their clothes and ornaments will disappear and be magically replaced with the three robes and bowl and they will become *arahats*.

After about four months the noble merchant prepared the wedding procession. As dowry for his daughter he gifted five hundred carts filled with gold coins; five hundred carts filled with gold plates, vessels, and cooking pots; five hundred carts filled with silver plates, vessels, and cooking pots; five hundred carts full of copper vessels, and copper cooking pots; five hundred carts filled with iron vessels and other cooking utensils; five hundred carts filled with silks, shawls, garments, and other textiles; five hundred carts filled with pots of ghee, containers of sesame oil and other kinds of oil; five hundred carts full of rice and other grains; and five hundred carts full of sickles, hoes, saws, axes, chisels, and other implements. He also gave ploughs and yokes and all else that was needed so that she would lack nothing wherever she happened to live. In order that wherever she went there would be someone to bathe her and wash her hair and comb it, adorn her with toe rings, beads, and other ornaments, he placed three handmaidens in each of the carts making a total of one thousand five hundred. Thereafter, wishing to give a gift of cattle he ordered his men thus, "Open the gates of the small cattle pens and in order to know which ones are to be given, stand at intervals of one league over a distance of three leagues in length holding three drums. Stand on either side of the road with your drums leaving a space of a hundred and forty *riyan*[25] in width. Do not stop them or allow them to stray until they fill up a space of three leagues in length and one hundred and forty *riyan* in width. When they have filled such a space, order the cattle herders to stand by [and stop anymore from leaving]." He then gifted that number of cattle

24. [s. *aṭapirikara*] (the eight requisites for a monk) They are three kinds of robes, a kerchief or small towel, a begging bowl, a fan, a razor, and a needle and thread.
25. [s. *riyan*] is equal to one and a half feet or eighteen inches.

contained in that space. The power of Viśākhā's Merit was such however, that though the men tried to stop them, sixty thousand [more] cows and sixty thousand bulls jumped over the fences and crowded in.

What Act of Merit had she done to have one hundred and twenty thousand cattle jump over the fences and crowd in, in spite of the herders trying to stop them? It was a consequence of the offering she had made [in a past life] even when they had tried to stop her.

In the time of the Buddha Kassapa, she had been born as the youngest of seven daughters of King Kiki and named Sanghadāsi [Servant of the Sangha]. She made an offering of the five kinds of milk products to twenty thousand monks and had continued to make offerings even when they tried to stop her. As a direct consequence of that Act of Merit the cattle jumped the gates and crowded in even when the herders tried to stop them.

When the noble merchant had given so great a dowry the nobleman's wife said to him, "You have given much because you are wealthy. But do you expect your daughter to fend for herself once she goes to that place? Why didn't you give her men and women servants?"

"It was not because I didn't intend to do it. It was in order to test who was most loyal to her. I will not force anyone to go with her if they don't wish it, nor will I keep back anyone who wishes to go. Therefore I will order anyone who chooses to go with her to accompany her. Those who wish to go will do so without further talk. You will know that they are the faithful ones. If some say they will go but don't do so, one can be sure they won't be loyal and faithful to her. It is not much use sending unfaithful or disloyal servants. That is why I did not command any to go," said the nobleman.

The next day was to be the wedding. He called his daughter to his room that evening and advised her saying, "My child you should live thus among your protectors [in-laws] after marriage."

The noble merchant Migāra who happened to occupy the next room overheard the advice given by the nobleman Dhananjaya. The person giving advice said, "My child while you live in the home of your in-laws do not give out live embers from within your home to those outside nor bring live embers from without into your home. Give to those who give generously. Do not give to the miserly. Give to those who give to you as well as to those who do not give to you. Live happily; eat happily; sleep happily. Be careful in your tending of the fire. Honor the gods within." He gave her these ten pieces of advice.

The next day he gathered together those who were to accompany Viśākhā and in the midst of the royal assemblage he called eight noble gentlemen and said, "Though she is mature in wisdom she is young in years. If you see any shortcomings on her part you should look into it."

He adorned his daughter in her bridal ornaments worth nine crores and gave her fifty-four million worth to buy perfumes for her bath and led Viśākhā into a carriage to send her to the city of Sävät. Then from his possessions around the city of Sāketa out of the fourteen rice-supplying villages each of which was as big as the city of Anuradhapura in Lanka, he called up his followers and said, "Anyone who wishes to accompany my daughter may do so." Thus he commanded. All who heard him wished to go, not so much because of the noble merchant's command but more because of the commanding power of Viśākhā's Merit. The residents of fourteen villages all left leaving none behind. This was the consequence of her having [in the past] involved others too in performing Acts of Merit.[26]

The noble merchant Dhananjaya then entertained the king of Kosol and the noble merchant Migāra on an even greater scale than before, paid his respects, accompanied them part way, and sending his daughter on, he stayed behind.

The nobleman Migāra saw the procession of people following behind and asked who they were. He was told they were servants who were part of his daughter-in-law's dowry. Because of his limited vision resulting from his lack of Merit he asked, "Who is going to feed so many? Beat them and stop them. Let only those who earnestly wish to come, follow," he commanded. Just as a king, however much territory he has, does not consider it excessive, and just as the sea does not overflow however many rivers may flow into it over however many aeons, and just as a fire does not stop burning however much firewood there is, so Viśākhā, because she was a woman of noble vision said, "Do not stop them. They will find food for themselves or do hired labor. Since they must live their allotted span they will find food for their survival."

But in spite of this the nobleman Migāra said, "Daughter-in-law, we have no use for so many. Do not be stubborn about it." As they did not stop following he beat them back and left taking only those he chose.

When Viśākhā reached the gates of the city of Sävät she thought, 'Should I ride in a palanquin or should I ride in a carriage? If I go in a palanquin the people of the city will not see the beauty of my bridal ornament. Although she was reluctant to parade her virtues she did not wish to hide the beauty of her ornament so she entered the city in a carriage. The people of Sävät saw Viśākhā, beautiful in her bridal ornament, virtuous both in terms of this world and in Spiritual Attainments, pure in mind, and since not many people had

---

26. It is specially meritorious to involve others in one's Acts of Merit. Thus even today, in organizing an alms feast, all friends, relations, and servants are invited to participate.

seen her when in the city of Sāketa, they now acclaimed her saying, "This Viśākhā is like a branch of the Parasatu[27] tree. Is this she? Her beauty becomes her." Thus she entered the home of the noble merchant Migāra in a great procession, like a flash of lightning piercing a white cloud.

The day she arrived the citizens said, "When we went to his city the nobleman Dhananjaya hosted us most generously." They therefore sent her wedding gifts each according to his means. Viśākhā did not hoard the gifts she was thus given. Instead she redistributed the gifts, giving what one had gifted her to another and what that one had gifted to the other one. She gave gifts to suit each one's age and status, saying, "Give this to our mother, this to our father, these to our nephews, these to our neices, these to our brothers, these to our sisters."[28] She inquired who had given the gifts and reciprocated accordingly with kind words. Thus on the very day of her arrival she won their hearts making the citizens all her kin.

On the night of her arrival a mare gave birth. Viśākhā asked her servants to bring lighted flares and went there herself, bathed the mare that had just given birth, in warm water, rubbed sesame oil on its body, and only then went to bed.

The nobleman Migāra who had arranged the marriage for his son decided, "We shall celebrate this wedding with a feast for our ascetics." Ignoring the Buddha who was residing in a neighboring monastery, like one who ignores a fire but tries to light a spark from a firefly, or as one who picks up gravel while there are gemstones lying around, so being a firm adherent of naked ascetics who were unashamed of sinning just as they were unashamed of going about without clothes, he invited them.

One day he had a preparation of milk-rice[29] made without the addition of any water and cooked in numerous new cooking vessels. He then invited the naked ascetics to his home and sent a message to Viśākhā saying, "Ask our daughter-in-law to pay her respects to these *arahats*." Viśākhā, because she was already a *sōvān* established in the pure faith, was thrilled to hear the word *arahat* and came to where they were eating. When she saw the indecorous and unrestrained manner in which they were eating, like a pack of hunting dogs fighting and champing on their food, she said, "Why do you ask someone like me to come before such shameless ones? You must not know the kind of person I am. It is unfitting."

She returned to her rooms. The ascetics saw her leave and like a pack of barking hounds, together they pounced on the noble merchant saying, "What

27. A tree that grows in heaven and does not die.

28. In addressing the people of Sävät in the terminology of kinship she displays yet another example of her intelligence and social skills.

29. Milk-rice cooked only in milk without the addition of water makes it special. It is also an auspicious ritual food.

is wrong with you, noble merchant? Are there no women in this large kingdom good enough for your son that you have to bring this miserable girl who is a follower of that monk, Gōtama? If you want your son to be happy throw this wretched creature out of your house immediately."

The noble merchant thought, 'She is the daughter of a very rich man. It is not right to throw her out for something as petty as this.' He replied, "Young people do not know how to act. Since Your Reverences are compassionate ones, forgive the girl." He then sent them away, seated himself on a couch with costly coverings, and began to eat the rich milk-rice off a golden plate.

At that time, a monk who was on his begging round going from house to house, came there, since that house too was along his route. Viśākhā was fanning her father-in-law as he ate. Since it was rude to say 'There is a monk at the door' and announce his presence to her father-in-law, she moved away so he could see him. The noble merchant saw the monk but being more greedy for his food than for any Acts of Merit he sat eating quietly as if he had not seen him. Viśākhā realized this and said to the monk, "Your Reverence, go begging to another house. Our father-in-law eats stale stuff."

Although the noble merchant had been patient and not thrown her out on the command of the naked ascetics, now, not understanding the true meaning of what she had said but interpreting it wrongly, he lifted his hand off his plate and said, "Throw out the food on this plate. On this day of celebration you have described the food on my plate as if it were feces. Are you suggesting that people like us eat feces? Get out of this house," he commanded.

He made this order but since all the people there [in that household] were Viśākhā's followers, who would dare to touch her in anger? Her father-in-law's command was irrational but she herself was rational so she said, "I did not come here like a serving girl picked up at a well and therefore will not go back alone. An orphan may leave like that but one who has parents does not walk out of the house merely because one is asked to go. When my father sent me here to you did he not also send eight noblemen for just such eventualities, to inquire into any faults or wrongs on my part? Send for them now and let them judge if I am at fault."

Though the noble merchant was not very clever, he was not impatient, so he decided to do as she requested. He called up the eight nobles and said, "Look, this child, as she stood fanning me while I ate, said I was eating feces when I was eating rich milk-rice. Is that not a serious insult? Confirm that she is at fault and send her out of this house."

They listened to what he said and asked if it was true.

"I did not say what he thinks I said. I saw a certain monk stand at the door begging and instead of asking someone to take his bowl or give him some rice my father-in-law sat there silently eating. I saw that and thought,

'Our father-in-law does not perform any Acts of Merit to stand him in good stead in the next world. He merely consumes the benefits of Acts of Merit performed in past births. Thus thinking about his past Acts of Merit I said this. What is wrong with that?" she asked.

"A single meaning can be expressed in many words and a single word can have many meanings. What she meant can be expressed in those words. Now that she has explained the meaning what fault can you find with our child?"[30]

"Good. It was my fault that I misunderstood her. But there is something else I wish to know. Once, in the middle of the night, she went to the back of the house with a few of her women. She did not inform us why she was going out and we did not know why she went. Like King Chūlani who found fault with Kevaṭṭa on the grounds that he stared at him with burning eyes, so although she did no wrong he found imaginary faults.

When the nobles inquired why she had done that, she said, "I did not go for any other purpose but that a mare gave birth to a foal that night. There was no one in this house who knew what to do. It would have been wrong had I too done nothing, so I got my women to bring flares and did all that had to be done for that mare. Tell me if what I did was wrong."

At that the nobles said, "Why Your Honor, the only wrong on the part of our daughter, who is yet so young, was that she did such demeaning work that even the servants in your household do not do. How can you fault her for what she did?"

The nobleman had to take back that accusation too.

Having nothing to say he agreed. "I accept that she was not at fault there. However, when she was about to leave, her father secretly gave her ten pieces of advice without any explanation. Since she neither examined nor questioned them I don't know what it was all about. I would like her to tell us their intention. First he said, 'Do not give out live embers from inside the home to the outside.' What if a neighbor comes asking for a live ember and one has a fire going in one's house, can one refuse as if hoarding a treasure?"

"What have you to say to that?" asked the nobles.

"Why would my father, who gave such lavish gifts, ask me not to give away embers? He knew I would understand so he conveyed a hidden meaning. He did not tell me to refuse to give out fire. What he said was, 'Look child, if there are shortcomings on the part of your in-laws or your husband do not report them abroad. There is no fire worse than carrying tales.' That was what he meant. Unless I understood wrong that was what he said."

---

30. This ironic characterization of the diplomatic handling a delicate issue occurs only in the SR.

"I accept that. But her father also instructed her not to bring fire into the house. If the fire in one's own house dies out how can one not get fire from outside?"

"What do you say to that?" asked the nobles.

"If that were the meaning would our revered father specifically tell me that? It would have been enough if he told it to those who accompanied me. What he said was, 'Look child, if your neighbors tell you about the faults of your in-laws and your husband, do not keep it in mind and repeat it for your own gain or to undermine their relations.' That was what he meant when he said not to bring fire from outside in. There is no fire more fierce than carrying tales from outside, inside. That was why he said what he did."

Instead of stopping from further questioning he disclosed his own stupidity by saying, "I accept she is not to be faulted for that but there were a lot more things he said. Her father told her to give only to those who give. When one gives gifts to children should one ask something back from them? Why did he say that?"

The nobles asked her what that meant.

"My father meant 'Child, if someone asks for a loan you should investigate the matter and give only to one who can pay back. The problems that arise from loans are many."

When asked what he had meant by saying, "Do not give to those who give not" she replied, "If when asking for a loan they say all manner of flattering things but when they have to pay back they cheat and do not pay, then by giving to such people one destroys one's wealth. One destroys one's friendship. No ill can result from not giving to such people."

"He also said, 'Give to those who give and don't give.' Since she has explained half the statement, that is to give to those who give, I accept that. But having advised her not to give to those who do not give what is the meaning of saying 'give also to those who do not give'? She must explain that too."

"What he meant was that when poor relatives and friends come to you for help whether they can pay back or not, one should give to them."

That too is accepted. But her father told her 'Sit well. We may not have seats prepared and ready everyday. How then is it possible to sit well?"

"He did not mean it like that. He meant, do not remain seated when in the presence of one's in-laws or husband. If one rises when one sees them, is that not being 'seated well'?"

"That too is just. I accept that. But he said 'Always eat well.' Even the king, on occasion, has difficulty in getting milk-rice. How then can one always eat well?"

"That too was not intended to mean what you think. He meant, 'Child, before you eat, first give your in-laws and husband to eat, then inquire who else has eaten or not eaten, satisfy them too, and thereafter when you eat you would have eaten well.' "

The noble merchant accepted that too. But he advised you to 'sleep well.' What does he mean? Does one have beds prepared and laid ready everyday?"

"That too is not as you think. What he said was, 'Child, after you eat you should not climb into bed before everybody else and sleep. You should perform the customary observances for your in-laws and husband and only thereafter go to sleep.'"

He accepted that too but said again, "He asked you to 'be careful and tend fire.' It is impossible to keep a fire going continuously. How can one do that?"

"What can I do about someone who does not understand a simple thing like that? It means one should treat ones in-laws and one's husband who provides for one with great care, as one would treat serpents or a flame of fire."

Since she had an explanation to all of his questions he accepted them. But he asked again, "What did he mean when he said 'Worship the gods within? Can you bring gods like Ishvara and Vishnu and keep them beside you?

"It is said that one has only as much intelligence as one has gained by Acts of Merit. Those who have done much Merit are born very intelligent. But even if one does not have too much intelligence how is it that one can be so unintelligent as not to know even that? One may not have done Acts of Merit in the past but if one has just simple human intelligence does one not acquire wisdom through discussion and conversation? Does he [Migāra] not have even that simple human intelligence? After having explained nine of the ten admonitions if I must still explain the meaning of the tenth one and he cannot figure it out for himself, then I shall have to explain it and make him comprehend. The 'gods within' are one's in-laws and husband whom one should treat as gods. That was what he said."

The nobleman Migāra having been told the meaning of the ten admonitions could find no further fault nor could he come up with any imagined fault, so he remained silent like the Pandit Sēnaka who had nothing to say once the Sirimevan question was explained to him.[31]

The eight nobles asked, "What have you to say, noble merchant? Do you find any further fault with our child?"

---

31. This is a reference to the *Ummaga Jātaka* where the Pandit Senaka debated with the Pandit Mahauśada on the Sirimendi issue—that is, whether it was better to be ignorant and rich or poor and wise. When he could not argue any further Sēnaka held his peace.

"No," he replied.

"If so what reason have you to expel her from your home if she is not at fault?"

Viśākhā then said, "If I had left the moment he asked me to go I would have been acting without restraint. Was it not for that reason that my father sent you eight nobles to accompany me? Have you not investigated the matter and know now that I am free of blame? It was not right to have left at that time. Now, it is not right I should stay. Therefore I will leave." She commanded her retainers to prepare the carriages for the journey.[32]

The nobleman Migāra got the nobles to support him and said, "Daughter-in-law, forgive me for my thoughtless words. By my speaking in that fashion the strength of your mind and your intelligence were revealed."

Viśākhā replied, "I am not stubborn so I do forgive you. I am the daughter and granddaughter of a family that have been firm believers in the Buddha's teachings. I cannot therefore live apart from the Three Refuges. The Three Jewels of the Buddha are of more value to me than all the gems on my wedding ornament. Therefore I will stay only if I can minister to the needs of the Buddha and his monks as I wish."

Though the noble merchant Migāra was not a believer at the time he wished to prevent Viśākhā from leaving, so he said, "You can minister to your *arahats* as you wish."

Viśākhā then invited the Buddha and on the second day conducted him to her palace for a meal. The naked ascetics heard that the Buddha was begging alms at the home of the noble merchant Migāra and surrounded the house. Viśākhā poured water for the Buddha to wash his hands and sent a message to her father-in-law, "The feast of alms is ready. Come and make the offering."

The naked ascetics stopped him from going. Since he was prevented from going he sent a message saying, "Ask our daughter-in-law to make the offering herself."

In the time of the Buddha Kassup Viśākhā had given alms to twenty thousand monks and so was well experienced in the art of giving alms. She made offerings to the Buddha and his monks and at the end of the meal sent a message [to her father-in-law] saying, "Although you could not participate in the offering of alms come and partake of the flavorful Doctrine."

---

32. Thoughout the investigation Viśākhā acts with tremendous dignity and answers with complete confidence. Her impatience with the stupidity of her father-in-law is clearly indicated in the SR text. The DA has a shorter paraphrased version of this section. The commanding manner and tone in which Viśākhā conducts the debate is lost in the DA version. Her decision to leave, of her own volition after she has been exonerated is a further indication of her confidence. She is no abject dependent but a woman of dignity.

'I have been called twice. It would be wrong not to go,' thought the noble merchant and hastened. The naked ascetics tried to stop him yet again but as he could not be stopped they said, "If you must go then do not go close to that monk, Gōtama; listen to him from behind a curtain." They went ahead and tied a curtain around to cut the Buddha off from view. Since Migāra had not yet reached the point when he could ignore their wishes he remained behind the curtain.

The Buddha thought, 'You may sit behind a curtain. You may sit behind a wall. You may sit behind a mountain of rock. You may leave this universe and if you can, you may go to another universe, but if there is a Buddha in the world it is I. There is no other Buddha. I can preach and make you hear wherever you are.' He then began to preach. Like one who takes hold of a Daṁba tree, two hundred leagues in height from its root to where the trunk branches, another two hundred leagues in height to the topmost branch, thus altogether about four hundred leagues tall, about four hundred leagues from the easternmost tip of the branch to the westernmost tip of the branch, and another four hundred leagues from the southernmost branch tip to the northernmost branch tip, about one thousand two hundred leagues around in girth, and just as one shakes the tree causing a rain of fruit to fall, or like one who creates a rain of ambrosia, so the Buddha began to preach.

> saddhamma desanā kāle piṭṭhibhāgādi nissitā
> puṇṇacandaṃ va gagane mukhaṃ passanti satthuno

> [When a Buddha preaches the Doctrine even those who sit behind him see his face as if it were the full moon in the sky.]

When a Buddha preaches, whether one sits in front or at the back, or at the sides, or whether they sit beyond hundreds, thousands, hundred thousands of universes, or as high as the Akhnita heaven of the Brahmas, each one says to himself or herself, 'the Buddha is looking at me and preaching to me alone.' By the power of the Buddha there is no one who will say that he did not look at them or see them. It is as if the Buddha looked at each one and spoke to each one alone.

The Buddha is like the moon. When the moon is up overhead, wherever one may be it seems to be above one. It is the same way with the Buddhas. Wherever one may be the Buddhas seem to be facing one. It is the result of the power that comes from the cultivation of the Thirty Perfections,[33] through such gifts as cutting off and donating a crowned head, the gifting of eyes that

---

33. [s. *samatis pāramitā*] consist of ten Perfections achieved by giving away material belongings; ten Perfections achieved by gifting one's physical body; and ten Perfections that involve sacrificing one's life.

shone with the five colors, the donating of blood, the donating of flesh, the giving away of a son of such pure intentions as the prince Jāliya, and of a daughter equally pure like the princess Krishnajinā, permitting them to be taken away as servants and the giving away of a wife like Queen Madri.

As the Buddha preached on and on the noble merchant Migāra though hidden from sight by a curtain could not be shielded from hearing. He heard the sermon and became a *sōvān* endowed with the thousand ways of knowing. Filled with pure faith, free of doubts about the Three Jewels, he lifted the curtain. Since he had attained [the Path to] *nirvāṇa* through the intervention of Viśākhā, but as he had only obtained the taste of it as a *sōvān* and that was but a little, wishing to have a drink of that *nirvāṇa* that Viśākhā had obtained, without going first to the Buddha [he went to Viśākhā] and as if sipping from a golden vessel he put his lips to Viśākhā's breast and said, "From now on you are my revered mother."[34] He placed her in the status of mother. He then went to the Buddha and as if adorning himself with red lotus, he placed his head at the Buddha's feet and worshiped him. From then on, Viśākhā was known as Mother of Migāra. Later she had a son and named him Migāra and so further established that name.

The noble merchant said, "Your Reverence I am the merchant Migāra." He repeated it thrice.

> sohaṃ ajja pajānāmi yattha dinnaṃ mahapphalaṃ
> atthāya vata me bhagavā suṇisa gharamāgata.
>
> [Alms given to whom is most beneficial—this I have indeed understood today. O blessed One, it is verily for my benefit that my daughter-in-law has come to this house.]

meaning, Your Reverence, all this time I did not know the power of the Three Jewels as I associated with naked ascetics. Today I know the worth of it because of my worthy daughter-in-law. Although I may be only partly free of the sorrows of *saṃsāra* at least I am now freed of the sorrows of hell. My daughter-in-law has come here to be my rescuer." Thus he praised Viśākhā. Viśākhā invited the Buddha on the following day also and gave a feast of alms on the second day too. On that day her mother-in-law became *sōvān*. From then on, all the wealth of that household was dedicated to the Buddha *sāsana*.

Thereafter the noble merchant thought, 'Our daughter-in-law has been of great help to us. Although it is impossible to reciprocate adequately I can do

34. This is an act of subjugation and great respect. It underlines the important status of a mother in the society.

something. Her bridal ornaments are very heavy and so she cannot wear them all the time. I shall have a lighter, smaller ornament made and adorn her with it. He had an ornament called a *ghanamaṭṭaka* made which was worth a hundred thousand. When the work was completed he invited the Buddha and his monks, made an offering of alms, had Viśākhā bathed in sixteen pots of perfumed water, placed the ornament on her in the presence of the Buddha, and worshiped him. The Buddha then placed the ornament of the True Doctrine on her, over the ornament named the *ghanamaṭṭaka* and thereafter, returned to the monastery.

From that day forth Viśākhā performed many Acts of Merit such as the giving of alms. She gave offerings of gruel, she gave alms to visiting monks, and gave alms again when they went elsewhere; she gave offerings of medicines to monks who were sick and thus obtained the boon of eight occasions to serve the Buddha, became known as the moon in the sky of the Buddha's *sāsana,* and grew old, rich in sons and daughters. That was how it was. Viśākhā had ten sons and ten daughters, a total of twenty children. Each of them had twenty children. Thus she had eight thousand four hundred and twenty children, grandchildren, and great-grandchildren in her lineage. She lived with her children and grandchildren for one hundred and twenty years. As they had performed Acts of Merit to obtain good health they all lived free of disease. All that time, over several lives, they had done Acts of Merit that acting like a dye, prevented their hair going gray.[35] All of them seemed always sixteen years old. When she went to the temple or someplace together with her children and grandchildren they seemed so much alike that people asked 'Which among these is Viśākhā?' If someone saw Viśākhā go by they would say, "Let her walk a little farther. Her walk is beautiful." If someone saw her stand they would say "Though her foot is still, she is lovely when she stands." If they saw her sit they would say "She is beautiful when she sits." If someone saw her lie down they would say "It is good if she sleeps a little longer. She looks beautiful when she sleeps." There was not anyone of the four postures that one could say was unbecoming. Moreover, because she did not have to walk any further in *saṃsāra* nor have to stay any longer in *saṃsāra*, was not caught up anymore in *saṃsāra,* and no longer had to sleep in the bug-ridden bed of *saṃsāra* her four postures were so pleasing.

Even though she was a woman because she had done much Merit she had the strength of five elephants. The king of Kosol heard about it and wishing to test her released his elephant just as she was returning after listening to a sermon. It raised its trunk and rushed toward her like a black

35. The use of the image suggests that dyeing of hair was not unknown in thirteenth-century society.

mountain. Her retinue of five hundred maidens were terrified and even though some were strongly attached to her, their love of life was even stronger and they fled. Some others embraced her and stayed.

"What is all this?" asked Viśākhā.

"The king wants to test your power and so released the elephant," they said.

'What is the use of running away at the sight of this creature? If I grip him too firmly he might die. How then should I hold him?' she thought. She held his trunk with two fingers and gripping gently bent it slightly. The elephant sat back as if struck with a goad, unable to stand. The people applauded. Viśākhā returned home safely. The king too was rid of his doubts.

Not one of Viśākhā's many children and grandchildren had ever been sick. They died of old age but not in midlife. It was the secondary *(karmic)* consequence of not having harmed living creatures. On auspicious occasions like the weddings of Viśākhā's eight thousand four hundred and twenty children, grandchildren, and great-grandchildren the citizens of Sävät were invited to their homes, fed, and only thereafter would they celebrate their weddings. At one such celebration the citizens decked in their finery, went to the temple since the sight of ascetic monks was also a form of celebration. Viśākhā too, adorned in her wedding ornament was on her way to the temple when she stopped midway. As she neared the temple she called a young woman who, like her, had the strength of five elephants and said, "Come here, girl. People like us should not go into the presence of the teacher adorned from head to foot in ornaments, like daughters of dancers going to festivities." She then removed her ornaments, tied them in a cloth, and gave them to the maidservant saying, "Give it to me to wear when I return from the temple." There was none but that young woman who could carry (the weight) of that wedding ornament. She gave that ornament to the maidservant and wore the *ghanamaṭṭaka* ornament instead.

She then went to the Buddha, heard him preach, worshiped him, and hastened home. The maidservant had absentmindedly placed the ornament in the monks' quarters. When those returning from listening to sermons leave something behind, the Elder Ānanda generally puts it away safely. On that occasion, seeing the wedding ornament he said to the Buddha, "Viśākhā seems to have forgotten her wedding ornament."

"Keep it aside," the Buddha instructed him.

The Elder also had the physical strength of five elephants. He therefore carried it and hung it near the staircase.

Viśākhā, together with the lay devotee Suppiya was in the habit of going to the monasteries to inquire who the newcomers were, who was leaving, or who was sick. When they went there the young monks would crowd around in order to get their plates and dishes filled with honey, crystallized sugar, and clarified butter. On this occasion too they crowded around her.

Suppiya saw a sick monk and asked, "What would you like to eat and drink?"

Ignoring the fact that as devotees of the noble *Āriya*[36] order they did not kill animals he said, "I would like to eat venison."

"Good, I will send some," she replied.

Unable to find any meat that had been inadvertently killed, and because it happened to be a time when rules were not specifically laid down, she cut a piece of flesh off her thigh, cooked it, and satisfied the sick monk's appetite for meat. By the power of the Buddha he was healed and the very next day the wound in her leg also healed.

Viśākhā too made her inquiries of the sick monks. While leaving from a side door but still within the monastery premises she said to the maidservant, "Girl, go fetch me my ornament to wear." The maidservant realized that she had unthinkingly placed it somewhere and said, "My lady, I left it somewhere without thinking."

"Then go and look for it where you left it and bring it to me. However, if the Elder Ānanda says he has kept it aside then let it be," she said knowing that he was in the habit of putting away what was left behind.

The Elder saw the maidservant and asked, "Why have you come?"

"I'm looking for the wedding ornament," she replied.

"I hung it near the staircase. Go and get it from there."

"I was asked not to bring it back if you had touched it," answered the girl. She went empty-handed to Viśākhā and told her what happened.

Viśākhā said [to her], "If the ornament has been touched by the hand of the great Elder Ānanda, my master, then I cannot wear it again. It now belongs to him. But he cannot care for it. I will sell it and bring him something that he needs."

"Go then and get it," he said.

She got it and gave it [to Viśākhā].

Without wearing it again Viśākhā took it home. She called the goldsmiths and had it valued. It was worth ninety million. She then placed it in a cart and said, "Take this and sell it."

As there was no one in any of the cities wealthy enough to buy it Viśākhā herself paid ninety million plus another hundred thousand and bought it back. Let alone buy it, there was no one in the whole world who could wear

---

36. Here the distinction is being made between nobility as a result of birth and true nobility that the Buddha ascribed to the *āriyas* or the caste of the "noble ones." *Āriya* meaning "noble" was used by the Buddha to define a moral category of goodness, not nobility by birth. It was intended as a counter to the brahmanic caste system that depended on birth.

it except for only three people. They were Viśākhā, Bandula Mallikā, and the daughter of the noble merchant at Benares.

Viśākhā placed the value of the ornament in carts, went to the monastery, and worshiping the Buddha said, "I did not want to wear the wedding ornament that had been touched by the Great Elder Ānanda so I decided to sell it and with the proceeds organize a sermon. I put it up for sale but up to now there has been no one in this city who could purchase it. Even if they were to buy it there is no one but me able to wear it. Therefore I myself bought it back and have brought the money to you. Of the Four Requisites[37] which one should I provide?"

The Buddha heard her and said, "Construct a building by the Eastern Gate and donate it to the monks." Viśākhā already knew that the Merit gained from constructing such a temple was very great and was happy. She purchased land from those who owned it for ninety million. With another ninety million she began construction of the monastery.

One day at dawn, when the Buddha was casting his eye over the world, he saw that a man named Bhaddiya who had left the world of the gods and had been born into a nobleman's family in the city of Bhaddiya, was now ready to attain *nirvāṇa*. He ate at the home of the nobleman Anēpidu and left in the direction of the North Gate.

Customarily the Buddha ate at Viśākhā's home and left by the South Gate for the Devraṃ monastery. Once the Pūrvārāma Monastery was built he would eat at the home of Anēpidu and leave by the Eastern Gate to reside in the Pūrvārāma monastery. But when he left by the North Gate they knew he would set out for the outer regions. Viśākhā, hearing that he was about to leave by the Northern Gate came quickly to the Buddha, worshiped him, and asked if he was going out to preach in the outer regon. When he answered that he was, she said, "I am spending one hundred and eighty million to build a monastery for Your Reverence so it would be good if you reside here."

"Do not stop me Viśākhā," said the Buddha.

Realizing that he had said this because there was someone who was ready and waiting to attain *nirvāṇa*, she added, "When you have gone on this journey that cannot be stopped, there is still work that I should and should not do. It would be good if you ask one of your monks to remain behind so he can instruct me in what I should and should not do." The Buddha agreed.

"If you wish a particular monk to remain behind then pick up his bowl," he said.

---

37. The Four Requisites [s. *sivpasa*] that a layperson should give a monk are robes, alms, a place to meditate, and medicines.

She had always had a personal liking for the Elder Ānanda. However, as the Elder Mugalan had great supernormal powers and with his powers she would be able to complete her work, she took his bowl. The Elder looked at the Buddha.

"Stay behind together with your retinue of five hundred monks," said the Buddha.

The Elder accepted the Buddha's request and stayed back. Because of his special powers anyone who traveled a distance of two hundred or even more than two hundred and forty leagues to look for timber would return that very day with whatever load he was carrying. Nor did they tire when they loaded the carts with timber and stones. Whatever load they put in the carts the carts would not break down. Before long a two-storied structure was completed. The lower story had five hundred rooms and the upper story had another five hundred rooms. The building thus had a thousand rooms.

Because the Buddha was preaching in the peripheral regions he traveled for nine months and then returned to the city of Sävät. The two-storied building that Viśākhā was having constructed was on such a scale that the work was not likely to be completed in nine years. However, because of the supernormal powers of the Elder Mugalan and the power of Viśākhā's Merit and the power of the Buddha it was completed in nine months. The pinnacle of the building was in gold and large as if it could hold sixty pots of water.[38]

Hearing that the Buddha was on his way to the Devramvehera monastery Viśākhā went to meet him while he was yet on his way. She conducted him to the monastery she had constructed saying, "Your Reverence, do not go elsewhere for these next four months but reside here in this new monastery I have built. I will perform the completion ceremony for you." The Buddha agreed to stay. From that day forth she did not let the Buddha and his monks go out to beg for alms but carried the food to the monastery instead.

One of Viśākhā's nieces brought a piece of cloth worth a thousand and said to Viśākhā, "I wish to lay this out on the floor of your building as a carpet. I ask your permission to do so."

"Niece, if I were to say that there was no space you would think that I was unwilling to grant you permission. Go yourself upstairs and downstairs into the thousand rooms and find a place to lay it." She took the cloth worth a thousand and looked around the building but found nothing there that was of lesser value. Disappointed that she was unable to perform this Act of Merit [by making the offering] she stood by weeping. The Elder Ānanda saw her weep and as in the *Sattubhatta Jātaka*[39] when he was born a brahmin and the

38. Pinnacles were often shaped like water pots, rounded at the bottom and tapering up to the top. Hence the image.

39. A birth story of the Buddha illustrating his wisdom.

Buddha was born as the Pandit Sēnaka and he had been asked by Sēnaka why he was weeping, so now he asked her why she wept.

When she told him the cause he replied, "Do not be disappointed. I will show you a fitting place for it. Put it in a heap by the foot of the staircase leading down from the upper balcony. The monks as they wash their feet [on entering] will wipe them on your cloth before they enter the inner rooms. You will get much Merit by that act." Thus he made her participate in the Act of Merit by having her put it in a place that even Viśākhā had overlooked.

For the entire four months Viśākhā gave alms to the Buddha and his monks within the inner monastery. On the last day she gave gifts of cloth sufficient for each of them to make their three robes just as in the time of the Buddha Kasub [Kashapa] she had given gifts for twenty thousand and kept what was left over for yet another monk. The youngest monks obtained cloth for robes worth a thousand gold coins as if gold was not scarce at the time. She filled the alms bowls of each monk with clarified butter made of cows' milk and sugar and medicines since clarified butter was not scarce for a person who possessed so many cows. If one were to put a value on it she had spent ninety million just on giving alms. She had spent ninety million for purchasing the land for the monastery, ninety million for its construction, and ninety million for the Feast of Alms at the conclusion of the work on the monastery. She spent a total of two hundred and seventy million for the Buddha and his *sāsana*. Up to that time there had been no one other than Viśākhā who, though born a woman and having to marry into a non-Buddhist household, had spent so much for the sake of acquiring Merit.

On the day the monastery was dedicated, in the afternoon, surrounded by her children, grandchildren, and great-grandchildren, she walked around the building and reminiscing that all she had fervently wished for had come to pass without the slightest inadequacy, she chanted the following stanzas:

kadāhaṃ pāsādaṃ rammaṃ sudhāmattikalepanaṃ
vihāradānaṃ dassāmi saṃkappo mayha pūrito

kadāhaṃ mañchapīthaṃ ca bhisibimabohanāni ca
senāsanabhaṇdaṃ dassāmi saṃkappo mayha pūrito

kadāham salākabhattaṃ suciṃ mamsupasevanaṃ
bhojanadānaṃ dassāmi saṃkappo mayha pūrito

kadāhaṃ kāsikam vatthaṃ khomakoṭumbarāni ca
cīvara danaṃ dassāmi saṃkappo mayha pūrito

kadāhaṃ sappinavanītaṃ madhutelañca phānitaṃ
bhesajjadānaṃ dassāmi saṃkappo mayha purito[40]

saying, "I used to think, 'When shall I construct a building that is like the celestial mansion Vijayot for the world of men, whose white-plastered radiance outshines Mount Kailaśa, and make an offering of it to the Buddha'—that wish has now been fulfilled. I used to think 'When can I fill such a building with beds, mattresses and pillows and all such necessities?'—that wish too has been fulfilled. I used to think 'When can I prepare meals made of pure and tasty foods and make ticketed[41] offerings to the *sangha*?—that wish too has been fulfilled. I used to think 'When can I make an offering of fine cloth and textiles, cut up and made into robes for the *sangha*?'—that wish too has been fulfilled. I used to think 'When shall I be able to fill the begging bowls full of clarified butter, honey, jaggery, and other things and make offerings to the *sangha?*—that wish too has been fulfilled." She chanted these five verses indicating all this.

The monks heard her and went to the Buddha saying, "Your Reverence, up to this day we have never ever heard Viśākhā sing. Today, accompanied by her children and grandchildren, she walks around the building singing like a little girl. What is happening? Exhausted by her efforts to complete the building to perfection has her bile become upset and has she gone mad? Or is she under some demonic spell"?

The Buddha replied, "Monks, she is not singing crazy songs. She is delighted that the Fervent Wishes she has made have been fulfilled and so sings in praise."

"When did she make these Fervent Wishes?" they asked.

"Do you wish to know?" he asked.

When they said "Yes, Your Reverence," he continued.

"Monks, in the 100,000th *kalpa* [aeon] prior to this Bhadrakalpa that was adorned by the five Buddhas and in which I too attained Buddhahood, there was born a Buddha named Piyumatura. Throughout the one hundred thousand years in which he lived apart from when he traveled through the air, if he ever traveled to someplace on the earth, white and red lotuses would spring up, their petals ninety *riyan* long, their pistils thirty *riyan* long, with

40. I have not given the translation for the Pali here as what follows in the text is an exact translation of the Pali.

41. [s. *lābat*] comes from the word *salāka batta* (ticketed rice). It refers to offerings made by lay devotees who selected an allotted day to make their offerings of food to the monks. It was customary for monks to get such "meal tickets" to specific homes of the laity on specific days. By this means everyone had a chance to make an offering and monks had a regular schedule of meals.

pots of pollen and stalks that were twelve *riyan* long. Since he walked stepping on these lotuses he was named the Supreme Lotus Buddha Piyumatura. The city of his birth was called Hansavatī, his father was King Ānanda, his mother was Queen Sujātā, and he had a permanent retinue of a hundred thousand monks.

If a woman were to attend on that Buddha, she would get eight Fervent Wishes. One such female lay devotee attended on that Buddha. She would go each morning and evening to pay him reverence. A friend of that lay devotee who went along with her to the monastery saw how closely she was devoted to the Buddha and thought, 'What Act of Merit must one do to be able to serve a Buddha as closely as this?' She went to the Buddha and asked, "Your Reverence what is my friend, this lay devotee to you?"

"She is my chief female lay devotee," he replied.

"Your Reverence, what Act of Merit must one perform to obtain that title?"

"She made a Fervent Wish performing Acts of Merit over a period of one hundred thousand aeons."

"Can I now make such a Fervent Wish and obtain that title?" she asked.

"Yes, you can make a Fervent Wish now and obtain such a title because I am not the only Buddha, and she is not the only chief female lay devotee."

"Your Reverence, in that case will you and your one hundred thousand monks accept my invitation and accept my offerings for one week?"

The Buddha agreed.

She then made a great flood of offerings for a whole week and at the end of the week made offerings of robes and cloths to the Buddha and his monks, and worshiping said, "Your Reverence, by making these offerings I do not ask for the luxuries and blessings of the god Sakra or the god Brahma. May I instead, attend on a Buddha such as you, obtain eight Fervent Wishes, have the status of a mother, and be foremost among the women to attend on him providing the Four Requisites?" She thus made a Fervent Wish.

The Buddha looked into the future with his special powers and saw that just as she had made a great offering so her Fervent Wish would come to pass and said, "One hundred thousand aeons from now a Buddha named Gōtama will be born on earth. The city of his birth will be Kimbulvat; his father will be King Suduvun; the queen-mother will be named Mahāmāyā. The chief disciple on his right will be Sariyut. The one on his left will be Mugalan. His two chief female disciples will be named Khēma and Uppalavannā. The great Elder Ānanda will be his chief attendant and see to his needs. A noble merchant named Anātapiṇḍika will be his chief lay attendent. At that time you, like a branch of the wish-fulfilling tree, will be named Viśākhā and will obtain the eight Fervent Wishes you have now wished, in his dispensation. You will have the staus of a mother, will attend on the needs of the Buddha and as chief of the [female lay] devotees, you will climb to that place of eminence, and attend on him."

Since it was revealed with precision that this was to happen in a hundred thousand aeons she felt as if it were going to happen the very next day. She continued to do Acts of Merit for as long as she lived and when she died was born in the world of the gods. Sojourning in the world of the gods and men she was once born in the time of the Buddha Kakusandha as the youngest of seven daughters of the king of Kāsi named Kiki. She sought no refuge other than the Three Jewels, and was named Sanghadāsi [servant of the *sangha*]. For twenty thousand years together with her sisters she performed many Acts of Merit and in the time of the Buddha Kasub too she made a Fervent Wish to obtain this position. Since that time because the Acts of Merit performed were many, she was not born in hell but was born in the worlds of gods and men and enjoyed many blessings and luxuries. On this round she was born as the daughter of the noble merchant Dananjaya, son of the great noble merchant Manda, and has performed many Acts of Merit in my dispensation. She does not sing in madness. All that she has wished for has been fulfilled so she is singing in joy.

Then as if giving gifts to messengers, he added, "O monks, just as a skilled garland maker selects flowers of varied colours from a heap of flowers and makes different garlands, some with stalks all in a single direction, some with stalks at the two ends, and some with stalks in alternate directions, so human beings perform different Acts of Merit such as feasts of alms, observance of precepts, meditation, transference of Merit, receiving of Merit, preaching sermons, listening to sermons, and serving one's teachers and virtuous persons and many other such Acts. However skilled the garland maker, if he is short of flowers he cannot make garlands in the way he wishes. Alternatively, if the garland maker is not skilled, even if he has a great many flowers he cannot make good garlands. If the garland maker is both skilled and has a great many flowers, he can make good garlands. Similarly, if one is skilled but does not have the resources and although one has faith one is poor, then one cannot perform such Acts. If one has great wealth but has no faith and is not skilled in doing such Acts then one cannot perform Acts of Merit. But if one, like Visakha, is both wealthy and desirous of performing Acts of Merit then such people perform Acts of Merit. Wealth that those without faith accrue is like a pond guarded by demons.

Therefore the wise, established in virtue should avoid Acts of Demerit, perform Acts of Merit, and purify their minds and actions.

3

Utpalavarṇā

Moreover, to illustrate the serious consequences of serious Acts of Demerit we shall relate the story of Utpalavarṇā.

How does it go?

In order to become the chief female disciple of the Buddha, the Senior Nun Utpalavarṇā did not have to make Fervent Rebirth Wishes over a period of four uncountable and one hundred thousand aeons, but only for one hundred thousand aeons. Thus, in the time of the former Buddha Padumattara she made a Fervent Rebirth Wish to become a chief disciple and obtained from him a Prophetic Declaration[1] that it would so happen. She performed meritorious acts over a period of one hundred thousand aeons during which time she was born in the worlds of gods and men. Then, in the time of our Buddha she left the world of the gods and was born to a noble family in the city of Sävät.[2]

Since the rank of second chief disciple, whether male or female, had to be filled by one of dark complexion[3] she was born as dark skinned as a

1. [s. *varaṃ*] is a term difficult to translate and the closest meaning one can come to is "a promise that it shall be so." In the ritual context it is often translated as a "warrant." I translate it as a "Prophetic Declaration."
2. To be born a human, especially in the time of a Buddha is preferable even to being born in heaven, because on earth one has the possibility of performing Acts of Merit that lead to *nirvāṇa*. In heaven one can only enjoy the consequences of one's past good acts and that for a limited time, because when that is over one will be reborn back in the *saṃsāric* cycle.
3. Of the chief disciples of a Buddha one was always dark complexioned, the other light. Thus of Gōtama's disciples, Sariyut (Sariputta) was light complexioned and Mugalan (Mogallana) was dark complexioned. While there are stories to explain why Mugalan was born with a dark complexion the symbolic significance was perhaps to emphasize the all-embracing inclusiveness of the Doctrine in the context of the varied peoples and castes of the subcontinent.

garland of blue lotus blossoms and was named Utpalavarṇā [Blue Lotus]. When she grew to be a woman every prince and nobleman in Daṃbadiva sent envoy after envoy to her father asking for her hand in marriage. There was not a prince or nobleman in all of Daṁbadiva who did not make the request. The noble merchant her father thought, 'If I give my daughter in marriage to any one of these princes the others will surely be disappointed. I must think of a better plan. So he called his daughter and said to her, "Little mother, will you join the Monastic Order?"

Since this was her last existence before attaining Enlightenment,[4] she gladly agreed to her father's suggestion and replied, "Yes Father, I will join the Order."

The noble merchant then organized a grand ceremony and had her ordained a nun.

Although only recently ordained, she was called upon to perform the ceremonies of the *pōyagē* [where the observances on the full moon were held]. She lit the lamp, swept the room, and concentrating on the lighted lamp as an object of contemplation she attained to the Trance State of Great Power, achieved the Higher Insight, and became an *arahat*. Without further effort she also attained the Four Analytic Powers and Higher Knowledge.

One day that Senior Nun Upulvan (Utpalavarṇā) returning from her travels in the outer regions entered the Forest of Distractions located on the outskirts of the city of Sävät. She herself was free of Distractions. In those days living in forests was not considered a hindrance [to the ascetic life] and there were no restrictions on it. The Nun Upulvan built a hut there, set up a bed, and drew a curtain around it. She would go to the city of Sävät to beg for food and then return again to her hut [in the forest].

The son of a cousin of hers, a young man named Nanda who had been in love with her when she was a laywoman, hearing that she lived in the forest and overcome with passion, entered her hut one day in her absence and hid under her bed. The nun returned, closed the door behind her, and lay down on the bed, blurry-eyed, having just come in from the sun.

The young man, his eyes blurred by a film of Delusion and unable to distinguish right from wrong, emerged from under the bed and leaped upon her. "Oh foolish one do not destroy yourself; do not destroy yourself,"[5] pleaded

---

4. [s. *pascimbhāvika*] means the final existence in *saṃsāra*. Utpalavarṇā had completed one hundred thousand aeons as an aspirant to the discipleship and is now at the point when she is about to achieve her goal and become an *arahat*. This would be her final birth in *saṃsāra*.

5. In the DA version the nun cries out, "Fool, do not ruin me." In the SR the nun, already an *arahat* and beyond passion, remains unsullied by the act. Her words convey rather her compassion for the man committing the crime, the consequences of which for him, she clearly sees.

the nun. Even as she spoke, as if having no thought of future destruction the foolish young man satisfied his evil lusts and left. He thus destroyed his chances both of this world and the next. She, though she did not share his evil passions, yet was unable to exercise her supernormal powers as an *arahat* to stop him. The earth then split apart unable to bear the weight and power of the nun's goodness. The man was dragged down through the parted earth and was reborn in Avīci[6] hell to reap the consequences of what he had done.

The nun related to the other nuns what had happened. They told it to the monks. The monks reported the incident to the Buddha. The Buddha called up the monks and preached to them thus:

> One may be a monk, a nun, a male devotee, or a female devotee, but if a person does not act according to the Laws of the Order of the Awakened One he or she will suffer the consequences of his or her acts whether in this world or the other world. Just as one who partakes of honey and sweet confections consumes them with intense pleasure so Acts of Demerit are savored with ever greater and greater satisfaction until one begins to suffer their consequences. Then, when one is subjected to dire tortures, whether in this world or in one's next life in hell, one realizes what such acts are really like.

Thus he preached and many attained *nirvāṇa* at the end of the sermon.

Good men may say, "What of minor sins? They are not serious." But just as a fiery spark though it be a little thing should not be ignored as trifling, so an Act of Demerit should not be ignored as being minor. Similarly they may say, "What use are minor Acts of Merit? They are not as significant as great meritorious deeds." Do not think that. Instead, avoid sinful acts however trivial, engage in Acts of Merit however insignificant, and endeavor to put an end to the sufferings of *saṃsāra*.[7]

---

6. The worst of the seven hells.
7. For the first time the DA has material omitted in the SR. The following discussion among the monks and the Buddha's sermon do not occur in the SR. I shall quote the DA text here in full.

> Some time later the throng which assembled in the hall of Truth began to discuss the incident: "Even those who have rid themselves of the Depravities enjoy the pleasures of love and gratify their passions. Why should they not? They are not Kola-pa trees or ant-hills but are living creatures with bodies of moist flesh. Therefore they also enjoy the pleasures of love and gratify their passions." The teacher drew near and asked them, "Monks, what are you sitting here now and talking about?" They told him. Then he said,"Monks, they that have rid themselves of the Depravities, neither like the pleasures of love nor

The Buddha then called King Kosol and said, "Great King, just as men of noble families join the Order so do noble women give up kinsmen and large families, abandon a life of luxury, join the Monastic Order, and live in forests. While there, sinful men caught up in lustful passions try to undermine the celibate vows they keep under difficult conditions. Therefore, arrange for nuns to live within the inner city walls."[8] The king agreed and instructed that a certain section of the city be used for the construction of dwellings for nuns. From that time on nuns resided within the inner cities.

> gratify their passions. For even as a drop of water which has fallen on a lotus leaf does not cling thereto or remain thereon but rolls over and falls off, even as a grain of mustard seed does not cling to the point of an awl or remain thereon but rolls over and falls off, precisely so twofold love does not cling to the heart of one who has rid himself of the Depravities or remain there."

This omission is unusual. The SR author generally expands on the original text by interpolating additional sermons into his text. The omission suggests two possibilities. Dharmasēna may have used another version of the DA text. The other is that the SR author made a conscious cut because the nun's response in the SR is very different from that in the DA version. The question would thus not arise and there would be no need for the subsequent sermon.

8. As with so many *vinaya* rules, the restriction on nuns living in uninhabited forests was a very practical measure arising out of specific circumstances; in this case adopted to avoid possible harassment. Seen in context the rules often cease to be merely gender restrictions resulting from the "lower status" of nuns vis-à-vis monks. In this story there is not the slightest suggestion of such status differentiation, either in the woman's abiltiy to realize the highest goals of a Buddhist, or in her status as a chief disciple within the Order.

4

The Mother of Kāṇā

In order to show how those of little intelligence though they may not be able to acquire knowledge on their own, can do so when they follow the instructions of the wise, we shall relate the tale of the mother of Kāṇā.

How does it go?

The lay devotee Kāṇā was about to return to her husband [after a visit]. It is said "one should not return empty-handed," so her mother prepared honey cakes for her to take. However, on four succesive occasions four monks came begging for alms and each time the honey cakes that had been prepared were given as alms to the monks. Kāṇā's departure was thus delayed. Meanwhile, her husband took another wife.[1] When Kāṇā heard about it she said, "Had those monks come begging for alms but once or at the most twice, I would not have delayed my departure by having to prepare so many honey cakes and my husband would not have taken another wife. The monks are the cause of my misfortunes." She ranted in this manner and abused every monk she met without any consideration for the true facts. Thereafter, unable to bear her abuse the monks avoided her street altogether. The Buddha learned of this matter and visited the home of Kāṇā's mother.

---

1. In traditional Sri Lankan society, if a woman returned to her parental home and stayed away for an extended period, the implication was that the marriage was unsatisfactory. After some time both parties considered the marriage dissolved. Divorce was therefore relatively common. The DA has an additional comment. "In accordance with the precept laid down by the Teacher in such cases" and thus gives the practice a religious sanction not considered necessary in Sinhala society where the implications were clear.

Kāṇā's mother greeted the Buddha and paid obeisance. Seats for the monks are always kept ready in the homes of devotees so she led him to the seat prepared for the Buddha and offered him porridge and honey cakes. The Buddha partook of the porridge and then inquired, "Where is Kāṇā?"

"She is much disturbed in mind, so although she saw Your Reverence enter she did not come to pay her respects and now sits weeping within."

When the Buddha asked why she wept the mother replied, "Your Reverence, when she sees monks she rants and raves against them. Now she weeps, perhaps remorseful for what she has done."

The Buddha sent for her and asked, "What is the matter Kāṇā? When you should be happy to see me why do you weep? Do you cry because of some great sorrow? Is not being born the cause of all sorrow? If we can but stop the process of our continuing rebirths then will not our sorrows end? Answer me." Since she could not speak the mother responded, "She was about to leave to go to her husband, and as it was not good to go empty-handed I cooked some honey cakes but we offered them as alms to a monk who happened to come begging. The second time she cooked some cakes we again offered them to another monk who came by. A third and a fourth time we prepared cakes afresh, and yet again offered them to a third and a fourth monk who came by. Since she had none left to take with her shc delayed her going and in that time her husband took another wife. She has been greatly upset by the news and blames the monks for it saying, 'The monks are the cause of all of this.' "

The Buddha then said to her, "What is it Kāṇā? Did my disciples accept the alms you gave them or did they take something from you against your will?"

"No Your Reverence; they took only what was given."

"If my disciples came begging for alms and merely accepted what you gave them how then are they to blame?

"Your Reverence, the monks did nothing wrong. It is the one who abused those blameless monks who has done wrong," said Kāṇā's mother.

The Buddha then explained to Kāṇā, "When my disciples went from house to house to beg for alms your house happened to be on the street on which they were begging. Your mother offered them the honey cakes. How are my disciples to blame for that?"

"Your Reverence, your disciples are not to blame. It is I who am to blame for thinking so," replied Kāṇā and worshiping the Buddha she begged forgiveness. Since the Buddha had not yet completed the task for which he had come he now preached to Kāṇā the Doctrine in its consecutive order. Kāṇā became a *sōvān* and was rid of sorrows.

The Buddha arose and left for the monastery. Although there were other roads he could take he chose to go by the king's large palace grounds. The king saw him and inquired, "Is that the Buddha who I see coming this way?

When they said it was, he added, "Go inform him that I am coming to pay my respects to him."

The king then went to where the Buddha was and inquired, "Where did you go Your Reverence?"

"I went to the house of Kāṇā's mother," he replied.

"For what reason did you go there?" asked the king.

"Kāṇā has been railing at the monks without considering the facts of the case."

"Your Reverence, did you say something to stop her rantings?"

"I did Your Majesty. I gave her a little taste of the blessings of Spiritual Attainments and from now on she will not abuse the monks. I am just returning from there."

"Your Reverence, you have given her the otherworldy blessings of Spiritual Attainments, but I will give this person who is depressed because she has lost her material benefits, the blessings of this world too." So saying he sent his courtiers with a conveyance to bring her. Although her mind was now adorned with the ornaments of a *sōvān* her body was unadorned. The king gave her rings for her fingers and toes, jewels, and all the other ornaments that women wear. Having adorned her thus he gave her the position of his eldest daughter. He then commanded that if there was anyone fit to marry his daughter let him ask for her hand and take her. A certain minister of good repute, said, "I will take her and protect her." He took her to his home and gave her in charge of all his wealth saying, "Use it to perform whatever Acts of Merit you wish."[2]

From that time forth, Kāṇā would place people at the four entrances to her residence to invite in any monk or nun who happened to pass, so that they came to her home and she did not have to go out to seek them. There was a great flood of alms flowing from her home.

Talk arose in the councils of monks. "The four monks who had taken to the robes late in life were unaware of Kāṇā's inner feelings when they accepted the honey cakes from her. In accepting the alms they upset her greatly. The Buddha explained what the giving of honey cakes meant and by doing so he stopped Kāṇā from commiting further acts of mental aggravation. Understanding how she felt, the Buddha preached to her and set her on the Path as a *sōvān*. Not only was she no longer abusive but he called forth devotion in her. Thereafter, wherever there were monks or nuns, whether they wished to preach or to obtain their daily needs, he arranged it so that they would go to her and obtain it from her in her own home. She did not

---

2. The incident suggests a degree of social egalitarianism introduced by Buddhism and also that it was not unusual to give women the control and management of wealth—a feature of Theravada Buddhist societies even today.

have to go to them. How great is the Buddha's power and how benevolent." Thus went the talk.

The Buddha arrived and asked what they were discussing. However, knowing the issue that was being talked about he related the story of the *Bandu Jātaka;* how in a past life Kāṇā had been born a rat and the four old monks who had upset her by begging for honey cakes had been born as cats and had harassed her then too. The Buddha then had been a stonemason. He made the rat a shelter cut from a crystal and thus helped prevent further harassment. "O monks, not only now, as a Buddha, have I been able to alleviate mental distress but even in earlier situations when I was trying to cultivate the Perfections to become a Buddha I have done so. Just as fish at the bottom of the sea are disturbed by currents for a depth of forty thousand leagues and winds whip up the waters of the surface of the ocean to a depth of about forty thousand feet, but apart from the eighty thousand leagues at the top and at the bottom there is yet another area of ocean about forty thousand leagues deep in the middle, which is like a pool, calm and undisturbed even by the forces of a fourfold army.[3] Similarly, the wise hear the teachings and just as that pond is calm because it is undisturbed and remains still because it is unmoving so by becoming a *sovan*, a *sakadāgāmin,* or an *anāgāmin* one's mind is freed of Defilements, is stilled, and achieves calm. Those who have become *arahats* are especially calm," he said. At the end of the sermon many attained to the state of a *sōvān* and the other Fruits of the Path.[4]

Therefore, just as the moon slowly matures during the first two weeks so the wise should lengthen life by cultivating Moral Conduct and Contemplation. And as the moon is the chief of the starry galaxies so be noble like the powerful moon. Just as the moon walks alone at night without escorts so find time for oneself. Apart from the sun and moon, the abode of gods from which one can see stars is the most prestigious of all abodes, so be renowned for the good qualities of Moral Conduct. Just as the moon is first glimpsed with difficulty and after much effort, so engage [tirelessly] in Acts of Merit, acquire material wealth, and finally attain nirvāṇa.

---

3. The thirteenth-century views on oceanography may not be scientifically accurate but the idea that the bottom of the ocean is disturbed by currents and the surface by wind and waves while in between is an area of stillness, does provide a powerful image.
4. The DA version ends here but the SR characteristically adds a further sermon.

5

Kuṇḍalakēsī

Moreover, to show that there is nothing to be gained from frivolous discourse we will relate the story of Kuṇḍalakēsī.

How does it go?

In the city of Rajagaha there lived a very beautiful young woman of noble family. She was about sixteen years old and extremely attractive. Young women of that age are often intoxicated with their youth and are sexually attracted to men.[1] To prevent any loose behavior, her parents shut her up in a room on the topmost floor of a seven-storied palace, with only a serving maid to attend on her. It was as if she was imprisoned for being born beautiful.

[One day] a certain young man caught thieving, was being dragged to his execution. His hands were tied behind him and he was being whipped as he went. Hearing a great commotion the young noblewoman looked out of her top story room. She saw the youth being taken for execution, fell in love with him, wanted none other for a husband, and refusing all food took to her bed.[2]

---

1. The Sinhala version implies that such infatuations are a product of youth and thus not unnatural. There is even a subtle criticism of the convention of confining young women in a top floor room—imprisoning them for being born beautiful!
2. The rejection of food is a powerful symbolic gesture in South Asian cultures. The response of the "audience" for whom the gesture is made is equally predictable. They will make every effort to prevent the person from "fasting to death." The idea of a "political fast" such as the one Gandhi undertook is an extension of this same symbolic act into the political arena. Its effectiveness depends on its producing the expected response.

Seeing her lie there depressed her mother asked what was wrong. The young woman told her she had seen the youth being dragged to his execution and had fallen in love with him. She said that if she did not get him for a husband life was no longer worth living.

"Dear child, why do you say that? Do you think we intend to keep you confined in the house now that you have reached maturity? We will find you a husband, a young man suited to you in birth and status."[3]

"I do not want anyone else. If I don't get this man I shall die," the daughter replied.

Although the mother said everything she could, she failed to dissuade her and so she conveyed the news to the father. He too tried, but failed to make her change her mind and wondered what he should do in such a situation.[4] Then, secretly, he sent a thousand gold coins to the executioner with the message, "Take this money and do not kill the man. Release him and send him to us."

The executioner agreed, sent the man to the nobleman, killed another in his place,[5] and informed the king, "I have executed the thief."

Since the nobleman's daughter was determined she wanted none other, the nobleman gave her in marriage to the young man he had saved from death. From then on, in order to win his affection, the young woman would adorn herself in all her jewelery, prepare his meals herself, feed him, give him drinks, wash his hair, and bathe him.[6]

After a few days, ignoring all she had done for him, the thief thought, 'When will I get an opportunity to kill this woman, steal her ornaments, sell them to some city drunk, and do as I wish with the money?' He decided on a strategem. He took to his bed and refused all food. The noblewoman asked

---

3. [s. *jāti*] means birth and can also mean caste. I have used "birth and status" as an inclusive phrase, because the issue of caste is not an important factor in this context.
4. The parents' genuine concern for their child becomes evident. The norms of society require that the young woman be married to a man of similar birth and status, but when the daughter falls in love with a common thief, the parents neither force her to do as they wish, nor throw her out of the house for refusing to obey them. When they realize she cannot be persuaded otherwise, they do everything they can to make her happy.
5. The cavalier attitude of the executioner who "kills another in his place" is stated without comment and suggests that such actions were so common as not to even register as morally wrong.
6. The DA version merely states, "From that time on adorned with all her adornments she prepared her husband's meals with her own hand." The SR expands on this and in doing so brings in a note of excess, as if the woman in her infatuation subjects herself to performing menial tasks unusual for a woman of noble birth.

if he was sick. He said he was not, and she asked again, "Have my parents offended you then?" When he replied it was not that either, she asked yet again, "If not, what then upsets you?"

"Love, when I was being taken for execution I escaped death because of a vow I made to the gods who reside on the rock from which robbers are hurled. Entirely by their grace and without any effort on my part I not only escaped death but I obtained you too. I am troubled that I have no oblation to offer them."

"If that is all then don't be upset. I will make the offering. What do you want for it?" she asked. He requested five kinds of flowers[7] and milk-rice cooked without a trace of water.

"Good, I will provide everything." Then, having made the necessary preparations she called out to him, "Come, let us set out."

"Wear your best clothes and adorn yourself in your richest ornaments," he said, "And since it is a pleasure trip, let's leave all your relatives and kinsmen behind." Determined to win his steadfast affection, she did exactly as he wanted.

When they arrived at the foot of the rock he said, "Dear One, from this point on only you and I should proceed. We must not take our retinue. If many people accompany us there, they will be sure to dirty and litter[8] the [sacred] area, and it will be impossible to stop them from doing so. Therefore, let just the two of us go. Besides, the offering is for the gods, so you yourself should carry it." She did just as he suggested.

The thief accompanied her to the top of the rock from which robbers are hurled. The rock had one slope along which people could climb while on the other was a sharp precipice. Thieves were led to the top and hurled down the cliff face on that side. They were smashed to pieces as they fell. The place was thus called "Robber's Rock."

The noblewoman stood on the summit of the rock and said, "Let us make our offering." He did not respond.

"Don't you hear me?" she asked again.

"I'm not interested in sacrificial offerings. I made the excuse of a sacrifice just to bring you here."

---

7. They are figuratively termed *flowers* but refer to five ritually used items: broken rice *(hunusal);* white mustard *(hela aba);* jasmine buds, a specific kind of grass *(itana)*; and parched grain *(vilanda)*. The five together are [s. *lada pas mal*]. These items are specific to the Sri Lankan world. The DA translator was probably unaware of this reference and so translates it as "five kinds of flowers including the *laja* flower."

8. This is an interesting touch of local flavor that does not come in the DA. The author no doubt had firsthand experience of pilgrim crowds who leave a lot of litter behind them. Keeping sacred areas clean must have been a problem then as now.

"Why did you bring me then?" she asked.

"To kill you, steal your ornaments, and run away,"[9] he said.

Terrified, she said, "Dear husband, I and my jewelery are all yours. Why do you need to kill me? Here take my jewels. Take them and accept service from me too."

In spite of all she said he was determined to kill her.

"Listen to me. There is nothing to be gained by my death. Take the jewels and take me too as your bond slave," she said.

"If I do that, you will inform your parents and they will destroy me," replied the robber.

The noblewoman thought, 'This fellow is truly wicked. Intelligence after all, is intended to be put to use. It is not there just to be consumed. Therefore, irrespective of what I may have thought or done in the past, let me now unflinchingly do to him what I must.'

She then said to him, "Dear husband, sometime back, when I saw you being taken for execution [I fell in love with you] and told my parents. They paid a thousand gold coins, saved you from death, and gave you to me in marriage. From that moment I have been totally devoted to you. Can I now be angry with you because you might kill me? Please do me one favor. Permit me, who am about to die, to make my farewell obeisance to you in whatever manner I choose."

"Very well, wife, make your obeisance," he said, and, unaware of the kind of obeisance she was about to make, he moved away and stood by the cliff face.

The noblewoman circumambulated him three times, making obeisance at each of the four cardinal points. Then she said, "Dear husband, this is my last obeisance. From now on you will not see me again, nor I, you." So saying she embraced him first standing in front and then standing behind. As he stood at the edge of the cliff, lost in thought, she went up to him from behind, put one arm round his neck, and one in the small of his back and hurled him over the precipice. Her shrewd intelligence proved a match for his physical strength.[10] He was smashed to pieces by his fall and died, becoming himself the sacrificial offering. The deity who resided on the Robber Rock witnessed the incident and remarked, "It is not men who always have the best strategems. In certain situations women too know what to do."

---

9. The cruelty and cold indifference of the robber comes out in the sparse, harsh words. The woman's slow reversal from a state of complete infatuation to cold cunning is thus both understandable and in character.

10. The SR constantly draws attention to Kuṇḍalakēsī's intelligence which is underlined by the deity's praise of female strategems and practical good sense. The author goes on to justify the woman's action using the *karma* theory.

The young woman hurled the robber down from the rock with the help of his enemy, his own bad *karma* and herself escaped death by the grace of her friend, her own past good *karma*.

She then thought 'If I go back home they will ask "Where is your husband?" If I say, "I have killed him" they will say, "Why you loose woman, you paid a thousand gold coins to obtain him and now you kill him!" If I say that he tried to kill me they will not believe me and say, "Why would he want to kill you?" Whichever way one looks at it there seems to be no point going back.' She realized too that it would be unsafe to travel alone wearing her ornaments so she left them there and set off into the forest.[11]

After wandering from place to place, she arrived one day at the temple residence of some female ascetics. She paid her respects to them and said, "Your Reverences, admit me to your Order." They ordained her in the manner that they had been ordained themselves and she became an ascetic. Since certain disciplinary practices are fundamental to asceticism, she wished to cultivate a specific one and inquired, "Your Reverences, what practices are most important to your doctrine?"

"O female ascetic, one can concentrate on the *kasiṇas*[12] and attain to Trance States, and one can study the thousand discourses. These two skills are considered important in our order.

"Your Reverences, I cannot attain to Trance States but I will study the thousand discourses," she said.

The ascetics taught her the thousand discourses. Thereafter they said, "We have taught you all what we know. You should now walk the length and breadth of this land of Daṁbadiva and search out those able to debate with you."[13] They gave her a branch of a *Jaṁbu* (Rose Apple) tree and said, "O ascetic, go forth. If you meet a layman who can defeat you in debate, serve

---

11. The confrontation with death transforms the infatuated young girl into a mature woman who from that point on makes clear rational choices that highlight her intelligence.
12. *Kasiṇas* are objects of concentration used as aids to meditation and to the achieving of Trance States.
13. The phenomenon of wandering monks and ascetics *(paribājika)* stopping to engage in debates and discussions was a feature of early Buddhist and Jaina practice. Laity occasionally engaged in such debates too, as in the case of King Milinda. These debates were more than discussions. They were verbal confrontations that ended in victory or defeat of one or other of the participants and his or her philosophy. This tradition of debate continued in Sri Lanka up to the late nineteenth century when Buddhist monks and scholars engaged in public debates with Christian missionaries, often drawing large crowds. (See K. Malalgoda, *Buddhism in Sinhalese Society* [Berkley, 1976] for a more in-depth account.)

him as his wife; if a monk wins in the debate, then join his Order."[14] So they advised her and sent her forth.

She was called the "Rose-Apple Mendicant" because she wandered around with the Rose-Apple branch in her hand. She traveled all over the land engaging in argumentative discussions with whomever she met. She encountered no one who could defeat her in a debate. Men living in those areas fled the moment they heard that the wandering female ascetic was approaching, afraid of her very name.[15] When she went to a village or a town to beg, she would make a mound of sand by the entrance to the village, stick the branch on it, and say, "Anyone who wishes to take me on in debate must trample this Rose-Apple branch." She would then go into the village to beg. Quite apart from taking her on in debate, nobody even came near the Rose-Apple branch. When the branch finally withered away, she would take up a fresh one and move on.

As she walked thus she came to the city of Sävät and planted the Rose-Apple branch by the gateway to the city and made the same declaration as before. She then went to the city to beg. Children gathered around the branch. The Senior Monk Sariyut [Sāriputta] having completed his begging and repast and about to leave the city, saw the children surrounding the Rose-Apple branch and asked what it was about. They told him what was going on.

"If that is so then trample the branch," he instructed.

"We are scared," they said.

"We[16] will take on the task of debate. You just trample the branch," the Senior Monk instructed. Encouraged by the Senior Monk's words the children trampled the branch, and shouting loudly jumped on the mound of sand and kicked up a lot of dust.

The female ascetic returned and scolded the children, "I have nothing to debate with the likes of you. Why did you crush my Rose-Apple branch?" she asked.

The children answered, "We did it on the instructions of the Senior Monk. Otherwise why would we do such a thing?"

---

14. This statement is a direct translation from the DA with one exception; the DA says, "if anyone who is a layman is able to match question and answer with you, become his slave" (Burlingame, p. 230). The SR version is "Serve him as his wife." This suggests that while both are roles of subjection there was a difference in status.

15. Note that this female ascetic's skill in debate is unquestioned and the respect she draws unqualified. Her being a woman is not a consideration. Gender is not an issue here.

16. The plural form is often adopted by monks very much as in the case of royalty.

Since the Senior Monk too happened to be there she turned to him and asked, "Your Reverence, did you ask them to trample the branch?"

"Sister, it is so. We asked them to do it," he replied.

"Since you had the branch trampled then you must debate with me," she replied.

"Good, we shall debate with you,"[17] he answered.

That afternoon the female ascetic went to the place where the Monk Sariyut resided in order to put her questions to him.

The city was agog like the city of heaven when the Asura demons invaded it. Eager to hear the debate the citizens accompanied the female ascetic to where the Senior Monk was and stood respectfully on one side.

The female ascetic now said to the Senior Monk, "I shall ask you a question."

"Why keep it for another day? Ask it," he responded.

She questioned him on all the one thousand discourses she knew. The Senior Monk answered them all. When he had finished answering her he asked, "Are these all your questions? Are there no more?"

They were all the doctrinal discourses she had learned from her teachers. She had acquired nothing new thereafter. They had proved sufficient so far. However, as she knew no new questions, only what had been taught her of old, she answered, "That is all."

"You have asked us a lot of questions and we have answered them. We will not question you at length but pose just one question," he said.

"Go ahead Your Reverence; ask," she replied.

Since he had said he would ask one question he now took up the word *one* and asked, "What is one?"

Though she had learned many other doctrines she had not studied the Buddha's teachings and so did not know the answer to the question that was asked.

"What is the answer Your Reverence?" she asked.

"Listen, O female ascetic, it is a question from the Doctrine of the Buddha."

She, eager for new knowledge, asked, "I am keen to learn so please tell me about it."

"When the young prince Rahul came asking for his inheritance the Buddha said, even to him, 'Join our Order and then obtain it.' If you too become one of us we will teach you this doctrine."

---

17. There is not the slightest note of deference on the woman's part or patronage on the part of the Monk Sariputta. It is one professional's acceptance of another's challenge. The citizens are equally eager to witness the confrontation.

"If that is so, ordain me," she replied.[18] The Senior Monk asked the nuns to ordain her.[19]

She was ordained, became a nun, and was known as the Nun Kuṇḍalakēsī.[20] A few days later she obtained the higher ordination, became an *arahat* possessed of the Fourfold Analytic Powers, and just as she had escaped death in the past, so now she escaped the sufferings of *saṃsāra.*

The monks who were gathered in the Preaching Hall said to each other, "Kuṇḍalakēsī didn't hear much of a sermon and yet she has become an *arahat.* Besides, she fought and overcome a robber."

Monks are expected to either engage in doctrinal discussion or remain silent, but as this discussion was not entirely unconducive to attaining Spiritual Attainments they stood around talking.[21]

The Buddha arrived, inquired what was going on, and knowing what was happening said, "Do not say that I have preached too little or too much. One may tell hundreds of meaningless stories full of elaborate descriptions of female beauty[22] merely because one is skilled in telling stories, but they will be of no use to anyone in the afterlife. However, that stanza is blessed if by hearing it human beings attain *nirvāṇa.* Some may think it a great achieve-

---

18. The female ascetic's total commitment to the intellectual life is demonstrated by the eagerness she displays at the prospect of new knowledge. She takes on the monk as an equal, but when she cannot answer his question she is not chagrined by defeat but instead, does whatever is required in order to learn the new philosophy.
19. The Order of Buddhist nuns was separate from the Order of monks. Monks did not ordain nuns. The Buddhist Order of nuns is likely to have existed at the time of writing the DA in the fifth century and possibly also during the thirteenth century. It has since died out. Ironically, it is the question of ordination that has stalled a revival of the Order of nuns. Since no monk can ordain a nun, once the Order died out there was no way to reestablish it. However, it is stories such as this that have kept the "idea" of an "Order of nuns" alive and have fueled the revivalist attempts of Buddhist women in the twentieth century.
20. It means "curly haired." As a Jain ascetic she had to pluck out her hair. When it grew back she is said to have had tight curls. Hence she was known as the Nun Kuṇḍalkēsī or Curly Locks.
21. The monks' murmurings about Kuṇḍalkēsī's past actions suggest that some of them were more than a little discomfitted by the speed with which she attained Enlightenment. It is perhaps why the SR author surfaces the issue and tries to justify it.
22. The author seems to be making a passing jibe at the erotic descriptions of female beauty so commonly found in classical Sanskrit literature. As scholars of Sanskrit, Buddhist monks were not unfamiliar with such works but they were dismissed as not conducive to the religious life and so of little value. The statement underlines the importance given to didactic literature in the Sinhala Buddhist tradition.

ment to battle a host of ten thousand foes and overcome them by prowess on the battlefield, but that is not an achievement. If one were to develop concentration both day and night wherever one may be and overcome the more than thousand enemy Defilements like Lust and Hatred and conquer the country of *nirvāṇa*, I consider such a one to be the greatest of all conquerors."

At the end of the sermon many attained to the states of *sōvān*, *sakadāgāmin*, *anāgāmin,* and *arahat.* Wise men should give up fighting for their beliefs and other such battles.[23] With the hand of Insight take up the sword of Knowledge of the Path and commit yourself specifically to battling the enemy of Defilements.

---

23. [s. *lädi satan*] and could mean either battles for things one desires or battles for one's beliefs. The Buddha dismisses them as not being conducive to true wisdom or Enlightenment. The central theme of the story is thus not one of gender; that was not an issue in Buddhism; but rather the futility of arid scholasticism, or contentious debates even on philosophical or intellectual issues.

6

The Nun Paṭācārā

Moreover, to illustrate how calamities can befall even those who may have done Acts of Merit in the past, if an Act of Demerit committed in the past has a chance to surface, we shall relate the story of Paṭācārā.

In the city of Savat there lived a noble merchant whose wealth was reckoned at over four hundred million. He had a daughter who was very beautiful. When she was sixteen years old [her parents] confined her to an apartment on the topmost floor of a seven-storied mansion in order to prevent any misconduct. In spite of this she became intimate with a young man of her own household.

Her parents made plans for her to marry a young nobleman who was her equal in rank and wealth and fixed a day for the event. As the auspicious day drew near the young noblewoman said to the young man with whom she was in love, "On such and such a day they are going to give me in marriage to a certain noble merchant. Once I'm married to him, even if you were to get an opportunity to come with some present, you will not be allowed to see me because there will be guards there too. Therefore, if you love me, before I go there, take me away now, to any place you wish." He agreed.

"Then I will be at a certain place near the city gate tomorrow. You must come there by some ruse or other without letting anyone know," he said.

The next day he went to the meeting place.

On that next day, wearing a dirty rag she had found somewhere—as unclean as her thoughts[1]—tying her hair loosely as servants do, her body

1. The parenthetical remarks do not occur in the DA. They suggest the Monk Dharmasēna's personal views (or those of the society of his time) on Paṭācārā's actions. In the content of the story itself no such negative views are expressed.

streaked with dust and dirt as if after exhausting work, the young noblewoman grabbed a water-pot, and like a servant going to fetch water, she left the house with a group of servant girls. She went to where the young man was waiting, also in servant disguise. As if secretly hiding a jewel in a piece of rag, the young man led away the young woman, for though ignoble in her actions she was a woman of birth and wealth. He took her away to a distant village and lived as a tenant-farmer, ploughing land, harvesting the crop, and fetching firewood. Like the Bōsat (Bōdhisattva) who, in his birth as King Kusa,[2] had to suffer a life of hardship because of his love for Pabāvatī, so the young noblewoman, as if to show that it is not only men who suffer hardship for the love of a woman but that women too do so for love of a man, fetched water, cooked, and cleaned. As one who formerly ate rice but now must live on *Amu* grain,[3] so she began to consume the ill consequences of her past Acts of Demerit.

With time she conceived a child. When she was due to deliver, she said, "I have no kinsmen here. Whatever the faults of their children, parents' hearts always soften toward them, like the mother in the *Padamānavaka Jātaka,* who though a she devil, died of a broken heart when abandoned by her son. Let me return there to have my child,"[4] she begged of her husband.

"What are you saying? You are their daughter so they may not say or do anything to you, but I am an outsider and they will kill me for the wrong I have done them. I cannot go there."

Though the young woman pleaded again and again, he was hesitant. One day, when he went out to work, she said to her neighbors, "When my husband returns, finds me gone, and asks for me, tell him that I have gone to my parents." So saying she closed the door of her house and left.

Her husband returned, found her gone, inquired of the neighbours, heard what had happened, and pursued her. He saw her and begged and pleaded with her to return but could not stop her. At a point along the way she went

---

2. In the *Kusa Jātaka* story the Bōdhisatva was born as the powerful King Kusa but with an ugly face. He fell in love with the beautiful and proud princess Pabāvatī who rejected him. He then left his kingdom and disguised himself as a servant in her household. After a series of incidents he finally overcomes her pride and wins her. The comparison with the Bōsat undercuts the negative implications suggested in the earlier parenthetical comment. There is a certain tension here between the author's sympathy for the woman and the overriding values of the time.
3. A grain that is less valued than rice and often the food of the poor.
4. It is customary in Sri Lanka for a daughter to go to her parents' home for the delivery of her child. This is so especially in the case of the first child. There is also the commonly held belief that parents' anger over an elopement disappears when a grandchild is born.

into labor. She crawled into a thicket and told her husband who had followed her, that she was in labor. Soon her pains became very severe. Trembling and gasping, suffering greatly she gave birth to a son. 'I was on my way to my parents' home for a particular reason. But now that has been accomplished,' she thought and returned to her own home.

As time passed she conceived again. The second time too she pleaded with her husband to take her to her parents for the birth. Since he did not agree she left, carrying the older child in her arms (as the child was still unable to walk), and the other in her womb. The husband went after her to persuade her to return but she did not stop and continued on her way. The husband followed her. As they walked on together a huge storm arose unexpectedly, and unseasonally. The lightning, thunder, and rain were so severe that the sky became completely overcast without a glimmer of light. At that very moment her labor pains hit her like the lightning that flashed again and again. She cried out aloud like the thunder in the sky and as the rain increased so did her pains. She said to her husband, "I'm in labor. It is too cold; I cannot bear the pains and the wetness. Construct a shelter so I can give birth without being rained on." He picked up a knife with which to cut some sticks and branches and went in search of wood. He saw a small grove of trees beside an anthill and went there to cut sticks. A snake living in the anthill, disturbed by the sounds of activity, came out and bit the man as he was cutting wood. Instantly, like a fire consuming a dead tree the venom from the bite rose and spread poisoning his blood. His body turned blue and he fell down dead.

The young woman in great pain, not only did not obtain a shelter from her husband who went to cut wood, but lost that husband too. Suffering greatly she gave birth to another son. The two children cried incessantly unable to bear the cold and the wind. The young woman placed them under her belly and crouching over them on her hands and knees spent the three watches of the night in that position. Rained on all night, wet through and weak, at dawn she placed the child born that night on her hip and holding the older son by the hand said, "Come children, your father went in this direction" and set out toward the anthill. There she saw her husband lying dead on the anthill.

"My husband died, here, on the roadside, because of me," she wept. Crying and lamenting she set out for her parents' home.

Because it had rained all night the Acīravatī River had risen and was running knee high, [then] almost breast high above the riverbank. Unable to think clearly, distracted by her pain of mind, she decided not to carry both children across at one time even though they were not very heavy. Those children were not destined to live long. She left the older child on this bank, carried the younger child across, collected some leaves and twigs and placed the child on them, and decided to return for the child she had left on the other bank. Anxious about leaving the infant, she kept looking back and hurried to get the older child.

As she reached the middle of the river, not too far from either child, a hawk saw the infant lying on the lcaves like a lump of raw meat and thinking it was a piece of meat swooped down on it. The young woman saw the hawk swoop down on her child. She clapped loudly making a big noise to shoo it away. Not hearing her cries the hawk carried off the newborn infant and she lost that child. The young child on the other bank, seeing his mother in the middle of the river raise her hands and cry out, thought 'I am being called' and destined by his *karma,* without waiting for his mother to come, stepped into the water. As he stepped in, the water was too strong for him and he was swept away. Thus she lost the son on the other bank too.

"My husband who provided for me died along the way. My younger child was snatched by a hawk. My older child was carried away by the water." Weeping and lamenting thus she proceeded. Along the way she accosted a person coming from the direction of the city of Sävät. "From where do you come?" she asked.

When he said he came from the city of Sävät, she inquired, "There is a nobleman's family living on such and such a street in the city of Sävät. Do you know them?"

"Yes I do know them but whatever else you may ask me do not ask me for news of them."

"I have no use for other information. That is the only information I want."

"Since you insist what can I say? Did you see how it stormed last night?" he asked.

"Yes. Did that rain fall elsewhere too or did it rain just for me? But more of that later. You covered up my question regarding the nobleman with your talk. Why have you said nothing? You must tell me," she said.

"In that case I will. Last night the nobleman, his wife, and his son, all three died when the palace they built collapsed in the storm. They now burn on a single pyre. The smoke you see over there is from that."

Her grief was so great that she went mad. Trembling and shivering she was unaware even that the clothes she had on had fallen off.

She cried out,

> ubho puttā kālakatā panthe mayhaṃ patī mato
> mātā pitā ca bhātā ca ekacitakasmiṃ dayhare
>
> [Both my sons are dead. My husband lies dead on the road
> Now my mother, father, and brother burn on one funeral pyre.]

"My two children are dead. My husband is dead. The parents and brother to whom I came for support now burn on a single funeral pyre." Thus weeping and lamenting she walked around naked as the day she was born since even the clothes she wore had fallen off. People who saw her, ignoring the troubles of this *saṃsāric* existence, called her crazy, threw mud and dirt on her head, and pelted her with clods and stones.

At the time the Buddha was preaching at the Deveramvehera monastery accompanied by the fourfold assembly of male lay devotees, female lay devotees, monks and nuns, the eightfold assembly of the [deities of the] Caturmaharājika heaven and of the Tavtisā heaven, the king's retinue, the assembly of brahmins, Māra's assembly, the assembly of farmers, the assembly of ascetics, and the assembly of the god Brahma. He saw the young noblewoman approach, unseemly to all appearance because she was naked and had lost all sense of modesty, but blessed because of a Rebirth Wish she had made one hundred thousand aeons ago. However, as she had still not attained the Path and the Fruits she was like a newborn child.

In the time of the Buddha Piyumaturā[5] she had seen that Buddha raise a nun versed in the Rules of the Order and as if placing her in the Nandana Garden of heaven, appoint her chief of the Order of Nuns versed in the Rules of Monastic Discipline. She had then made a Rebirth Wish, "May I too, like you, achieve such a status in the dispensation of a future Buddha." The Buddha Piyumaturā looked into the future and knowing that her wish would be realized said, "One day in the future, in the dispensation of the Buddha Gōtama you will be famous as the Nun Paṭācārā, the chief of the nuns versed in the Rules of Monastic Discipline."

The Buddha [now] saw this person of great Merit who had made such a Rebirth Wish approaching from a distance. 'There is no one but me who can help this person and she needs help,' he thought and willed that she would not go elsewhere but would come to the monastery. The assembly saw her come.

"Don't let that crazy woman come here," they said.

"Do not stop her," said the Buddha. When she came near he added, "Though your sorrows were great and have led you to this state, you are not one who is lacking in reason and so you will get back your reason." That very instant, by the power of the Buddha, she got back her sanity. She realized immediately that she had no clothes on and shrank in modesty. Someone wrapped a shawl around her. She wore it and went up to the Buddha. Thereafter, freed from her many griefs, she adorned her head by worshipfully laying it at the lotus feet of the Buddha, [feet that were] adorned with a

5. Sinhala name for the Buddha Padumuttarā.

multitude of auspicious signs, ornamented with its petal-like toes, lotus-colored stamenlike nails, and stamen-filament hairs.

"O Most Revered Lord who helps all creatures, please help me. I have lost the husband who provided for me and am childless having lost the unfortunate children I bore. I have lost my parents and so have no support from them, have no siblings and so am bereft of kin support. My home was lowly and I lost caste[6] because of my bad actions. It would be a blessing if you will establish me in the noble caste of the *Ariyas* and thereby provide this servant, bereft of all worldly blessings, with the blessings of the Path and the Fruits." Thus she pleaded.

The Buddha listened to her and because her robe was of *paṭa* (silk) and because now as *ācārya* (teacher) she had regained her status that she had lost when she lost her clothes, she was to be known to posterity as Paṭācārā. As if giving her the name himself, he addressed her saying, "O Paṭācārā, do not grieve. You have come to the One who can provide a powerful refuge. Just as in this life your young child was carried away by a hawk, and your older child was washed away, and your husband died along the way, and your parents and brother died when their house collapsed, so as long as you remain in *saṃsāra* the tears you will shed for the death of parents and others are greater than the waters of the four oceans." He then recited the *Anamatagga-pariyāya sutta*:

catusu samuddesū jalaṃ parittakaṃ
tato bahuṃ assūjalaṃ anappakaṃ
dukkhena phuṭṭhassa narassa socanā
kiṃ kāranā samma tuvaṃ pamajjasi

[The tears you have shed are more copious than the waters of the four oceans. Such is the lament of the human being afflicted with grief. Why then O friend do you remain indolent?]

and even as he recited it as rust disappears from sharpened steel, her sorrows eased. Seeing that her grief had eased the Buddha called Paṭācārā and said, "Listen Paṭācārā, you could not be of help to your dead parents and kinsmen even when they were alive. The wise engage in discipline and meditation and are a help to themselves." He then preached a sermon on the last two verses of the twentieth chapter. At the end of the sermon Paṭācārā rid herself of more Impurities than there was sand on the earth, became a *sōvān,* and by that was established in the clan of the *āriyas*. She thereby regained her lost

6. The references to "caste"—the losing and regaining of it do not occur in the DA.

caste and rid herself of the evils that arise from *saṃsāra*. To make up for the worldly happiness she had lost she achieved a small taste of the blessings of the Path and the Fruits. Many others too became *sōvān*.

Paṭācārā saw no further joy in the householder's life and asked to be ordained. The Buddha sent her to the nuns to be ordained. The nuns ordained her as an Elder. As she was ordained an Elder having already attained the status of teacher she obtained parents from the *sāsana* for the parents she had lost and became known as the Elder Paṭācārā. One day she poured water out of a pot to wash her feet. The water flowed a little way and was soaked into the ground. The second day when she washed her feet, the water flowed a little further than the already soaked area and only then soaked into the ground. On the third day when she washed her feet the water flowed further than on the two previous days and then soaked into the ground. Paṭācārā did not look further for an object of meditation but contemplated the water with which she had washed her feet as it had disappeared on the three successive days. She thought, 'Just as the water first went a short distance and disappeared so human beings die within the first thirty-three years of their birth. Just as on the second day the water flowed a further distance and disappeared, so human beings die in middle age between the years thirty-three and sixty-seven. Just as the water disappeared on the third day so human beings die between the ages of sixty-seven and a hundred. Thus all creatures that are born, die. She sat contemplating in this manner.

The Buddha from his perfumed chamber sent forth a ray of light and as if standing beside her and addressing her said, "Look Paṭācārā, of the five Aggregates[7] that are of a Form and Formless nature, the Aggregate of Form is born of Ignorance, Craving, Karmic Forces, and Material sustenance. The characteristic of its origination is called "Becoming." Of the three other Aggregates—Sensation, Perception, and Conditioned Phenomena each is born of Ignorance, Craving, Karmic Forces, and Touch. Their origination is also called "Becoming." The (fifth) Aggregate of Consciousness is born out of Ignorance, Craving, Karmic Forces and Individual Nature *(nāma rūpa)*. Its origination is also called "Becoming." Thus the Characteristic of Becoming exists in five ways in respect of each Aggregate making a total of twenty-five.

Similarly the Characteristic of Cessation exists in five ways in respect of each of the Aggregates, thus making a total of twenty-five. For example, with the Cessation of Ignorance, Cessation of Form occurs. So with the other Aggregates. If a person does not understand Becoming and Cessation in their fifty characteristics just mentioned, even if he were to live a hundred years

7. [s. *skandha*] The elements or substrata of sensory existence. They are enumerated as Form, sensation, perception, mental formation, and consciousness.

it would be of no use. But were he to comprehend them, then even if he lived only for a single day, his life would be meaningful."[8]

At the end of the sermon the nun Paṭācārā became an *arahat* possessing intuitive knowledge. Her grief was assuaged and her suffering in *saṃsāra* ended. Therefore the wise should avoid Acts of Demerit, engage in Acts of Merit, and strive to destroy the pain of birth that is the root of all suffering.

8. Yet another display of scholarly erudition.

7

Kisā-gōtamī

Moreover, to illustrate that wisdom becomes a refuge in every situation we shall relate the tale of Kisā-gōtamī.

How does it go?

The home of a certain noble merchant in the city of Sävät together with his entire wealth of about four hundred million all turned to charcoal as a result of what was left of some past bad *karma*. Greatly depressed by what had happened the noble merchant refused all food and took to his bed. A friend came to visit him and inquired, "My good friend why are you depressed?" He learned the cause and added, "Friend, do not be upset. What is now become charcoal was once your wealth. By some expedient is it not possible for the charcoal to turn again into wealth? I know a way to turn that charcoal into wealth. Even what is not gold or silver can be turned into gold and silver by certain devices. Do as I tell you."

"What shall I do?" he asked.

"Order some mats for your store, spread them out, heap that charcoal on the mats, and sit there as if you were selling it. If people come up and say, 'Others sell oil, honey, jaggery, clothes, and such things. You sell charcoal,' reply 'If I don't sell what I have what should I sell?' Now if someone else comes along and says, 'Others sell clothes and such like goods. You sell gold and silver,' reply, 'What gold and silver?' When they say, 'Why, like this you have here,' say, 'Then give it to me,' and get them to bring it to you. Thus whatever they bring when it reaches your hand will (as if secretly) turn to gold. Now if the person who gives you the gold is a young woman, then bring her to your household (since the association will be beneficial) and give your son in marriage to her and also your four hundred million in wealth.[1] Live on what she gives you. If the person who gives you the gold and silver happens to be a man, then marry your young daughter to him and give the four hundred million to your son-in-law, just as with a daughter-in-law. Take what he gives and live on it. Don't try to keep ownership of your wealth or enjoy it except in this way."

He took the advice, heaped the charcoal outside his shop, and sat as if selling it. At that time a very poor young woman who was named Kisā-gōtamī because she was physically lean (though she was very strong in Merit) came to the fair to buy something. She saw the noble merchant and said, "Others keep cloth and such things for sale but why do you sell gold? These are things one should buy even if one sells all else?"

"My child, where is the gold?"

"You are like one who while traveling along the road asks where the road is. Those piles you have there are gold."

"If that is so my child, give me some in my hand."

As the young woman picked up a handful of charcoal it turned to gold by the power of her Merit just as the Venerable Pilindivacca's garland turned into a golden necklace by the power of his psychic powers and by the merit of those in the monastery. Even what was put in the merchant's hands remained gold, did not turn back into charcoal.

"My child, where do you live?" asked the noble merchant. When she told him he inquired if there were suitors for her hand and when he learned there weren't any he then paid all the expenses and gave her in marriage to his son. He gave the four hundred million as a dowry as the piles of charcoal had all turned into silver and gold.

Some time after her marriage, she conceived a child not destined to live long. After ten months she gave birth to a son, who was like a visitor come for a limited time. Just at the age when he began to take his first steps he died. Kisā-gōtamī had not seen a dead person before so she stopped those who came to take her son for burial or burning, saying, "I'll go ask for some medicine for my child."

Carrying her dead child on her shoulder she set out. She went from house to house asking, "Do you know of a medicine to cure my child?"

Those she spoke to would answer, "Child, are you crazy to seek medicine for a dead child?"

In spite of whatever anyone said, she kept asking for the medicine she was seeking.

One wise man saw her and thought, 'This is perhaps her firstborn so she has not seen a dead child before. I must try to be of help to her.' He said to

---

1. The assumption is that he regains his lost wealth through the magical powers of the woman.

her, "My child, I do not know of such a medicine but I do know of a place where you can find such a medicine."

"O Father, who is it who knows such a medicine?" she asked.

"Child, the Lord Buddha, teacher of the Three Worlds[2] knows everything. Therefore would he not know of such medicines and cures. He knows cures for everything. Go there and ask him," he said.

"Good," she said and went to the Buddha. She worshiped him in greeting and standing on one side she said, "Your Reverence, do you know a cure for my child?"

"I who know the deathless state and the cure for birth, decay, and the sufferings of life, why would I not know that? I do know," he said.

"What then is needed [for the cure?]," she asked.

"A pinch of fresh mustard seed," he replied.

"Isn't it easy to find that? From what sort of place should I get it?" she asked.

The power of her intelligence could be gauged from the fact that she did not set off to look for mustard seed merely on being told to get it but asked some basic questions.

"Listen Gōtamī, I do not want it collected from any household at random. If there is a household that has not lost a daughter or a son, get it from such a house," he said.

"Good," she replied, and worshiping the Buddha and carrying her dead child on her shoulder she left for the inner city. At the first house she asked, "Do you have any mustard seeds? It is for a medicine for my son." When the people replied that they did, she asked them for some. As they brought it to her she asked, "Have you lost a son or daughter in this household?"

"My child what can I say? There are as many more who have died here as there are living."

"In that case your mustard seed will not be a cure for my child," she said and gave it back.

In this manner she walked to every house in the village inquiring but could not find what she wanted from a single house. Toward evening she thought, 'Alas, it seems impossible to do. I think only of my son dying. But in this village there seem to be more sons and daughters who have died than there are living.' As she thought thus she realized that there was no other cure for the disease of death and her ailment of overpowering affection for her child eased somewhat. As the grief arising from her strong affection eased little by little her heart became strong. Just as ashram-dwelling yogis discard

---

2. Refer to the formless realm (*arūpa*) or heaven, the human world of form (*rūpa*), and hell or the spirit world of (*kāma*) lust.

a corpse once it passes the swollen stage so she buried the corpse of her son and went to the Buddha, worshiped him, and stood on one side.

The Buddha knowing that she had not obtained it asked, "Did you find the handful of mustard seed?"

"Your Reverence I did not. There were as many dead sons and daughters in this village as there were living."

"If you cannot find the medicinal ingredients we need what then can we do? Just as you could not obtain such mustard seed so there is no cure for the dead. What one can do is find a medicine to stop one from dying," and he recited a stanza from the twentieth *Magga* (Path). At the end of the stanza Kisā-gōtamī became a *sōvān,* partook of the medicine of *nirvāṇa,* and rid herself of the three ailments such as the belief in the body as a personal possession. Many others too attained to the state of *sōvān* and other states.

Having become a *sōvān* she asked to be ordained so she could find the cure for the ills of birth and suffering through the monastic order. The Buddha sent her to the nuns and she was ordained and conferred Higher Ordination. Having obtained the status of seniority she became known as the Elder Nun Kisā-gōtamī.

One day when it was her turn to do the observances at the temple she made the offering of lights and as she saw the flames die down and rekindle again she thought, 'We beings, if we cannot stop the continuous rebirth process will be born again and again. Since death is inevitable, all creatures born must die. Only those who attain *nirvāṇa* become extinct leaving no residual matter. She made the lighted lamp, like a weapon come to hand, an object of meditation.

The Buddha, seated in his perfumed chamber, sent out a ray of light to her and as if he were talking to her in her presence, said, "Gōtami, it is so. Other than Designatory Form and Characteristic Form all other types of Form have a life span of not more than seventeen mental moments. Formless entities are also subject to the three characteristics, namely, birth, existence, and destruction. Hence these beings die an instant death or by death as a [sequential] process. Those who die are born again. That does not happen even after a long time when one attains *nirvāṇa*. Therefore if one were to live a hundred years (which is the longest one can live in this era) without understanding *nirvāṇa* it is of no use. But to live for one day having seen *nirvāṇa* is blessed, because such a one has no fear of hell and fear of *saṃsāra* is lessened."

At the end of the sermon Kisā-gōtamī, even as she sat there, reached the final stage of *arahat* with the Fourfold Analytic Powers. Though she was physically lean she filled out in goodness.

Thus good men though they be lacking in physical fitness should acquire mental fitness, free themselves from Acts of Demerit, perform Acts of Merit, and cultivate goodness.

8

The Nun Bahuputtika

To encourage efforts at practicing Discipline, we will relate the story of the Nun Bahuputtika.

How does it go?

In a certain noble family in the city of Sävät there were seven sons and seven daughters. When they came of age, they married, established their separate households,[1] and lived happily. After some time the father died. The mother did not divide her wealth. The fourteen children then said, "Revered Mother, now that our father is dead what is the use of your keeping all this wealth yourself? If you divide the wealth among us will we squander it like throwing a burned-out firebrand? Will we not safeguard it?" She listened to all they had to say but said nothing herself. Since all of them kept pressing her to divide her wealth she realized that it would be too much hassle not to do so. She therefore decided to distribute her wealth among her children and thereafter to live with them. She divided her wealth in two parts, gave one to her sons and one to her daughters.[2]

After a few days she went to her oldest son's house to see how he would look after her. The daughter-in-law said to the mother-in-law who had just arrived, "Our mother-in-law has chosen to come to our house. One would

1. Note the nuclear family, not the extended family was the unit (and still is so) in Sri Lanka. Also, the widow has the right of inheritance.
2. Note how property is distributed. On the death of the husband, the widow not the children gets full control. When the mother in turn divides her wealth she does so equally between her sons and daughters. It is a sharp contrast to Hindu inheritance patterns.

think she had given her eldest son the biggest portion of her wealth." The wives of the other sons too said the same thing when she went to visit, almost as if they had talked it over among themselves.

Since that was all the hospitality she got from her sons she decided to visit her seven daughters. Apart from the words of greeting she got on arrival they treated her no better. She received no welcome and was deeply shamed. 'Why should I live with such children? I will live as a nun,' she thought and went to a nunnery and asked to be ordained. They ordained her. She obtained full ordination and was known as the Elder Bahuputtika.

"I have become a nun late in life so I must make haste," she said. "I will perform the Disciplinary duties heedfully, and throughout the three watches of the night I will practice meditation." So saying she held on to a pillar on the lower level and walking around it performed her meditative exercises. As she walked she [mindfully] moved the branches of trees away from her lest she knock her head against them. Thus she meditated, not permitting herself to be distracted by pain, suffering, sloth, and so forth. Doing as the Buddha instructed, she performed her meditative exercises with no thought of physical comfort.

As if sending a messenger to inquire into how the meditation was progressing, the Buddha sent forth a powerful ray of light from his perfumed chamber, and as if talking to her in person said, "Bahuputtika, if one ignores the Threefold Law, the understanding of the Doctrine, the practice of it and the realization of it, and does not act accordingly, even if one were to live a hundred years it is of no use. It were far better, even for one instant, to live according to the Doctrine since it is the source of everything." At the conclusion of the sermon the Nun Bahuputtika became an *arahat* with the Fourfold Analytic Powers.[3]

Therefore, the wise should not be attached to however much wealth and possessions they may have because they are a hindrance not a help [to salvation]. Just as termites when they go in search of food cover themselves with earth and by creating anthills hide while they move, so one should cover one's Acts of Demerit with Acts of Merit like Generosity and Moral Conduct. Moreover, just as cats constantly search for rats wherever they go and think only of that, so should one always think about Acts of Merit. And just as a scorpion makes a weapon of his own tail thus one should take in hand Wisdom as one's weapon. Just as a mongoose rubs himself against medicinal plants when he goes to hunt snakes, similarly use the medicine of compassion against the snakes of hatred. As jackals are not repulsed by any object however unclean so do not despise any person. Just as deer run and hide when one hurls a spear, so should one hide from Acts of Demerit and just as deer fear even a moderate

3. The DA version ends here.

sound so should one fear even a moderate wrong act. Just as cattle do not abandon their herd so should one not abandon Right Action and just as those same cattle once yoked, do not break out until they are released, so until death one should not abandon Moral Conduct. Just as pigs seek a water hole to cool their bodies when the heat becomes unbearable, so when the heat of anger becomes too strong, seek the water of compassion and cool off the heat of rage. Just as elephants crush the earth beneath them as they walk so crush all Acts of Demerit, and like elephants who carefully examine everything they see so examine each thing with Wisdom not in Ignorance. As elephants sport in ponds with lotus, waterlily, and *Ipul* blossoms, so step into the pond of full Awareness filled with the pure waters of the Doctrine and the five flowers of Freedom and engage in the sports of Wisdom. And as elephants mindfully take each step so act always with Mindfulness and Wisdom. Just as lions are clean in their habits so be constantly clean in your thoughts, and as a lion even if he were to die will not succumb to another so do not in any way succumb to Acts of Demerit. As a lion will prey on an animal for food but will eat only what he has caught there and for the rest of that day he will not hunt anything and everything, so live on what you happen to come by and that you obtain by harmless means and do not engage in wrongful acts because of selfish desire for personal possessions. Just as the *sakvālihini* birds as long as they live, do not go about in the sky alone but in pairs, similarly, until the end of life one should not live divorced from goodness. And just as those *sakvālihini* birds do not harm any living creature so do not harm any creature by word or deed, or indulge in the Five Acts of Demerit. As pigeons, wherever they live, are not attached to the comforts of that place so do not desire what belongs to another. As owls hate crows and hunt them all night and kill a great many, so hunt and destroy Ignorance with Wisdom. As the *kā̆rala* bird by its cry fortells the good or bad fortune about to befall men so preach sermons about what is good and bad without seeking profit and reputation. As bats fly into a house, circle around and leave but have no fondness for anything in that house, similarly consider what you see as what you see and do not let desire for it arise. Just as bats live in the houses of others but do no harm to it, so, do not seek to harm those with whom one associates. As a leech, once it attaches itself to something, will suck blood only from that bite and will not move here and there, similarly, if you attach yourself to a particular place, unless you see something unsuitable, do not break that association. Just as snakes have no other means of movement except by crawling on their stomachs so one can progress only with Wisdom, and just as snakes avoid medicinal [herbs] as they move about, similarly avoid

---

4. The Four Forms of Activity or four postures are sitting, standing, lying down, and walking.

wrong deeds during the Four Forms of Activity.[4] As snakes are afraid when they see men so seeing the consequences of wrong acts, fear them. Just as pythons have huge stomachs which they can never hope to fill and so are satisfied with less, similarly seek not to satisfy your Desires. Just as the tarantula weaves a web across the road and eats flies and other creatures caught there so weave a web of Awareness across the four gateways such as the eyes and with the mouth of Meditation munch the flies and caterpillars of Impurities caught in there. Finally, having devoured them experience the taste of *nirvāṇa*.[5]

---

5. This sermon does not appear in the original DA. It was clearly added on by the author-translator of the SR and is typical of the style of Sinhala sermons as they are still preached by monks in rural temples today. Images are drawn from the familiar world of the village and used to illustrate everyday moral and ethical values. However, the author's choice of images in this sermon and the manner in which they are piled on suggests almost a researcher's obsessive interest in, and careful observation of, the insect and animal world around him.

9

The Goddess Lada

Moreover, even if one were blameless oneself, if censure results from one's actions, then one should avoid that too. To illustrate this we shall relate the story of the goddess Lada.

How does it go?

This present story took place in the city of Rajagaha. The Elder, Mahasup [Great-Kassapa] who had a long life span was residing in the Pulila cave near Rajagaha. He attained the Trance State of Cessation[1] and sat for seven days without food. On the seventh day because it was right that he should obtain some rice and because were anyone to offer him food that person would obtain great blessings, he cast his Divine Eye[2] around to see who was fit to make that offering. He saw a certain woman gather some ears of *hal*-grain from a plot she was tending, clean it, and dry roast it into puffed rice. He considered whether she was or was not a devotee and realizing that she was, he reflected yet again, 'Is she able to make an offering to me or is she not?'

Then aware that this woman of good family would make an offering, and that though she would not live long enough to enjoy the benefits of that act in this life, she would obtain great blessings in her next life, he retied his robe, took up his bowl, and appeared at the edge of the *hal*-field. The good

1. [p. *nirōdha samāpatthi]* Another of the many categories of Trance States that can be achieved by concentrated contemplation.
2. [s. *diväsa*] *Arahats* have the power of supernormal vision.

woman saw the Elder and her mind was suffused with the five kinds of joy.[3] With a serene mind she said, "Please stay."

She gathered the puffed rice, brought it quickly to the Great Elder, offered it, and making the five-point gesture of worship uttered this Fervent Wish: "Your Reverence, just as these grains of rice became light when roasted so may I be lightened of my Impurities and achieve *nirvāṇa*."

The Great Elder replied, "Just as you have acquired the Merit of Giving, so may you acquire the Merit of Contemplation" and proceeded to preach a Sermon for the Transference of Merit.

Worshiping the Elder she contemplated the Act of Giving she had engaged in and just as she had cleansed her mind of its initial, and secondary thoughts she purified her final thoughts.[4]

In a certain hole along the path that led to and from the field there lived a snake. It could not bite the the Great Elder's calf because it was covered by his robe. The good woman arrived there, still thinking only of the offering she had just made. The snake hastened out of its hole and bit her as if to enable her to [immediately] enjoy the heavenly blessings that were her due because of the offering she had made. She was struck down right there. She died with a serene mind, undisturbed by the power of the venom.[5]

Like one who awakes from sleep she was reborn in the Tavtisā heaven as a goddess, in a golden mansion one hundred and twenty leagues long, with a divine form three leagues tall, adorned with golden ornaments. She was dressed in a shawl about forty-eight leagues long that when folded was as fine as a *tŭmba* blossom or a *poda* flower. She had a similar shawl over her shoulders. She was accompanied by about a thousand heavenly maidens and in order to indicate the nature of her Act of Merit in the past, the halls were decked with golden plates filled with golden puffed rice placed on shawls of pearls. She stood at the entrance to her chamber contemplating her heavenly blessings and asked, "What Act of Merit have I performed to obtain these blessings?" As she looked with her Divine Eye she saw that it was the reward for the puffed rice she had offered to the Elder Great Kassapa. She had given to one who was blessed with the Divine Eye and so had obtained such heavenly blessings. "With such a minor Act of Merit I have obtained such great blessings. Life in *saṃsāra* is infinitely long, much more than the thirty-

---

3. The five kinds of joy are momentary joy *(ksanika)*, joy that causes horripilation *(khuddaka)*, joy that lifts the body *(udvēga)*, joy that rises like the ocean wave *(okkantika)*, and joy that pervades the entire body *(pharana)*.
4. Thoughts pertaining to the Act of Giving.
5. Buddhists believe that it is one's state of mind at the point of death that conditions one's immediate next rebirth.

six million years I spend in this heaven, so it is wrong to delay further. If I were to perform the major and minor rituals and services for the Elder Mahasup that would be no trifling Act of Merit. I will therefore perform that more serious Act of Merit. Just as with repeated readings one firmly fixes in one's mind an already studied text, so I will do more Acts of Merit and ensure further blessings."

Very early in the morning, at dawn, taking a container for refuse and a broom made of gold (since they were divinely created) she swept the Great Elder's temple premises, threw out the sweepings, and filled the containers with bathwater and strained water for drinking. The Elder noticed all that but without observing too closely, he thought that someone had come very early and performed those tasks. On the second day too the goddess performed the tasks in the same manner. The Great Elder thought as he had the day before. On the third day the Elder heard the sound of sweeping and saw the light from her body that had entered into the inner chamber through the keyhole. He opened his door and asked, "Who is sweeping out there?"

"Your Reverence, It is I the goddess *Lada* who am your servant," she replied.

"Do I have a servant by that name?" he asked.

"Your Reverence, in a former life I was tending a field of *hal-rice* and prepared some puffed rice to eat. However, I offered the rice to you instead and did so with a serene mind in the hope that even though it was an insignificant act it would stand me in good stead for a long time. I am now come again. I died at the hands of a snake as if he had called me saying 'Is the Act of Merit you have done not worth more than tending fields? Come, enjoy the golden chambers of heaven,' and I was reborn in the Tavtisā heaven. Your Reverence I obtained these blessings because of you. I have come in the hope that by continuing to serve you I can further extend those blessings."

"Was it you who performed the Acts of service on the two previous days too?"

"Yes Your Reverence," she replied.

"Goddess, the services you have rendered have been rendered. But do not do so in future."

"Your Reverence, don't say that. I cannot again find a Field of Merit[6] such as you. This Act of Merit I now perform is not minor. The blessings obtained from such Acts of Merit are also not minor. Do not hurt my chances of increasing my blessings by such instructions."

---

6. [s. *pin keta*] (merit-field) The image is often used to describe the disciples of the Buddha. What is given to them is of great Merit so they are an arena for Acts of Merit by the laity.

He heard her and responded, "Goddess, are there no better ways to improve your blessings than this? However much one seeks to extend such transient blessings they die and cannot be lengthened. What lasts is *nirvāṇa* that does not die. Do whatever Acts of Merit you can in order to obtain *nirvāṇa*. In future times, when monks sitting in specially prepared seats, holding their palm leaf fans, preach the Doctrine, do not have them say, 'In the time of the Buddha a certain goddess swept the temple premises and provided water for the Elder Mahasup. If people were to hear that it would go contrary to the praise I have received from the Buddha. From now on do not perform these services or come here." Even after he said that the goddess remained standing there, carried away by the force of her devotion, thinking only of the benefits to her, ignoring the impropriety that might accrue to him.

As one who is angry, the Elder said, "Even when told to go you remain. Do you not know your place?" and snapped his fingers [to shoo her off]. She could no longer stand there and leaped into the sky. With both hands held to her forehead in worship she cried out, "Your Reverence, please allow me to strengthen the blessings I have obtained," and stood in the sky weeping and lamenting.

The Buddha was in his perfumed chamber at the monastery of Deveramvehera about one hundred and eighty leagues away. He heard the sound of the goddess weeping and sent out a ray of light. Then as if he were standing right there he said, "Listen goddess, it is right that you should stop the service you render my son Kassapa because it might do him a disservice. Those who wish to perform Acts of Merit acquire more and more Merit. They think, 'Such Acts can benefit us.' Even though they are stopped again and again from performing such Acts of Merit the [thoughts] are in themselves beneficial, just as one's stomach is filled by the rice one eats even though disturbed again and again." He added, "Listen goddess, when one performs an Act of Merit, do not say, 'I have done one Act of Merit. That is sufficient for me.' Do not stop at that but do more and more Acts of Merit. Even when there is no material good and wealth and no opportunity to perform Acts of Merit one should always think, 'How can I find a way to perform Acts of Merit?' Why so? Because whether by deed or by thought[7] to gather Merit is of benefit both for this world or the otherworld. That is the reason," he said.

At the end of the sermon, the goddess though she was a hundred and eighty leagues away became a *sōvān*. Whatever her material blessings she was now ensured of the blessings of *nirvāṇa* that leaves no residual matter. She made firm the blessings of the Spiritual Attainments and put an end to her existence in *saṃsāra*.

---

7. The story emphasizes that a person's good thought is as important as the action itself.

10

Viśākhā's Companions

To illustrate the benefits of association with good people we will relate the story of Viśākhā's friends.

How does it go?

Some five hundred noblemen of the city of Sävät each entrusted his wife to Viśākhā's care on the grounds that just as leaves used to cover a scent absorb that scent so the association with her would be beneficial to them. Whether they went to parks or to temples these five hundred [women] now went in the company of Viśākhā.

During a certain season, it was ordered by royal edict that a drinking festival be held for the duration of one week. They [the women] prepared the intoxicating liquor *rā*[1] for their husbands. The husbands participated in the drinking festival for seven days and on the eighth day they returned to work, having been recalled by royal messengers and the beating of drums to their respective agricultural and commercial tasks.

The five hundred women then said, "We could not get to drink when our husbands were present. There is liquor left over. Let us drink it without letting them know." They went to Viśākhā and said, " O respected Viśākhā, we would like to go to the park."

---

1. [s. *rā*], popularly translated as "toddy" is an intoxicating drink made from fermented coconut sap. It is the local drink in Sri Lanka today and was obviously popular even in the thirteenth century. The text specifies the particular drink as *rā*, giving the story, even though ostensibly set in the time of the Buddha in North India, a very Sri Lankan context.

"Good, if that be your wish, attend to what is needful and let us go," she said.

They secretly brought the liquor with them and taking Viśākhā along, like cats who close their eyes when they eat curd, they drank and became intoxicated in the park. Their actions though hidden from Viśākhā were apparent to the next world.

Viśākhā, though she did not know it at the time, came to learn of it later and thought, 'What these women did was wrong. The *Tirtakas*[2] will now say that the female devotees of the monk Gōtama go around drunk and thus disparage us all, including me.' She called them up and said, "What you did was very bad. By being associated with you I too have been disgraced. Your husbands will also be very angry. What will you do now?"

"We will pretend to be sick."

"I did not tell you to drink nor will I now tell you to fake illness. One who sows rice will reap rice; those who sow *amu* grain will reap *amu*.[3] You will be known by your own deeds, but don't bring me into it as if trying to hide rotten fish under *ītana*[4] grass," she said.

They went to their homes and pretended to be sick. When their husbands returned they inquired after their wives and were told that they were sick.

'What could have caused the illness? A disease might hit one or two of them but how could all of them be sick at the same time?' they thought. They knew then that in spite of their attempts to keep their wives from evil ways they had drunk the remaining liquor. They created a big row and beat them.[5]

They [the women] suffered the blows but on yet another occasion they wanted to drink again. They said to Viśākhā, "Please accompany us to the park."

"Once before I accompanied you to the park and you brought shame on me. Am I to do so again and be disgraced? If you wish to go, go by yourselves. I will not accompany you," she said. They decided not to go but said instead, "We wish to pay our respects to the Buddha. Take us to the temple."

"Now if there is something worth doing that is it. Prepare the offerings to take with you," Viśākhā said and left. They took baskets of scents and flowers, and as if carrying jars of water to sprinkle on the flower offerings, they carried pots of the liquor, wrapped themselves in large robes [to hide the pots], and taking Viśākhā with them they went to the temple. [Once there] they ran to a corner, put the pots to their mouths, and drank the *rā* like those

2. A rival sect of ascetics who lived during the time of the Buddha.
3. Rice is a valued grain while *amu* is not.
4. A wild coarse grass.
5. The casual remark suggests that wife-beating was not uncommon, also that intoxicating drinks though permitted to men were considered "evil" for women.

who put their lips to blow on a conch blackened with dirt. Then they threw their pots away, went into the assembly, and sat in front of the Buddha.

Viśākhā said to the Buddha, "Your Reverence, these women are my companions. It would be good if you were to preach to them." They, however, were drunk. Worship was not their intention. They decided to dance and sing. Spirits who were supporters of Māra thought, 'We will take possession of these women and perform all manner of comic jokes and tricks in front of the monk, Gōtama.' They did so. Possessed by demonic spirits and overcome with the liquor some of the women began to clap their hands and laugh in front of the Buddha. Others began to dance. The Buddha wondered what was going on and realized what had happened. "I will not permit Māra's suporters to do this. I did not fulfil the Perfections to permit them room for such actions."

In order to instill fear into the minds of those who had lost all fear in their state of demonic intoxication, he emanated a blue ray from his eyebrow. A great darkness fell as happened at the time when the Buddha Mangala died and attained *nirvāṇa*. Not laughter and dancing but fear overcame the women. With the fear their intoxication vanished. The Buddha then disappeared from his seat, appeared on the top of Mount Mēru, and shed forth a white light from his eyebrow. That very instant, as if a thousand suns and a thousand moons had arisen, the exterior darkness vanished, although the darkness of their delusions did not disappear. Thereafter he preached to those women from the top of Mount Mēru.

"Your heedless behavior in our presence was wrong. Because of your [drunken] condition Māra's spirits were able to come into our presence and do what they should not have done. Viśākhā was not intoxicated so they could not get her to do likewise. Rather than drinking *rā* try to quell the fires of lust that burn and destroy lives," said the Buddha. He then preached his sermon.

"This world is continuously burning in the eleven fires such as lust. As you burn, waiting for someone to quell those fires, what use is laughter, what use is happiness? One must try to quell those fires:

na vaṭṭati hasantena gantuñceva nisīdituṃ
vatthusmiṃ hasanīyasmiṃ mihitamattantu vaṭṭati

[It is not proper for a person to be seated or to go about laughing.
When an occasion arises that causes mirth one should be restrained.]

That being so, there is a proper time for laughter. Excessive laughter, more than what the occasion demands, is wrong.[6] You who are shrouded in the

6. There is a slight shift in the Monk Dharmasena's translation of this text. It is excessive laughter that is forbidden.

darkness of Delusion why do you laugh and dance instead of looking for the lamp of Wisdom to disperse that darkness? The darkness of Delusion will not go away by dance and laughter. If you wish to dispel it, make wicks of good deeds, soak them in the oil of faith, light up the lamp of Knowledge of this world and the worlds beyond, and dispel the darkness of Delusion." Thus he preached. At the end of the sermon the five hundred women became *sōvān*. Thereafter, let alone thoughts of drinking *rā* even if it were put in their mouths they would not swallow it.

The Buddha established them in the steadfast faith of the Path, climbed down from the top of Mount Mēru, and sat again in the Buddha's seat. "Your Reverence, this liquor *rā* is a very bad drink," said Viśākhā. "Even these women who associated with me and had come so far along the Path, could sit in the presence of a Buddha such as you and show their lack of restraint, and laugh and sing and dance. They behaved like that because of the [intoxicating] drink but they are not really like that."

"O Viśākhā, that is indeed so. Those who drink *rā* suffer the sorrows of hell. Therafter, they will be born as demons for five hundred births and for five hundred births as dogs[7] and wander mad through countless births. Thus *rā* is very belittling. Many are led astray because of it."

"Your Reverence when did this *rā* originate?" asked Viśākhā. To relate the origin of *rā* in detail the Buddha related the Khuṁbha Jātaka.

Thus good men should consider the drinks and intoxicants as worse than an instant killing poison. They should rid themselves of the five kinds of Demeritorious Acts[8] including this one, perform Acts of Merit, and cleanse their minds.

7. Here the connection between being born as demons and then as dogs is that both categories wander around mad. Rabid dogs were probably a familiar feature of the landscape as they still are.

8. These are the five basic acts that Buddhists are asked to avoid: killing, stealing, adultery, lying, and drinking of intoxicants.

11

Sirimā

Moreover, to teach men not to be attached to the human body by revealing its disgusting nature, we relate the story of Sirimā.

How does it go?

The story of how Sirimā heard the Buddha's sermon and became a *sōvān* is related in the Tale of Sirimā that appears in the seventeenth section of the *Kōdhavagga* (Stanzas on Anger).

She was an extremely beautiful courtesan of Rajagaha. After she had become a *sōvān* she had invited the Buddha to a meal the following day and prepared a great Feast of Alms. She also arranged for eight "ticketed offerings" to be given to the monks. From that day, eight monks regularly visited her house. She filled their begging bowls with ghee, bees' honey, cane sugar, and treacle and spent sixteen *kalan*[1] daily on an offering of rice. Whatever may have been her mode of earning that income,[2] she spent it in a worthy manner.

One day a monk came to her house, partook of the ticketed offering, and proceeded on to a temple about twelve leagues away.

That evening at the time of the customary monastic rituals, one of the resident monks asked, "Monk, where did you go for your food today?"

"I ate of the ticketed offerings provided by Sirimā," he replied.

1. A *kalan* was a measurement of weight. It was the equivalent in weight of twenty *maditi* seeds or 1/80th of a pound.
2. The profession of courtesan was clearly accepted in the society of the day. The remark however suggests a certain reservation on the part of the monk-author of the text.

"Monk, is she generous with the food?" he asked.

"Why do you ask? She is most generous. One might think that because the quality is so good the quantity is likely to be small, but it is not so. What she offers to one monk is usually enough for several. Besides, though there may be others who make as generous offerings, the attraction is more than the food. Her beauty is such that one cannot tear one's eyes away. Thus he engaged in talk,[3] unsuited to a monk.

A monk who was not yet firmly fixed on his meditative practice, hearing the talk was attracted to her and fell in love with her without ever having seen her. He was quite unlike the monk, Tissa Thera, of Mihintalē,[4] who on seeing but the teeth on a smiling face, immediately perceived the skeleton behind it, invoked the meditation on bones, and thereafter, became an *arahat*.

'I will go there on the pretext of obtaining the ticketed offerings and with luck see her,' thought this monk. In order to attend the ticketed offerings he discussed with the monk who was returning from the meal the question of his own seniority and inquired about the seniority of the monks who were to go there the next day.

"If you get there before the other monks you have sufficent seniority to obtain the ticketed offerings," replied that monk.

Unable even to wait till dawn, the (young) monk instantly took his robes and bowl and even though it was not a journey undertaken for the purpose of meditating on one of the ten inauspicious objects, completed the twelve-*gav*[5] journey that very night.

At dawn he arrived at the place where the ticketed offerings were being made. There were already eight monks there. But he took his place in the queue according to his seniority and caused the monk at the end to be left out. He thus obtained the ticketed offering.

The previous day, shortly after the first monk had eaten and left, Sirimā had been stricken with a fatal illness. She had asked to be relieved of the weight of all her ornaments and lay down. When the monks arrived the next day for their offerings the servants informed her but too weak to attend on them herself, she instructed them thus, "Maids, invite the monks in. Take their bowls, offer them gruel and sweets, and when it is time, fill their bowls with rice just as I would have done." They did as instructed and informed her when the gruel, sweets, and rice offerings were made.

---

3. There were thirty-two topics of conversation that were listed in the *vinaya* as unsuitable for monks. The discussion of Sirimā's beauty would fall into this category.
4. Another reference to a specifically Sri Lankan context—the monastic complex at Mihintale.
5. [s. *gav*] was a measure of distance often roughly translated as a "league."

"Now take me to greet the monks," she said. They supported her hands and feet and took her to them. But *karma*, that enemy, wracked her body and she trembled with pain and weakness even as she greeted them.

When the monk who went eager to meet Sirimā saw her, he thought, 'If one so weakened by sickness and ill health can be so lovely, how much lovelier must she be when healthy and adorned in all her ornaments, just as a highly polished statue when touched with gold becomes even more beautiful.'

As his thoughts wandered more and more along these lines, Defilements fostered over interminable periods in *saṃsāra* caused his mind, that had been set on meditative practices, to veer now in the direction of Sirimā.

As the veil of Delusion gradually closed in, the Eye of Wisdom[6] slowly failed and he could not see the birthmark of Defilements on the body of his Discipline *(sīla)*. Thus, unable to consume the good rice he was heir to,[7] he took his bowl back to the temple, put it aside, covered himself with a corner of his robe, and lay down disconsolate. A monk-friend seeing that he had eaten nothing tried hard to persuade him but could not make him eat. Just as he was neglectful in keeping the rules of the monkhood so he was neglectful of eating and was in despair.

Like a garland that fades Sirimāvō died that same evening. The king informed the Buddha that Jīvaka's younger sister had died. The Buddha instructed that the body should not be cremated for a while yet. He asked that it be taken to the cemetery and be placed on a high platform so crows and dogs could not get at it and that it be guarded. The king did as instructed.

Three days passed. On the fourth day the body had swelled so much that it could be seen from afar. Worms spilled out of the nine openings. The entire body looked like a pot of boiled, broken rice-bits. It was enough to destroy all desire for living.

The king sent out a drummer to announce that apart from children and those looking after households, anyone else who did not come to view Sirimā would have to pay a fine of eight gold coins each. He informed the Buddha that the monks too could be sent to view the inauspicious object.

"Let us go visit Sirimā," said the Buddha. "Come with us," he said to the grieving monk.

Just as a person consumed by grief cannot eat however much another may try to persuade him, so the young monk who had traveled twelve leagues to see Sirimā, lost his appetite. He fasted for four days as if engaging in a therapy for the disease of Defilements. The rice in his begging bowl rotted,

6. [s. *nuvaṇäsa*] Knowledge that is attained through disciplined meditation.
7. Rice, being the staple food of Sri Lankans is greatly valued. The good rice here refers to the Fruits of the Path that he was foregoing because of his attraction for Sirimā.

as did Sirimā's body, and the bowl began to fill with mould. His monk friends announced that the Buddha was going to see Sirimā. Though he had been fasting for four days, on hearing the name Sirimā he sat up instantly, as if the very name were some kind of food. When the monks asked if he were joining them, their words were like a drink of water. He got up, energetically scrubbed and washed his bowl, and joined the other monks.

Like the moon accompanied by stars the Buddha and his monks stood on one side of the corpse; the nuns stood on the other side. The king stood on another side, and the lay devotees stood on yet another. The Buddha then addressed King Bimsara [Bimbisāra].

"O King, who is that?" When the king replied that it was Sirimā, the Buddha added, "Formerly those who came to seek her paid 1,000 gold coins. Ask anyone who so wishes, to pay 1,000 gold coins as they did in the past and take her now." Not only was there no one to take her but no one to even hear the order. The king reported this to the Buddha.

"O King, if that be so, lower the price," said the Buddha. The king lowered the price by half to 500 and then halved it again to 250, and again to 125 and then to 62 and 5 *aka;*[8] and then to 31 and 2 *aka* and then to 15 and 5 *aka,* then 8 and 1 *aka,* and half that to 4 and 10 *aka*, to 2 and 5 *aka;* and to 1 and 2 1/2 *aka*. He then said take her at 80 *hamu,* at 40, at 20, at 10, at 5, at 2 1/2, or 1, but they were all reluctant even at that price. He then ordered that she be given for nothing, free, gratis. The corpse might have been of some use to one engaged in meditating on the impermanence of the body but no one else had any use for her. Let alone take her, no one would come near her. In fact, they would not have been there at all had it not been for the king's command.

The king informed the Buddha that there was no one to take her. The Buddha then addressed the monks, particularly the monk who had come eagerly to see Sirimā.

"Monks, Sirimā, once so loved by so many who would pay as much as 1,000 gold coins for but one day with her, now has no one willing to take her even without payment. How did she look, monks, when she walked around this city then and how is she now? Her hair that was like a black river flowing down a golden mountain was once described by poets as bees swarming around the stamens of her lotus blossom face. How does it look now? Where is that forehead that was like a half moon appearing from behind a blue-black cloud? Where are those brows considered by the ignorant to be a pair of heavenly bows? Where are those eyes described as the sapphire-blue windows

---

8. These are units of calculation. The display of mathematical dexterity is typical of the kind of elaboration that monks indulged in to awe the listeners and perhaps to drag out a sermon.

of a gem-studded palace? People now wrinkle up their noses at that nose once described as a golden hook. Where are those lips that were like a beaded ship sailing on the ocean of her face? Where are her teeth that appeared from inside her mouth like the sixteenth part of a moon? Her ears once seen as traps to entice young men, now exude mountains of worms. Her neck compared to the neck of a golden pot is now so swollen that there is no top or bottom end to it.[9] No one has any use for her except as an object on which to meditate in order to arrive at Trance States and obtain the Path and the Fruits."[10]

So the Buddha preached. "Look on this human form, fed, given drink, bathed, washed, groomed, adorned with ornaments; what has it come to now? This corpse, vomiting worms from its nine openings, built of three hundred bones, constantly changing posture from moment to moment, from birth to death, thus constantly ailing, adorned as if one decorates a pot full of feces, is looked upon by many in a variety of ways. But even if it were to exist on earth for an uncountable number of years it must finally die. Contemplate this body with wisdom, realize that it is empty, is confined to sorrow, and obtain what Fruits one can from contemplating this body that now has come to this.

Just as no desire arises when one sees a body in this state, so no one can obtain the Path and the Fruits without getting rid of desire." Thus spoke the Buddha.

At the end of his sermon eighty-four thousand people saw the sullied corpse and attained to the unsullied state of *nirvāṇa*. The monk who had been fasting for four days, like one who breaks a fast but is still unable to eat much for some time thereafter, was unable to attain all the Paths and partake of *nirvāṇa* fully. He reached only to the state of *sōvān* and was to enjoy *nirvāṇa* later. Thus the wise should not celebrate the body but celebrate goodness and substitute for impermanent life the permanent state of *nirvāṇa*.

---

9. The tone shifts from a lingering admiration for her beauty (described in lavish imagery) to one of repulsion as the description proceeds. This entire passage does not appear in the DA and implies that the translator was carried away by his subject.
10. Contemplation of a disintegrating corpse was one way of understanding the impermanence of life. Many monks engaged in what was termed, *cemetary meditations* and attained *arahat* status thereafter.

12

The Nun Uttarā

Moreover, even though one may have practiced other meditations it is important to practice also the Meditation on the inevitability of Death. In order to illustrate that we shall relate the story of the Nun Uttarā.

How does it go?

That nun, though she was one hundred and twenty years old, did not just curl up and remain inside the nunnery, but would go out to the street to beg for alms. In one of the inner streets she saw a monk and asked him if he wished to have some rice. Since he did not refuse it she gave him all she had. While there was time for a friendly chat after the partaking of alms, there was no time left to go begging again. Had she time she would have obtained more food but now she went hungry.[1] On the second and third days too she met a monk she didn't even know, but she offered him her alms and again went hungry. On the fourth day as she went begging for alms, she saw the Buddha at a narrow point in the street and trying to make way for him she tripped on her robe. Being very old and therefore feeble, and weak from not having had any food for three days, she could not keep her balance and fell. The Buddha went up to her and said, "O nun you are indeed very feeble. When one is old the body does not hold up." But because he wanted her to obtain the permanent state of *nirvāṇa* he preached to her.

"O nun your body has deteriorated with old age. Though enfeebled, you are fortunate if it remains free of disease for as long as it lasts. But it will

1. Monks and nuns are supposed to complete their one meal for the day by noon. Hence the lack of time to beg for more alms.

succumb to disease. Just as a jackal, though young is called *jarāsigala* [decaying jackal]; just as the *raskinda* [medicinal vine] even when tender is called *pūtilata* [rotten-vine]; in the same way, though newborn and golden, one calls the body *pūtika* [rotten]. Even though that body is rotten, if it remains intact one is lucky. But like a thin clay pot, it breaks apart. It breaks because life must end in death; that is why. Death originates with Birth and since it is a part of Becoming it cannot be stopped. But one must try to destroy the root, which is Becoming."

The nun, though well matured in years was not yet fully matured in her faith and in her control of the senses and so at the end of the sermon she became only a *sōvān*. Many others obtained the blessings of this world as well as Spiritual Attainments.

Therefore, just as when it rains the dust gets settled, so to end the cycle of births the wise should settle the dust of Impurities with the rain of Meritorious Acts; and just as rain cools the summer heat so one should cool the heat of Hatred with the cool rain of Compassion; and just as grains such as rice sown in the mornings and grains such as *ura* lentils and *mung* lentils sown in the afternoons sprout with the rains, so with the seed of faith let seedlings of Meritorious Acts sprout; and as rain, a product of the seasons, nurtures grasses and other plants that sprout in that season, so let the good deeds that spring from within oneself protect one. And just as rain when it falls, fills the rivers, lakes, ponds, and mountain streams so make the rain of the Doctrine fall, and with the waters of Meritorious Acts fill the lakes and ponds of human minds and make existence productive.[2]

2. It is useful to compare this text with the version in the DA. The SR version is filled with images drawn from the agricultural world of the villager and was clearly intended as a sermon directed at a village audience. The images also help personalize the old woman around whom the sermon is woven.

13

The Nun Rūpanandā

All beings may not have the same mental capacities but to illustrate how one can preach to each according to his or her capacity and the wonder of leading them toward understanding, we will relate the story of the nun Rūpanandā.

How does it go?

That nun, while she was still a layperson, thought, 'My older cousin has given up his royal pleasures, become a monk, then a Buddha. His son Prince Rahul [Rahula] has become a monk too. Prince Nanda, who was my husband, has also become a monk. Our mother,[1] Prajāpatī Gōtamī too has joined the Order. When so many of my relatives have joined the Order what is the use of my remaining a layperson? I too will join the Order.' She went to a nunnery and joined the Order. She became a nun not from any conviction but because of her kinsmen. She had earlier been known as Janapada Kalyāni [Beauty Queen of the Region] and as she was still very beautiful she was called "Rūpanandā" [Delightful Lineaments].

She set great store on beauty. The Buddha, however, stressed the Three Characteristics [impermanence, suffering, and the absence of a soul] in his sermons, and that was not to her taste. As a result she never went to see the Buddha, thinking, 'If I go there he will speak of beauty such as mine as subject to decay, as unclean, and destined to die, and it will only cause me anguish.'

1. The reference here is to her mother-in-law as she was married to Prince Nanda, the son of Prajāpatī Gōtamī. However, mothers-in-law are often addressed as "mother" *amma* rather than *nändamma* that is the specific kinship term.

Early in the morning the citizens of Sävät would commence their observances of the Eight Precepts, make offerings of food, and at dusk, covering their upper bodies with shawls, bearing flowers and incense, they would gather at the Devramvehera monastery to listen to the Buddha's sermons. The nuns too, since they resided in the inner city, would gather at the monastery and hear him preach. As they walked back to the city after the sermon they would talk among themselves, praising the Buddha's goodness.

Of the four categories of people who live in this world, if there be one who looks on the Buddha and is not convinced [of the truth of the Doctrine], such a person must surely be rare. The reason being that those for whom beauty is appealing feed on the Buddha's golden form complete with all the major and minor [auspicious] signs, and thereby become believers, as happened with the Thera Vakkali. Those for whom sound is appealing, hear of the Buddha's goodness as related in the *Jātaka Tales,* and hear his voice, complete in the eight tonalities that penetrate the directions like the voice of Brahma and thereby are convinced. Those for whom austere qualities are a paramount attraction are convinced by his austerities such as the wearing of austere robes. Those for whom goodness is appealing say 'the Buddha's moral discipline is such, his contemplative qualities are such, his wisdom is such, his goodness, meditative powers and intelligence are incomparable,' and so are convinced. Thus, when these people began to sing the Buddha's praises it was as if their mouths were not big enough for the purpose.

The nun, Rūpanandā, who was loth to go to the Buddha heard her fellow nuns and lay devotees speak of the Buddha's goodness and thought, 'All these people speak very highly of my cousin's goodness. Well, he may see me and preach of the faults of beauty, but though he may do so once, how many times can he repeat it? I will go with the other nuns, sit so he will not see me, then I too can see the Buddha and hear him preach.' So thinking she said to her fellow nuns, "I too am coming to hear the sermon." The nuns were delighted, saying, "After all this time Rūpanandā has finally expressed a desire to see the Buddha. Today, he is sure to preach a wonderful sermon specially for her" and they took her along.

From the time she set out she kept thinking, 'Though I go, I will not let myself be seen by the Buddha.' The Buddha on his part thought, 'Today Rūpanandā comes to see me. How shall I preach something suited to her? She values beauty greatly. Her love of self is strong. Just as one uses a thorn to take out a thorn, it is necesssary to use beauty to wean her away from her infatuation with beauty.' So he decided and about the time that she was to arrive at the monastery, he created the phantom of an extraordinarily beautiful young woman of about sixteen years, dressed in gorgeous garments, decked in jewelery, with a fan in her hand to stand by fanning him. She was visible to no one but the Buddha and to Rūpanandā.

Rūpanandā stood behind her fellow nuns, and greeted the Buddha with the five point gesture of worship. Though she belonged to the *ksatriya* [warrior] caste, since she came nowhere near the *āriya* [noble] caste[2] of the Buddha, she hid behind the nuns as if ashamed. Rūpanandā gazed on the Buddha's person, adorned with the thirty-two marks of a Great Being, shining also with the eighty minor marks, enveloped in untold brightness, his face soft as a full moon. Then Rūpanandā saw the woman beside him. She saw the beautiful phantom. Glancing at her own body and comparing herself with that beauty she thought she looked like a crow beside a golden swan. The moment Rūpanandā saw the figure her eyes began to dance. "O how beautiful is this woman's body,' she thought and as she stared at the woman her love of self gave place to a powerful love for this woman.[3]

The Buddha knew that, and because he wished to turn that powerful attraction into a desire for *nirvāṇa*, he made the sixteen-year-old woman now appear as a twenty-year-old, even as he preached. Rūpanandā looked at the woman and thought her not as beautiful as before, and her attraction for her diminished a little.

The Buddha then gradually changed the woman's appearance, first to that of a mother of one child, then to a middle-aged woman, then to an old woman. Rūpanandā saw each change and while her love for the woman did not completely disappear, it lessened. However, as she saw that form change into old age, decayed, with broken teeth, her youthful hair turned gray like a heap of wood-ash from her burned out youth, her back bent like a curved gable, trembling and unstable, supporting herself with a stick, the form became extremely distasteful to her.

Rūpanandā had been intoxicated with the beauty of appearance. By showing the process of decay the Buddha had turned her away from it, but in order to cure her of the infatuation with health, he then made the old woman's body succumb to disease. At that very instant, the woman let go of her stick and her palm-fan and crying out aloud fell to the ground. Defecating and urinating she rolled this way and that. Rūpanadā saw it all and was utterly disgusted. The Buddha then made the form he had created appear as in death. The woman died and instantly swelled. Worms and pus exuded from the nine orifices. Ravens and other birds gathered and began to pick on it. Rūpanandā who was fixated on the beauty of form, not knowing the Buddha's powers and unaware that it

2. A distinction is being made between the brahmanic caste divisions and that introduced by the Buddha. The *āriya* caste (noble ones) were the followers of the Buddha whose nobility depended on goodness not birth.

3. Physical attraction or love between two people of the same sex is here, as in the story of Soreyya, described not as an aberration but as one of many forms of attraction that tie one to the *saṃsāric* cycle.

was all a creation of his magic, saw it all happen and thought, 'When I came here this woman was as beautiful as a goddess. In this very place, she has gone from carefree youth, through the processes of decay, disease, and finally death. If one so beautiful as she experiences decay, disease, and death what then is there left for us others?' She considered the fact that life, since it begins and also ends is impermanent, that it is subject to birth and destruction and so is full of suffering, and since one has no control over such processes, it is soulless.

Thereafter, she felt as if the Three Modes of Existence[4] were on fire and ablaze. Her mind turned toward meditation. The Buddha wished her to be a refuge to herself. However, because she had not practiced meditation before, he knew that without help she could not help herself. He therefore preached the following stanza specially suited to her:

> āturaṃ asūciṃ pūtiṃ passa nande samussayaṃ
> uggharantaṃ paggharantaṃ bālānamabhipatthitaṃ
> yathā idam tathā etaṃ yathā etaṃ tathā idaṃ
> dhātuto sunñato passa ma lokaṃ punaragāmi
> bhave chandaṃ virājetvā upasantā charissasi

> [Nanda, behold this assemblage called the body, diseased, impure, and putrid; it oozes and leaks and is desired only by simpletons. As is this body so also is that; as is that body so this body will be.]

The nun, Rūpanandā, heard the sermon and became a *sōvān*. Moreover, like a mother who feeds a young child repeatedly as he cannot consume everything at once, so, in order that she might obtain the Path and the Fruits sometime in the future, the Buddha preached to her giving her objects of meditation.

"Just as those in charge of a village, in order to store their paddy, rice, black gram, *mung* gram, sesame, *kollu* [a kind of lentil] and other grains, build houses, wrap the timbers with strong vines, and cover it in clay, so in order to store decay and death, pride, and hypocrisy in human minds one constructs houses of their bodies, with timbers of bone, tied up with the vines of veins; one takes the clay of flesh and mixes it with the water of blood, plasters it with sandy clay and the finished clay of life, and constructs a city. Whatever mental or physical ailments one may have they come from within that very city of the body. Apart from that, there is little else one can get from it," he preached.[5]

---

4. The three Modes of Existence are the worlds of Lust, Form, and Formlessness.
5. This is a typical elaboration by the Sinhala author of the SR of what is a very brief sermon in the DA. The images are all drawn from the world of the village and describe in detail the way they built their granaries to store their crops. The images give immediacy and body to what must have been the bare bones of a sermon text.

At the end of the sermon the nun, Rūpanandā, destroyed not just her lust for beauty but also for the five upper-level fetters of Existence[6] and became an *arahat*. Many others also achieved *nirvāṇa*.

Thus the wise should obtain the very best for the body by revering the Three Jewels; obtain the very best for birth in the world of men by observing at least the Five Precepts; obtain the best of wealth and riches by generous giving; and finally obtain the very best that is *nirvāṇa*.

6. [s. *uddhambhagiya sanyojana*] They are lust after material form, lust for incorporeal form, pride, distraction, and ignorance.

14

Queen Mallikā

To illustrate the evils of lying we shall relate the story of Queen Mallikā.
How does it go?

One day Queen Mallika went to her bathhouse, washed her face and mouth, and bent over to scrub her feet. The dog who lived in the palace and had accompanied her there, saw the queen bend down and started to perform an indecent act with her. Though she took no active part, it was not a fitting thing. However, since there are none who reject such gratification, the queen endured the pleasure.

King Kosol, looking out of the window of the upper story, saw her unseemly behavior and when she returned to the palace said, "You despicable woman, you deserve to be killed. Why did you do such a thing?"

To cover up what she had done she said, "Your Majesty, what did I do?"

"What else but that you engaged in intercourse with a dog," he replied. Although she had taken no active part she had let it happen and hence was greatly ashamed.

"No such thing occurred," she said.

"Is it not enough to sin with your body must you now sin in your speech too? I saw it with my own eyes so don't lie to me and add to your sin."

"Your Majesty, anyone looking down from up here on someone who goes to that bathhouse sees the image doubled. So it appears as if they were engaging in unseemly acts." She lied to pacify the foolish king.

"You sinful woman; say what you like but I will not believe you."

"Your Majesty, if you don't believe what I say, you go down to the bathhouse. I will watch you from up here." Since the king was very foolish, he took her at her word and went down to the bathing place. The queen looked out of the window and cried out, "O foolish king, as king you have access to so many queens and yet must you engage in acts of dalliance with a she goat? Does such an act befit a king?"

Though the king said "I did no such thing," she replied, "I saw it with my own eyes. Whatever you say I will not believe you." The king heard her and thought, 'When a person goes to that bathhouse the image must surely appear doubled.' He decided that the incident involving the queen also had not happened.

Queen Mallikā thought, 'The king is foolish and has believed what I said to deceive him. I may not have committed an act of adultery, since the creature was an animal, yet a sin is a sin. That being so, I also commited the sin of lying that is the gravest of all the sins. I may foolishly try to hide my action, but the Buddha who knows the past, present, and the future, and his eighty senior monks will all know of it. Not just them but anyone with the power of divination will know of it. Alas, what I did was very wrong. What I said was even worse. I had better do something to mitigate my Acts of Demerit.

She participated in the vast Alms Feast that King Kosol gave to the Buddha that was superior to all other Alms Feasts, and on the final day she made an offering of one hundred and forty million. She also made offerings of a white umbrella to protect the Buddha's head, a seat for him to sit on during a meal, a stand on which he could place his begging bowl, and a rug on which he could place his feet after washing.[1] These four gifts were invaluable.

When Queen Mallika was about to die she did not think of all the offerings she had gifted to the Buddha but thought only of the Acts of Demerit she had committed and so she was reborn in the Avīci hell.[2] Since she was very dear to the king, his grief at her death was very great. After cremating her body he went to the Buddha thinking, 'I will inquire where she has now been reborn.' The Buddha decided it were better that the king should not ask that question and directed the discourse accordingly. The king talked of many things with the Buddha and then returned to the palace. There he remembered the question he meant to ask and thought, 'I went to the Buddha to inquire where Mallikā had been reborn and did not do so. I will ask him tomorrow.'

1. Monks in Sri Lanka traditionally walked barefoot. Since they traveled distances through dust and mud it was customary to wash and wipe a monk's feet before he entered a home for an alms feast. The washing of the feet by a lay disciple is still done in Sri Lanka, even though now it is more a symbolic gesture.
2. Unlike in Christianity where remembering one's sins helps one to repent at the moment of death, Buddhists believe that it is the final thought at the point of death, which determines one's immediate next birth. In this case the queen thought not of her Acts of Merit but of the sin she had committed and so was born in hell.

He went again on the second day. The Buddha, for seven consecutive days, willed that he should not remember the question.

Since Queen Mallikā's Acts of Demerit were mitigated by her Acts of Merit, she burned in hell for seven days, not according to the time frame in hell but in terms of human time. On the eighth day she left that place and because the lie she had said was not seriously damaging and because her Acts of Merit were many, she was reborn in the Tusita[3] heaven.

We may ask; why did the Buddha will that for seven days the king should not remember his question? That queen was very dear to King Kosol. The Buddha knew that had he been told she was born in hell, he would have thought, 'If even one such as Mallikā, who performed so many Acts of Merit and gave so generously is reborn in hell, then what is the use of my making these offerings?' Losing faith in the positive returns of offering alms he would stop the offerings laid out for the five hundred monks, engage only in evil deeds, and end up in hell. So, out of compassion, the Buddha willed that he should forget for seven days. On the eighth day, while on his begging rounds, he went himself to the king's palace.

The king heard the Buddha had arrived, took his begging bowl, and led the way to the upper story. The Buddha said he preferred to remain on the lower floor where the chariots were kept. The king then made a seat for the Buddha right there, ordered gruel and sweets to be served, and after he had eaten asked, "Your Reverence, for seven days I came to see you wanting to inquire where Queen Mallikā had been reborn. But I forgot and did not ask. Where has she been reborn Your Reverence?" he asked.

"O King, she has been born in the Tusita heaven," replied the Buddha.

"Had she not been born in the Tusita heaven who else would be fit to be born there? Apart from Viśākhā and a few others, who among women can compare with her? When did she ever engage in any activity other than the offering of alms? Your Reverence, ever since her death I can't contain my grief."

"Great King, do not grieve. All things that are born must die." He then asked, "Whose is this chariot?"

"This belonged to my grandparents, Your Reverence."

He pointed to the next chariot and asked, "Whose is this one?"

"It belonged to my father," the king replied.

The Buddha pointed to yet another and asked, "Whose is this one?"

The king answered that it was his.

"Your Majesty, your grandfather's chariot could not [function long enough to] become your father's chariot. Just as your father's chariot could not last long enough to be used as your chariot. Even wooden objects such as these

3. Another of the six heavens in Buddhist cosmology.

are subject to decay. What then of human life which is all subject to decay." So saying he preached a sermon.

"O King, even the decorated chariots, from the moment of their construction, fall apart, little be little. Not just the chariots but this body that we consider ours, from the very day of its birth, moves toward decay. What then is not subject to decay? The doctrine of the Ninefold Spiritual Attainments of good men like the Buddhas, since it remains unchanged throughout all time, does not decay. Sages like the Buddha, when they speak, speak specially to those who are intelligent. There is no use talking to those foolish ones who do not think of death and decay and so he does not address them."

At the end of the sermon many achieved Enlightenment.

Therefore since death and decay come to all men, good men should perform Acts of Merit whenever possible, before they become unfit to do so, enjoy the material comforts that result from such meritorious acts, and finally achieve the blessings of *nirvāṇa*.

15

The Mother of the Elder Kumāra Kasub

One should not seek refuge in others; one should be one's own refuge. To illustrate this we relate the story of the mother of Kumāra Kasub.

How does it go?

She was the daughter of a wealthy nobleman of Rajagaha. From the time she could discriminate between good and bad she knew that she must be her own refuge and so pleaded with her parents to let her become a nun. She did not get her parents' permission, though she begged them to let her go. When she came of age she was given in marriage. She then became a devoted and faithful wife, treating her husband almost like a god. Shortly after marriage she became pregnant. Unaware that she was pregnant she convinced her husband of the benefits of ordination and obtained his permission to become a nun. He conducted her in a great procession, with much ceremony, and unwittingly had her ordained by nuns of the Order of Devidat.

After some time the nuns realized that the young nun was pregnant and asked, "How did this happen?"

"I do not know. I have not broken my vows of chastity," she replied. The nuns of Devidat's Order then took her to Devidat and said, "This woman took ordination of her own wish and choice. Up to now we have not known her to do anything like this. Nor do we know when she became pregnant. What should we do?"

Devidat, not being a Buddha, was concerned only with the disgrace to his Order, and unaware of that nun's good standing, said, "Disrobe and expel her."

At that, the young nun who had taken orders because of her strong faith, said, "O nuns do not destroy me. I did not become a nun because of Devidat. My allegiance is to the Buddha. That Buddha who knows what happened in the past and what will happen in the future will surely know what is happening here. If the Buddha in his wisdom so decides, I will give up the robes. If not I will remain a nun. Take me to him at the Deveramvehera monastery."

They agreed, took her to the Deveramvehera monastery, and informed the Buddha of the case. The Buddha with his powers of foreknowledge knew that she had become pregnant while still a householder but wishing to silence all talk he invited the king of Kosol, the noble merchant Anēpidu, senior, the merchant Anēpidu the younger, Viśākhā, and several other prominent people. He asked them all and appointed the Elder Upāli Thera, preeminent in the practice of the Doctrine, to be the judge.

"Upāli, in the midst of this Fourfold Assembly[1] question the young nun and clear her good name," he said.

The Elder Upāli called Viśākhā and gave her the task of determining whether the nun had become pregnant when she was still a laywoman or after she took the orders. Viśākhā drew a curtain around the nun and examined her hands, feet, navel, and stomach. Since Viśākhā herself had borne twenty children she could calculate the days and months of the pregnancy and assess it in relation to the time she joined the Order. "Had the pregnancy occurred during her time as a nun, then her hands, feet, navel, and stomach would not be like this. It is because the fetus is fairly well developed that it looks like this," she concluded and informed the Elder Upali that the nun had become pregnant while still a householder. Amid the Fourfold Assembly the Elder cleared her name saying, "This woman is innocent of the gravest of transgressions.[2] Since she was declared innocent in the Fourfold Assembly, disreputable talk [such as] 'What Devidat had expelled as unclean the Buddha has taken in as clean,' did not arise.

When her pregnancy reached full term, the nun gave birth to a son of great good fortune, power, and much Merit, who, in the time of the Buddha Padumattara had made a Rebirth-Wish to achieve Enlightenment as a monk. One day King Kosol happened to pass by the nunnery and heard a small child's cries. When he asked how this came about he was told of the nun and her child. He then took the child to the palace and gave him over to foster mothers to care. On his name day he was called "Kaśyapa" and since he had been brought up in the palace like a prince he was called "Kumāra Kasub," or "Prince Kasub."[3]

In the playground one day, when the young boy got into a fight with his small friends they said, "Only one who has no parents would do that." When

---

1. Consists of monks, nuns, and male and female lay devotees.
2 [s. *mūlāpattiya*] For a monk or nun the act of sex is considered the first and most serious transgression of the Rules of Conduct.
3. Kasub or Kasup is the Sinhala short form for the name Kaśyapa.

he heard that Kasub ran to the king and said, "O King, my friends call me the 'one who has no parents.' I think Your Majesty is my father. Who is my mother?" The king showed him one of his foster mothers and said that she was his mother. "This woman is not my mother. There must be another who is my mother," he answered. The king realized he could not hide it from him and said, "Your mother is a nun. I brought you here to care for you."

The boy was a person of great Merit so with just that word, he lost all desire for the comforts of the lay life and said, "O Father, please ordain me." The king agreed, took him with great ceremony to the Buddha, and had him ordained. He soon obtained the higher ordination and became well-known as the Elder Kumāra Kasub. Not satisfied with that, he obtained a meditation exercise from the Buddha, went to the forest, and worked very hard at it. But just as one cannot reap a harvest on the very day one sows the seed, so, because his intellect was still not fully developed he was unable to achieve any special Attainment.[4] He thought. 'I will ask him to clarify it further.' He went to the Buddha and thereafter continued to live in the Anada forest. The god Brahma who had been a fellow monk with him during the time of the Buddha Kasup, had now reached the stage of an *Anāgāmin* and was living in the world of Brahma gods. He came down and asked him fifteen questions. "These questions can be answered only by the Buddha, none other. Go to him and get the answers to these questions," he advised. Kumara Kasub did as he was told, went to the Buddha, and when the questions were answered, he became Enlightened, an *arahat*.

Ever since he had been taken away, for twelve years now, his mother, the nun, had walked around with her eyes full of tears. Grieving with a mother's grief, yet staunch in her commitment to her vows of ordination, she would go on her begging rounds to the inner city, her face streaked with tears. One day she saw the Elder and she ran to clasp him, saying, " My dear little son, my little son." But as she ran she tripped and fell. She stood up, her robe all wet with the milk that had come flooding to her breasts, and she clasped the Elder. He on his part thought, 'If she were to hear a soft word from me, she will not be able to rid herself of her affections and will wither away. I will talk to her firmly.' So he said, "Affection is not good for one who practices the ascetic life. A farmer will not have a successful harvest if he does not dig up the grass that suffocates the rice plants. Similarly, if one does not rid oneself of affection, not just the ascetic life but life itself will be destroyed."

"My dear son, what are you saying?" asked the nun. He repeated the same thing again.

---

4. There are eight Attainments, endowments, or modes of abstraction induced by ecstatic meditation.

'For twelve long years, day and night, eating and sleeping, I have shed tears for this man. Alas, he has a hard heart. In this long *saṃsāric* cycle of rebirths, who has not been my child? What use is this son to me?' she thought. With that, the affection that had so powerfully gripped her for twelve years vanished in an instant. That very day, desires that had existed over an infinite time period during her journey in *saṃsāra* were all extinguished and she became an *arahat.*

In the congregation of monks one day the talk went thus: "Look at Devidat's ignorance. In one moment both Kumāra Kasub and his mother would have been destroyed had the Buddha not rescued them." The Buddha heard them and said, "Monks, this is not the first time that I have been of help to these two. In the past too I have helped them. Once when I, Devidat, this nun, and Kumāra Kasub were born as deer, there was an order that each day one deer from his herd and the next day one deer from my herd should die. Once when it was her turn to put her head on the block because she was with young she requested that she be allowed to miss her turn and that he send another in her place. He refused. That day I went myself and put my head on the block and so saved her and her son the young foal. I saved not just them but all the deer, other four footed creatures, birds and fish, and all things. At the time I saw to it that they each went on to their natural deaths instead of being killed. Now, I have obtained the strength to save all from the sorrows of *saṃsāric* rebirth."

So saying he related the Nigrōdha Jātaka story and explained it saying, the Kola deer at the time was Devidat. His followers were his herd. The deer whose turn had come was this nun. Her son was Kumāra Kasub. The king of the Nigrōdha deer who gave his life for the pregnant doe was me. He then praised the nun for helping herself by breaking the bonds of affection that tied her to her child.

"When born a human being one can perform Acts of Merit such as the giving of alms to get to heaven or cultivate the Path and the Fruits and achieve Enlightenment. Thus one must be a refuge to oneself. If one does not become a refuge for oneself who else can be one's refuge? If one disciplines oneself well, one can obtain the blessings of the Nine Spiritual Attainments so hard to achieve." At the end of the sermon many attained *nirvāṇa.*

Those that are wise must not waste time protecting others. Just as a fisherman lifts a fish out of the water, one must lift oneself up with wisdom and just as a fisherman gets much profit even from small sprats, so with small Acts of Merit one can obtain much bliss. In culmination try to obtain the blessings of *nirvāṇa.*

16

The Weaver's Daughter

We shall relate the story of the weaver's daughter in order to illustrate the benefits of practicing meditation on the inevitability of death.

How does it go?

One day when the Buddha arrived at the city of Alavi the citizens invited him for an Alms Feast. When he had eaten, the Buddha, as was his practice, preached a sermon for the Transference of Merit.

"Life is not permanent; death is inevitable. Life has death as its end. Therefore meditate on the inevitability of death. If a person has not practiced the Death-Meditation,[1] when he is about to die, he will be like one who sees serpents, is terrified, and dies, bawling and screaming. But if a person has practiced this Meditation, when he is about to die he will see the serpents of his fear of death from afar, hold them down with the stick of this Meditation, fling them far away,[2] and die unafraid. Therefore, practice this Death-Meditation," he preached.

Most of those who heard the sermon thought, 'Death-Meditations may be good for some, but what of it?' and went about their own affairs. One sixteen-year-old weaver's daughter thought, 'The revered Buddha will never tell us anything that is not for our good. I had better practice this Death-Meditation.' She practiced it day and night. [After the sermon] the Buddha returned to the Deveramvehera monastery.

1. A meditative exercise that focuses on the inevitability of death.
2. The image would be familiar to villagers who trap serpents in this manner even today.

The young woman practiced this Meditation for over three years. One morning, at dawn, as the Buddha cast his mind's eye over the world, the weaver's daughter [floated into his vision] and was caught in the net of his wisdom. He considered what might be of use to her. 'From the day she heard my sermon, for three years now, this young woman has practiced the Death-Meditation. I will go there and ask her four questions and when she answers them I will applaud her and recite a doctrinal stanza. When she hears the stanza she will develop understanding and become a *sōvān*. Because of this young woman many will benefit.'

With that knowledge the Buddha, attended by five hundred monks, left the Deveramvehera monastery and proceeded to the Aggālava monastery. The residents of the city of Alavi heard the Buddha had come, went to the monastery, and invited him. The weaver's daughter too heard the news of the Buddha's arrival and delighted, thought, 'My father, my Lord, my teacher, with a face like the full moon has come. It is three years since I saw that golden Buddha. Now I shall see the Buddha's golden, fragrant body. I shall hear his sweet sermons.'[3]

Just then her father who was leaving for the weavers' workshop said, "Child, I have undertaken to weave a piece of cloth for someone. It is almost done but there is about a span more to complete. I must finish it today. Spin the flax quickly and bring it to me."

The young woman thought, 'I want to hear the Buddha's sermon but now my father has asked me to do this for him. What shall I do? Should I go hear the sermon or should I spin the flax my father needs?' Then she thought, 'My father will kill me[4] if I don't get the flax to him. I will do that first and then go listen to the Buddha.' She sat down in the chair and began to spin the flax.

The citizens of Alavi offered alms to the Buddha and thereafter invited him to preach a sermon for the Transference of Merit. The Buddha thought, 'I have walked twelve leagues and come here for the sake of a certain young woman. I see she has still not had the leisure to come. When she finds the time to come I will preach my sermon for the Transference of Merit.' So he sat in silence. If the Buddha sits in silence and does not preach, no one, not even Brahma or the gods have the power to do or say anything.

The young woman spun the flax, put it in her weaver's bag, and on her way to her father passed by the outer edge of the crowd around the Buddha.

3. The woman's youthful enthusiasm is clearly conveyed in her reaction to the news. It contrasts dramatically with the maturity exhibited in her answers later on before the assembly.
4. In Sinhala, as also in English, the phrase is often used in conversation and not to be taken literally.

She kept looking at him as she went. Just then the Buddha lifted his head and looked the young woman in the eye. As if he had looked at her and spoken, she on her part thought, 'While such a large gathering of monks and laity are waiting he has picked me out as if he knew I wished to hear him.' She put down the bag she was carrying and went to the Buddha. Why did the Buddha look her in the eye as if wanting to talk to her?—Because he knew that this woman was destined to die that day. Were this woman to proceed on her way and not come to hear him, even though she had practiced the Death-Meditation for three years and would be fearless at the point of death, yet she would die without her next rebirth being determined.[5] But if she were to come to him, listen to his sermon, and become a *sōvān,* she would immediately be reborn in the Tusita heaven.

The young woman went up to him as if the Buddha had called her to preach to her in person. As one who decks herself in ornaments in preparation for attaining *nirvāṇa*, she entered the aura of his radiance, decked in the rays emanating from the Buddha,[6] worshiped him, and stood on one side.

The Buddha, who all that while had sat silent despite the invitations of the lay devotees to preach, now addressed the young woman who was reverentially standing by.

"Young woman, where have you come from?" he asked.

"I do not know, Your Reverence," she replied.

"Where are you going?" he asked.

"Your Reverence, I do not know where I am going," she said.

"Do you not know?" he asked.

"Your Reverence, I do know," she replied.

"Do you know?" he asked.

I do not know, Your Reverence," she answered.

Thus the Buddha asked her four questions. Where have you come from? Where are you going? Do you not know? Do you know?

Several people who were there said, "Look at the insolence of this weaver's daughter! She walks up to the Buddha and says things off the top of her head. When he asked her 'Where are you coming from?' why didn't she say 'From the weaver's house,' and when he asked 'Where are you going?' why couldn't she say 'To the workshop where they weave cloth.'"

The Buddha heard their comments and putting a stop to the recriminations said, "Young woman, when I asked you where you came from why did you reply that you did not know?"

---

5. For Buddhists, future rebirth is always a cause of fear as it is unknown. However, if one attains to the first stage of the path and becomes a *sōvān,* then Enlightenment is assured and rebirth holds no fears.

6. The Buddha is often depicted as surrounded by a halo of light that has all the colors of the rainbow. The Sinhala term is *budu räs* or "Buddha-rays."

"Your Reverence, you who know the past, present, and the future, who, without any external aids, but by your own intellect and insight understood the transient nature of conditioned existence, you surely knew that I came from the weaver's house. Therefore, when you asked where I came from you must have meant, 'Where were you before you were born here in this world?' Since I do not know from where I came I said I did not know."

The Buddha knew that that was in fact his question and that her answer to it was correct. He applauded saying, "Indeed that is so." He continued, "When I asked where you were going why did you say you did not know?"

"Your Reverence, you knew that I was carrying my weaver's bag and was headed for the weavers' workshop. If knowing that, you still asked me where I was going, it was because you were asking the question, 'When you die and leave here where will you go?' I do not know where I will go when I die, so though I knew I was going to the weavers' workshop I said I did not know."

"Well said young woman. You have answered the question that I asked," said the Buddha and applauded her a second time saying, "Woman, that is good. But when I asked the ordinary question, 'Do you not know?' why did you say you did know?" he asked.

"Your Reverence, I know that since I was born I must also surely die, so I said 'I do know.' "

To that too the Buddha said, "You have answered the question just as I asked it." He applauded a third time saying, "That is good. But when I asked if you knew, why did you say you did not know?"

"Your Reverence, I know that I will die but I do not know whether it will be at night, or during day, of a morning or an afternoon, so I said I did not know."

The Buddha responded, "You have interpreted the question just as I asked and answered well." He applauded again for a fourth time. Then he turned to the gathering of worshipers and said, "You, all of you, though you consider yourself learned enough to blame others, did you not fail to understand my questions, unlike this sixteen-year-old young woman? Do you now blame this young woman for insolence when she has understood and responded rightly? If a person does not acquire the Eye of Wisdom, the Eye of Faith alone is of no use. That person is still blind. Only one who has acquired the Eye of Wisdom has good vision."

He then preached thus: "These worldly persons do not have the Eye of Wisdom, do not see what they should see, and therefore are blind. But if one contemplates the Three Characteristics[7] such as Impermanence one is humbled.

---

7. The Three Characteristics are Impermanence, Sorrow, and Soullessness.

Just as a snarer of birds who is skilled at his task throws his net and snares them all, letting not one escape, so the snarer Death with his net of Attachment ensnares all within his mesh."

At the end of his sermon the young woman became a *sōvān*. If asked the question 'Where are you going?' she now had the strength to answer 'I am going to heaven.' Many others also found this sermon of great use.

The young woman took the bag of flax and went to where her father was weaving cloth. He had fallen asleep at his seat. As she unthinkingly put down her bag it struck the end of the loom with a loud clatter. The weaver awoke and tugged at the string that worked the shuttle that he was holding. It struck hard against the body of the young woman standing in its path. She fell down dead right there. Her father stood up to look and when he saw her body smothered in blood he was consumed with grief.

He went to the Buddha and told him about the death of his daughter and his great grief at the loss adding, "O great and revered Lord, you who are free of all sorrow, make me also sorrowless." The Buddha, to comfort him said, "Do not grieve. In this endless journey of *saṃsāra* the tears you have shed at the death of this same daughter, none other, are more than the waters that fill the four vast oceans." He then recited the *Anamatagga sutta*.[8] The weaver's grief was eased, he became a monk, grew old in the Order, and after some time achieved Enlightenment as an *arahat* and became sorrowless.

Thus, like the weaver's daughter, good people should look on the fears of rebirth with the Eye of Wisdom, and free themselves from it, perform Acts of Merit, and win the blessings of Enlightenment.

---

8. A sermon on the endlessness of the cycles of existence.

17

The Young Woman Ciṇca

In order to illustrate the consequences of harming the harmless, we will relate the story of the the young woman Ciṇca.

How does it go?

Just as the mouths of all rivers come together in the ocean, so when the Buddha attained Enlightenment many disciples were drawn to him, many attained *nirvāṇa,* and because the nine virtues of a Buddha[1] were now displayed on earth, he received tremendous respect and support.

The *Tirtakas* became like glowworms in the face of a rising sun that was moving ever higher. Just as fireflies have no luster once the sun rises, so the *Thirtaka* fireflies lost their public appeal as the sun of the Enlightened One displayed the light of his person and his Doctrine. They lost all support and respect and like packs of dogs who howl when deprived of their food, so they stood at street corners and alley-ways and shouted, "What? Has the monk, Gōtama, now become a Buddha to all of you? Are we not Buddhas too? What is it? Do the gifts given to him bring special rewards in the afterlife? Does what is given to us not bring rewards as with a barren woman? If what you give to the Monk Gotama brings rewards in the afterlife, what is given to us does so too. Therefore give to us. Support us."

---

1. The nine attributes of perfection that characterize a Buddha are described in this manner. He is the worthy one; the perfectly enlightened one; endued with higher knowledge and good conduct; the blessed one; the one who has comprehended the universe; the guide of men; the teacher of gods and men; the awakened one; and the exalted one.

However, though they walked about declaiming, they got neither respect nor support. Sitting alone [without a following] they plotted, "How can we cause some disgrace to the monk, Gōtama and deprive him of support and respect?"

At the time, in the city of Sävät, there was a wandering female ascetic called the "young maiden Ciṇca." She was very beatiful. Her body glowed like that of a goddess. One wily member of the *Tirtakas* said, "Let us create a scandal about the monk Gōtama using the young woman Ciṇca as its source." The others all agreed. "Let it be so," they said.

Sometime later the female ascetic, the young maiden Ciṇca, went to the monastery of the *Tirtakas* and respectfully saluted them. The *Tirtakas* did not talk to her. Afraid that she might have done something wrong, she said three times, "I greet you, your Reverences," but getting no response from them she initiated the conversation herself.

"Your Reverences, what have I done wrong that you do not talk to me?"

"Why, female ascetic, do you not know that the monk Gōtama has fooled the world and has appropriated for himself all the support and respect due to us and goes about disgracing us?"

"Your Reverences, up to now I had not heard it. I now know it. What should I do about it?"

"Well then female ascetic, if you wish to help us, use whatever means to create a scandal about the monk Gōtama, and just as a river at high tide flows upstream so turn the flow of support toward us."

As feces mixes with urine[2] she agreed with their filthy ideas. Saying, "Do not be upset," she departed.

Though lacking in intelligence she was skilled in female wiles. From that day forth, every evening, when the citizens of Sävät were returning home after listening to sermons, she wrapped herself in a red garment like a red ladybug, and bearing scents and garlands, walked in the direction of the Deveramvehera monastery. When people asked, "Where are you going at this hour?" she replied, "Why should you question my comings and goings? What is that to you?" Thus by her loaded speech she would arouse doubt in the minds of those who, like her, had evil thoughts. She would then spend the night at the monasteries of the *Tirtakas* near the Deveramvehera monastery, and early the next morning, at the time when devotees, eager to be the first to worship the Buddha, hastened to the Deveramvehera monastery, she would walk toward the city as if she had spent the night at the Deveramvehera monastery. To those who asked, "Where did you sleep?" she would reply, "What is it to you where I sleep? Must you inquire into that?" and depart.

2. This image appears only in the SR. Images of feces and urine occur often in the SR signifying filth and repulsion.

After about a month or two quarters had passed she would reply to those who questioned her, "Where else would I sleep? Those who are beautiful are led astray. I'm returning from the Deveramvehera monastery where I shared the same bedchamber with the monk, Gōtama." Thus she caused doubts in the simpleminded. After three or four months had passed she wrapped rags around her stomach to make it seem big, covered herself in a red robe as if to suggest she was with child, and said, "I have conceived a child by the monk, Gōtama." She created much Demerit for herself by making the ignorant accept her word. When eight or nine months had passed she wrapped a bundle of faggots around her belly, covered herself in a robe, made her hands and feet swell by beating them with ox bones to seem as if the time of delivery was near, and went one evening to the assembly where the Buddha was preaching. She stood before the Buddha and said, "Monk, you preach to large numbers of people. Your voice is so powerfully attractive as to be never enough for your listeners. Your appearance is even more attractive. There is a child now in my womb fathered by you. The time of the delivery is near. I have no place in which to give birth. Up-to-date no provisions, whether it be oil or chili spices, have been given me. Even if *you* do not do it, you might say to your devotees the king of Kosol, or the rich merchant Anāthapindika, or Viśākhā, 'That young maiden Ciṇca is with child. Since it is also our child, I am bound to do something. Do what you can for her without delay.' Why do you not command them thus? Just as you needed no persuasion to cohabit with me, so you should have commanded them without my having to ask you to do so." Thus, as if flinging excrement on the body of a clean and pure person, she continued, "You cohabited with me, fathered a child, and now you must do what is needed." Like one who tries to fling a fistful of dung at the moon even though it can never touch it, so she berated the Buddha seated in the middle of the Fourfold Assembly. She was able to berate him thus because her past evil acts were about to reach fruition. They encouraged her to speak thus. Unable to resist that compulsion she berated him.

The Buddha concluded his sermon and like a lion roaring, said, "Female ascetic, only you and I know whether what you say is true or false."

"Monk, that is so. It is because only you and I know it that it happened," she replied.

At that moment Sakra's seat heated.[3] He realized that just as there are no flowers on the *Diṁbul* tree so the young maiden Ciṇca was accusing the Buddha with baseless allegations. 'I will convince them that this is false,' he thought and arrived with four gods. The four gods transformed themselves into mice and together bit through the ropes that bound the faggots around

3. Sakra's seat heats up when some grave injustice is committed in the world of humans, and he then intervenes.

her belly. A gust of wind arose to lift up the robe with which she had covered herself. As the faggots fell they pierced her feet. The toes of both feet were cut off.

The people saw it all and said, "You wretched girl, why did you say and do this to the Buddha who is faultless?" They spat on her head, beat and kicked her, and drove her from the monastery. As she went out of sight of the Buddha, the earth, as when it has been dried and cracked for the past eight or nine months and then splits apart, now split and opened. At the same time a flame from *Avici* hell rose up through the crevice and as if wrapping her in a robe, enveloped the young maiden Ciṇca, and hurled her into hell. As for the *Tirtakas* even the little gain and honor they had received dried up. Respect and support for the Buddha increased, as a wick when dipped in oil burns ever brighter.

The next day, the monks gathered at the preaching hall commented, "Monks, what a disaster overtook that female ascetic, when she thus falsely accused the Buddha." The Buddha heard them and added, "Monks, it is not just on this occasion that she has spoken falsely and been destroyed. In the past too when I was born as the Great Prince Padumā, she wished to cohabit with me. Though she has gone through numerous transformations of births during four incalculables and one hundred thousand aeons there has been no change in her evil nature. When my mother the queen died, she became my father's wife and since she could not have me she tried various strategems to have me killed and made various accusations against me. But no harm came to me. Then too, it was she herself who was destroyed. The only difference between what she did then and now is that this time she has achieved nothing by her words. At that time, because of what she said, my father had me flung down a cliff from where robbers are hurled. The god who lived on that rock did not allow me to hit against the rock but bore me and placed me on the hood of a snake-king. The snake-king took me to his snake abode and gave me half his kingdom. I stayed there a year. Then, wishing to become a monk I came to the foot of the Himalayas, became a monk, and attained psychic power.

A hunter saw me and informed the king my father. The king came to see me, inquired how I had escaped death, and invited me back to rule the kingdom. I said, 'I no longer wish to rule. Do you continue to rule the kingdom in accordance with the Ten Practices of good rule.'"[4] Sad and mournful he was returning to his kingdom when along the way he asked his ministers, 'Who was it who estranged me from such a good son?' When they told him it was his chief queen's doing, he had her thrown down the rock and there-

4. [s. *dasarājadharma]* They are generosity, morality, magnanimity, straightforwardness, gentle nature, practice of austerities, absence of hatred; nonviolence; forbearance; and avoidance of contrariness.

after, ruled the kingdom well. Then too her attempts to kill me resulted in her own death," said the Buddha relating the Jātaka Tale of the Great Prince Padumā. "Now in attempting to slander me she has died."

He then preached to the gathered assembly, saying, "Even if one were to keep talking for an entire day, if one does not speak the truth but only what is false, that person cannot obtain the blessings of heaven, of this world, or of *nirvāṇa*. There is no wrong however bad that cannot be done by persons who have no hopes for a better existence in the next birth. Evils befall those who lie." At the end of the sermon many attained Enlightenment.

Thus good people should avoid falsehood like avoiding poison and consider true words to be like a good friend. They should live in goodness and attain *nirvāṇa*.

18

The Three Daughters of Māra

Moreover, in order to show how the Enlightened One, whatever insults he may have received, ignored them, and concerned himself only with what was of benefit to others, we shall relate the story of the three daughters of Māra.

How does it go?

In the country of Kuru there was a brahmin named Māgandi who had a daughter called Māgandiya. She was extremely beautiful.[1] Many brahmins and kings approached Māgandi requesting the hand of his daughter. He refused them saying, "Though you may all be wealthy none of you are good-looking enough for my daughter.

Some time after, as the Buddha cast his glance over the world one dawn, the brahmin Māgandi was caught in the net of his wisdom. And, with his Buddha-knowledge as he contemplated what would be of use to this man, he knew that both the brahmin and his wife were soon to become *anāgāmins*.

The brahmin was in the habit of leaving the village each morning and going out to perform rituals to the fire-god. The Buddha, took his robe and begging bowl and came, very early in the morning, to where the brahmin was worshiping the fire-god. The brahmin saw the Buddha's infinitely compassionate, handsome, appearance and thought, 'There is no one in the world as handsome as this man. He is surely fit for my daughter and my daughter is fit for him. I will give her in marriage to him.'

1. This story is a repetition of the Māgandi story of the Udēnī cycle. It gives a fuller context however, for the negative antifeminist image used earlier.

"Monk, I have a very beautiful daughter," he said. "I've been looking for a man good enough for her but so far I have found none and so have not given her in marriage. You alone are fit for her. I will give you my daughter in marriage. Do not leave this place. Stay here till I bring her to you."

The Buddha heard him but said neither 'Very well' nor 'I don't like it.'

The brahmin went home and said to his wife, "Good woman, today when I went to worship the fire-god I met someone fit for my daughter. I will give my daughter in marriage to him."

He had his daughter adorned and went with her and his wife to that place. A large crowd of people followed amazed, expecting something very unusual to happen.

The Buddha, instead of staying where the brahmin had told him to wait, moved to another place leaving only his footprint, like the auspicious mark on the forehead of the earth-goddess. If the Buddha leaves his footprint with the intention that a particular person see it, then it remains to be seen by him alone. It will not be visible to anyone else.

The brahmin's wife who was accompanying him looked around and said, "Where is the man now?"

"I asked him to wait here," said the brahmin, and looking about saw the footprint. "Here is his footprint," he said. The brahmin's wife, knew the science of signs well.

"Brahmin, this is not the mark of one who lives a lay life," she said.

"Good woman, you see crocodiles in the water-pot. I mean to give my daughter to this man. He too has agreed. If he did not like it he would have said so."

"Brahmin, you know only to light the fire;[2] you know nothing else. Just as there are no women in the Brahma-world, so this footprint is that of one who has rid his mind of all lust and desire."

"Good woman, stop talking, be quiet and come with me," said the brahmin. Just as he moved away he saw the Buddha. "There's the person I spoke of," he said and went up to the Buddha.

"I have brought my daughter to give her in marriage to you. Take her," he said. Without saying, "I do not like your daughter" the Buddha said, "There is one thing I wish to say to you. Will you listen?" When they agreed, he continued to give in brief the story of the "Great Renunciation."

"Listen then; at twenty-nine years of age I gave up my life of royal pleasures, mounted Kanthaka, that king of horses, and left accompanied only by the charioteer Channa. At the city gates Vasavat-Māra[3] accosted me saying,

---

2. To tend the sacred fire is an important ritual task for a brahmin.
3. Another name for Māra.

'Prince Siddartha, stop. In seven days the wheel symbol of a universal monarch will descend for you.'

'Māra I know it. I will not stop.'

'Why do you not stop?'

'Because I am going to be a Buddha,' I replied.

'If so from today do not even think an evil thought. If you so much as think an evil thought I will know it, however silent it be.'

From that day for seven years he tried to find an opportunity. I too, for six years engaged in the strictest forms of asceticism. In the fifth week after I had become a Buddha I was seated under the ficus tree called "Ajapāla." At that moment Māra said, 'All this time I have unceasingly sought for some [negative] information about you and got none. You have survived my poison.'

Frustrated he stood by the roadside. His three daughters, Tanhā (Desire), Aratī (Infatuation), and Rāgā (Lust), said, 'We do not see our father. Where is he?'

Then they saw him standing on the roadside looking angry and said, 'Dear Father, why are you upset?'

When he told his three daughters the reason for his frustration they said, 'Father, do not be upset. We will arouse him, conquer him, and bring him to you.'

'He is not one to be subdued by anyone. Daughters, you will not succeed,' replied Māra.

'Father, we are women. We will bind him with the flowers of lust specially intended for capturing young men, and we will bring him to you. Do not be upset.' "[4]

They went to the Buddha and said, "Monk we will be your wives," and each sister in turn displayed her female charms. The Buddha though he heard what they said paid no more attention than he would to the howl of vixen who have lost their teeth. He desired them no more than he would a burned-out, shrunken old she-monkey. He did not raise his eyes to look nor did he speak. He sat unmoving like a stone statue. Again the three daughters of Māra said, "Men have many different ideas of what they desire. Some desire ten- and twelve-year-olds. Some desire very young children. Some desire mature women, others older women. We will arouse him in one way or another. Each one took one of the six forms, that of a young bride, of a pregnant woman, of the mother of one, the mother of two, a mature woman, and an old woman, and transforming themselves into hundreds and hundreds of guises, went up to the Buddha and said, "Monk all three of us sisters will be your wives." But they could not arouse desire in the Buddha. Since they

4. Note the author/translator's unconscious slip into third-person narration.

would not go away however long he remained silent, he said, "You evil women, leave. Why do you try so hard? You should focus your attention on one who has Impurities. The Enlightened one has no Impurities like lust just as you have no goodness in you." He then preached a sermon.

"An Enlightened One whose Impurities have been destroyed by means of Attainments such as becoming a *sōvān*, can no longer be aroused by desire. Therefore nothing can destroy him and none of the destroyed Impurities can again prevail. In what way then can you entice the Enlightened One, of infinite power, who has reached the ultimate wisdom, who has destroyed all the Impurities such as lust? Moreover, how will you ever bring under your sway an Enlightened One who has completely destroyed the one hundred and eight desires to go wherever he wishes, and who has no desire because all desires have been destroyed? So he preached and many gods *(dēvas)* attained *nirvāṇa*. The three daughters of Māra fled and hid themselves.

The Buddha then said, "Māgandi, in the past, I saw those three goddesses whose bodies were golden because they had only five of the thirty-two Impurities found in a human body. They did not have the other twenty-seven Impurities. Yet no desire arose in me just as no plants grow in a fire. Though your daughter's body seems to her and you to be beautiful it is filled with the thirty-two forms of decay. It is like a pot of feces, decorated on the outside. If there were some dirt on my foot and she were like the rag on which to clean it, I would not use her body even to clean the dirt on my foot. He then recited the following verse:

disvāna taṇhaṃ aratiṃ ragañca
nāhosi jhando api methunasmiṃ
kimevidaṃ muttakarī sapuṇṇaṃ
pādāpi naṃ samphusituṃ na icche

[Even after seeing Aratī [infatuation] Ratī [lust] and Rāgā [passion]
no passing thought of lust crossed my mind.
What then of this container [the human body] full of feces and urine,
I would not desire it even to wipe my feet.]

At the end of the recitation the brahmin and his wife both became *anāgāmin*. Just as nectar for some can be poison to others, so that sermon became poison to the young brahmin woman Māgandi. It will be useful to relate that elsewhere. Just as the Buddha ignored the unseemly words and vows of vengeance made by the brahmin woman Māgandi and considered only the good that would befall the two older people, so the wise should ignore worldly pleasures, live heedfully, and think only of achieving *nirvāṇa*.

19

Viśākhā's Questions

In order to show how different are the views of different people we will relate the story of Viśākhā's questions to the female lay devotees about the Special Observences on the Full Moon Day.

How does it go?

One full moon day, many citizens of the city of Sävät went to the temple together with about five hundred female lay devotees who were observing the Eight Precepts on that day. Viśākhā went up to the older devotees among the five hundred and asked, "Mothers, what do you hope to get by keeping these observances?"

"What use is all else to us? We hope only for the blessings of heaven," they replied.

This did not seem to be a satisfactory reason for Viśākhā so she went to the middle-aged women and asked them, "Elder and younger sisters, why do you perform these special observances on the full moon day?

"We want to free ourselves of our anger against our cowives," they all replied.

That did not satisfy her either.

She then went to the even younger women and asked, "Friends, what do you hope to get by performing these observances?"

"We hope to have a son as our firstborn," they said.

That wish seemed too petty[1] so she went to the young adolescents and asked them, "Children what do you hope to obtain by performing these observances?"

---

1. Viśākhā's response runs counter to the brahmanic norms of the time.

"We wish to marry young and not grow old confined to the home," they replied.[2]

Viśākhā heard the replies of the old women, the middle-aged women, the younger women, and the children and took them all to the Buddha so he could tell them not just that but much more. She told him their answers in sequence.

The Buddha listened and responded, "Viśākhā, these people's lives are like those of cowherds who try to use the stick of life to control their flock. Birth moves toward old age and decay. Old age heads toward sickness and disease. Disease heads toward death. Death cuts off all as if with an ax. Even so, the power of Delusion is so strong that they wish only for the [perpetuation] of the self. There is no one here who wishes to attain *nirvāṇa*."

He then continued, "O Viśākhā, just as a cowherd skilled in controlling his herd, beats with a stick the cattle that run astray and guides them to pastures that have grass and water, so life and decay, like a cowherd drive the cattle of life's process to the pastures of death. Thus birth drives both beauty and ugliness to decay. Decay drives them to disease. As streams and rivulets move to the rivers and from there on to the sea, so disease moves inevitably to death. Death, as if caught in a giant whirlpool destroys everything. This is what happens to those who wish for the pleasures of life. It were far better to wish for *nirvāṇa*." At the end of the sermon many attained to the Path and the Fruits such as *sōvān*.

Thus the wise should realize that decay, disease, and death arise from life. Life that is the root cause can be overcome only by becoming an *arahat*. Thus aim at becoming an *arahat*.

2. These comments provide us an interesting account of the prevailing social values and popular expectations of women.

20

Princess Rohiṇī

Moreover, to illustrate the ills that result from impatience we shall relate the story of Princess Rohiṇī.

How does it go?

At a certain time the Elder Anuruddha, son of the Sakya king Amitodhana, arrived at the city of Kimbulvat. His relatives heard of his arrival and went to engage in [religious] discussion with him. His sister the lay devotee Rohiṇī, did not go. The Elder asked, "Why has Rohiṇī not come?"

"She has a skin rash covering her entire body and so she was ashamed to come," they replied.

"Bring her to me," said the Elder.

She covered her body in a silken garment and came.

"When so many others came to talk to me why didn't you come, Rohiṇī?" asked the Elder.

"Your Reverence, my entire body is covered with a skin rash and I am ashamed to even step outside," she replied. It was not out of any disrespect but because I was ashamed that I did not come," she said.

"Whatever you may suffer from now, in order to be free of disease in future, do not neglect to perform Acts of Merit and Giving," he replied.

"What Act of Merit should I do?" she asked.

"Construct a refectory for the monks," he said.

"How can I pay for it?" she asked.

"Why, do you not have the jewelery that you wear?"

"I do," she said.

"How much are they worth?

"Over ten thousand," she replied.

"If that is so, sell the jewelery and with the money construct a refectory for the monks," he said.

"Your Reverence, I'm young and a woman. Who will do the work for me?" she asked.

The Elder said to her relatives who were gathererd there, "Help her to get this done."

"Your Reverence we will help her but in what way will you help?" they asked.

"Then gather the timber," he ordered and they did so.

The Elder too gave instructions for the construction of the refectory and said to Princess Rohiṇī, "Rohiṇī, build a two-storied refectory and as soon as the floor of the lower level is covered with planks, finish it with cowdung paste[1] and arrange seating for the monks. Set up pots, containers, and cauldrons and fill them with strained drinking water for the monks who will frequently be eating there."

She agreed, sold her ornaments, constructed the two-storied refectory, and from the moment the floor was covered with planks she set about finishing it with a coating of dung. She did this often and the monks too, often visited the refectory. By the power of the merit from this act of rubbing cowdung paste and preparing seating for the monks her skin rash began to disappear.

When the refectory was completed she invited the Buddha together with his retinue of monks and filled the hall with them. As one who gives charmed water to those suffering the pangs of labor,[2] so she made offerings of honeyed foods to them because her skin disease was now cured.

At the end of the meal the Buddha asked, as if he did not know, "Who was it who made the offering today?"

"Your Reverence it was given by the sister of this Elder, the princess Rohiṇī" they said.

"Where is she now?" asked the Buddha

"She is inside," they said.

---

1. Before the use of cement for flooring, all houses in Sri Lanka had earth floors finished with a smooth layer or paste made of cowdung. Once dried and hardened it was smooth, cool under foot, and could be swept and kept clean easily.

   The princess Rohiṇī is required to perform the act of rubbing cowdung paste on the floor of the refectory. Psychologically it is equivalent to the action of rubbing soothing ungents on her own skin, and yet it is also an act of humility as it is dung, not perfumed ungents she is handling.
2. It is a common among Budhists even today to administer charmed water to women in labor to ease their pain. The water is made magically potent by the recitation of certain stanzas (in this case the *Angulimāla pāritta* stanzas).

"Bring her to me," said the Buddha.

Although her skin disease had gone away her beautiful complexion had not yet been restored so she was reluctant to come out. Though she did not want to come, the Buddha insisted that she be brought. When she came and stood by, having greeted him, he said, "Why Rohiṇī, did you not come until they had to bring you here?"

"Your Reverence, although my skin disease is cured the new skin has not yet been fully restored, so I was ashamed to come out," she said.

"Rohiṇī, do you know why you got that skin disease?" he asked her.

"No," she said.

"Listen then. It was not because of something that was done to you by another. It was something that you did yourself." So saying he described it in detail.

"Long ago the chief queen of the king of Baranas was jealous of a certain courtesan and intending to cause her hurt she gathered some leaves of *kasabiliya*[3] and secretly crushed the leaves and scattered them in her bed amid her bed linens. She invited the courtesan to visit her and playfully, laughingly, she threw *kasabiliya* dust onto her. Instantly the woman's entire body reddened and came up in hives. The patches of rash grew large. Unable to bear the powerful discomfort she took to her bed. But with each toss and turn the *kasabiliya* leaves on the bed rubbed against her skin and her pain was unbearable. Rohiṇī, you were that chief queen of the king of Baranas. It was anger that made you throw *kasabiliya* on another and reap such ill consequences. Therefore anger should be avoided at all costs," he said. "An enraged person knows not what he does in his anger. Therefore shed all anger. The nine kinds of overweening pride only lengthen one's days in *saṃsāra* so avoid them completely. Until all doubts and falsehoods inherent in human beings and described in both the *suttas* and the *abhidamma*[4] texts are completely rooted out, one must at least temporarily try to subdue them. If one has shed the sense of 'I-ness' with regard to everything, that person is not attached to anything. A being who is not attached to anything will not suffer from the kind of grief and pain you had to suffer." Thus he spoke.

At the end of the sermon many attained Enlightenment. The princess Rohiṇī too feasted on the ambrosia of the Doctrine, rid herself of the three afflictions known as Impurities, became a *sōvān,* and was destined to achieve the deathless state *[nirvāṇa]*. Even though there was no medicine for her body, the medicine of Meritorious Acts entered her mind, soothed, and cured

---

3. A plant much like poison ivy or poison oak that can cause severe itching if one touches it.
4. Two of the three sections of the *Tripiṭaka* or Buddhist Canon.

her body and it became golden. Later, she died and was reborn in the Tavtisa heaven in the border between the heavenly abodes of four gods.

Like a lacquered image whose color increases as it matures, the consequences of her Acts of Merit in her previous birth reached their point of maturity and she was exquisitely beautiful. The four gods saw her and became fiercely enamored of her but since she was born in the marginal area between their four abodes they debated who should claim her. Unable to decide they finally came to Śakra, king of the gods and said, "Lord, investigate our claims and give your decision." The god Śakra saw the goddess Rohiṇī and fell even more in love with her than had done the other four gods. He asked the four gods, "What did you feel the moment you saw her?" One god replied, "I felt my heart pound like a war-drum." Another said, "I felt my mind that was like a rock become a river of molten fluid." The third said, "From the moment I set eyes on her my eyes that could see ahead went in all directions like the eyes of a crab." The fourth god said, "From the moment I saw her my mind fluttered like a banner tied to the crest of a *dāgoba*[5] and could not be stilled." At that the god Śakra said, "What all four of you say is good. But you can continue to live. I, if I cannot have her, will die. If I am to live I must have her."

At that the four gods said, "What good is it to us if your Lordship dies? It is better you should live." They left the goddess Rohiṇī for Śakra and departed. She was greatly beloved of Śakra. If the goddess Rohiṇī said, "Let us go to this or that amusement park," Śakra would not object.[6]

Thus the wise should control their anger. When anger arises, as if applying the necessary medicine for a disease and curing it, they should call to mind the necessary doctrinal remedies, rid themselves of hatred, do Acts of Merit, and attain *nirvāṇa*.

---

5. These are large burial mounds in which relics are enshrined. Many have gilded pinnacles that are sometimes decorated with banners.
6. In both the DA and the SR versions the story of Rohiṇī's past is part of the Buddha's sermon on anger and jealousy. The DA ends with the verse from the *Dhammapada* that this story is meant to illustrate. The sequel about Rohiṇī's future birth and how five deities (including Śakra the king of the gods) vie for her hand seems to be a charming comment on lovesickness even among the gods!

   The two parts are cleverly tied together, however. The story of the past illustrates the bad consequences of Rohiṇī's Acts of Demerit while the story of her beauty and the power of that beauty over Śakra illustrate the consequences of her Acts of Merit. The story is then rounded off with an additional doctrinal comment on remedies for controlling anger that is the central theme.

21

Uttarā

In order to illustrate the evils of anger and the benefits of forgiveness we shall relate the story of Uttarā.

How does it go?

In the city of Rajagaha there lived a poor man named Puṇṇa[1] who was the vassal of a noble merchant named Sumana. Apart from his wife and a daughter named Uttarā he had no other dependents.

One day there was an order from the king that there should be a week of auspicious celebrations in the city of Rajagaha. On hearing which, that very morning, the noble merchant Sumana called the poor man Puṇṇa and said, "Child,[2] our workers say that since we, [the landowners] are celebrating they wish to do so too. What do you want to do? Join in the celebrations or continue with your work?

"Master, festivities are for the rich. As for those like us, let alone riches, we do not even have the wherewithal to buy a measure of rice. Therefore what use are celebrations for us? If I can get a pair of bullocks I will go plough."

1. Note the name can be the same for both sexes but if it is a male there is no accent on the terminal "a."
2. The term by which the rich man addresses his vassal is *daruva* (child), suggesting the paternalism that was a part of the feudal relationship between master and servant. The vassal on the other hand addresses the master not as father, but as lord *(svamini)*. The same paternalism is seen in the readiness with which the workers' request to celebrate is granted. However Puṇṇa's response emphasizes the deep economic rifts in the society.

He took a pair of bullocks and his plough and before leaving said to his wife, "Dear One, city people are celebrating. We, because we are poor go to perform our labors. However that may be, please cook a little extra rice and curries, more than you normally do, and bring the food to me in the field." So saying he left to go plough his field.

The Captain of the Doctrine, the Great Elder Säriyut had spent the previous week in the Trance State of Cessation. The week was completed on that very day. He rose from his Trance, cast his Divine Eye over the world, and asked himself, "Whom shall I benefit today?" He noticed the poor man Puṇṇa, who, though trapped in *saṃsāra* was now caught in the net of his [Säriyut's] Wisdom, and thought, 'Let us see if he has sufficient faith to entertain me even though he has nothing himself.' He saw then that Puṇṇa did have the faith and would entertain him and that as a result of that action he would gain great wealth. So he took up his double robe and bowl, went to where the man was, and sat on a bank looking out over the forest.

Puṇṇa the poor man, saw the Great Elder and since he had already cultivated Mindfulness and Wisdom he now stopped his other cultivation, stood on one side, and greeted the monk, bowing down and making the five-point gesture of worship. 'This monk sits gazing at the forest because he probably needs some teeth-cleaning twigs,'[3] he thought. He cut some twigs and offered them to the monk. The monk then handed him his bowl and straining cloth. 'Though he has not requested it with words he must need some water,' thought Puṇṇa and filled the bowl with water, strained it, and gave it to the monk.

The Great Elder thought, 'This man works for another so his home must be in a corner of the yard behind the main house. If I were to go begging to the house his wife may not see me as she lives at the back. However, she is likely to come here bringing his meal of rice so I shall remain here till then.' He thus remained awhile and knowing she was on her way he began walking in her direction toward the inner city.

Puṇṇa's wife saw the monk approach and though she had no gold or silver she had a mind suffused with faith, so she thought, 'When we do have some little thing that we can offer we never find that Field of Merit, a monk, to offer it to. When, unexpectedly we meet a monk we never have anything to offer. Today I have found a monk full of goodness. I do also have some rice. It may not be that flavorful but the thoughts that went into the preparation of the food were clean and good thoughts. It is as if he has come to be of benefit to us poor folk in the same manner in which he favors the rich.'[4]

---

3. [s. *däviti dandu*] were the twigs of a particular plant that were used to brush one's teeth. Monks in rural areas of Sri Lanka still use them even today.
4. Monks were often invited to alms feasts *(dana)* at the homes of the rich. The poor have an opportunity to make offerings when monks go on begging rounds, as in this case.

Thus thinking she looked at her pot of rice, then worshiped the Great Elder in greeting and said, "Do not consider the rice I'm about to offer you as unfit, but in consideration of the Merit that will accrue from this act to that poor man and me his wife, and the Fruits of the Path that we might enjoy because of it, accept our poor food offering."

The Great Elder allowed her to serve about half the amount and then put his hand over the bowl to indicate that it was enough, knowing that they too would need some of it. The lay devotee understood his gesture and said, "Reverend Sir, if you divide in two the rice I brought for one person you will not have enough. For vassals like us, far more important than the food of this world are the blessings of the next world. Therefore I would like to offer it all." She thus served all the rice saying, "Though this rice may not be tasty, may I, by this Act of Merit, enjoy the extremely sweet taste of *nirvāṇa*."[5]

"May it be so," said the Great Elder.

Even though she believed the rice to be unfit, her thoughts were good so he preached a sermon accordingly. He then sat down in a place where there was some water and ate his meal using that good thought as the accompaniment to add flavor to the rice. The lay devotee returned home, took some more rice, and cooked it.

Puṇṇa, the poor man, fatigued after having ploughed almost two *ammunums*,[6] unable to bear the pangs of hunger, released his bullocks, sought a shady place, and waited expectantly, watching the road. His wife, who was delayed in bringing the meal, saw as she approached that the bullocks used for ploughing had already been released, and thought, 'Since he did not have a meal before setting out in the morning he must be hungry, tired, and anxiously watching the road. Therefore, not knowing the cause for the delay were he to get angry and beat me with a stick, I too will get angry. Like rice that has been cooked and then burned, the effects of the Act of Merit I just performed will then be diminished and that will not be good. I will therefore not get close but explain everything from a distance. So saying she shouted, "Husband, set your mind at ease on this day. Do nothing to spoil the Act of Merit I performed today. I was coming early morning with your rice cooked and ready but on the way I met the Captain of the Doctrine [the Monk Sariyut] and offered him the rice I was bringing to you. I then returned home, got some more rice, cooked it, and am now bringing it to you. That was the reason for the delay. Think now of the gift that was given and let your mind be happy."

---

5. The wife performs her Act of Merit in the expectation not of material benefits but of *nirvāṇa* or "Enlightenment." By contrast her husband sees the Act of Merit as intended to bring them wealth and retinues.
6. An extent of acreage. It is calculated on the amount of rice needed for sowing a given area.

Puṇṇa's hunger was so great that he could not understand what she was saying, so he questioned her again. When he heard the story he said, "It was a very good thing you did to offer the rice you brought for me to the monk. Now, for as long as we are in *saṃsāra,* our anxieties regarding food have been taken care of. I too offered him some teeth-cleaning twigs this morning. By that act, as long as we stay in *saṃsāra* may we never lack the benefits of companions and a retinue." He said this with a calm mind. Thus, even though she had not done it on his instructions, he was pleased with her actions, and ate his meal. Then, as the meal was eaten late and he was very tired, laying his head on his wife's shouder, he slept.

The land that he had ploughed and the clumps of earth broken up that morning began to turn golden and gleamed like clusters of *kinihira* flowers. Puṇṇa awoke, saw the piles of gold, called to his wife, and said, "Dear One, I see the two *ammunums* that I ploughed this morning as golden. Perhaps my eyes are dazed because I ate my meal so late."

"I did not eat a late meal but I too see it as gold," said his wife.

Puṇṇa then got up, took one lump, and hit it against the plough head, realized that it was indeed gold, and said, "The offerings we made to the Captain of the Doctrine have borne fruit, not sometime in the future, but this very day. So much gold is not something we can hide and make use of just by ourselves. He then filled the pot in which his wife had brought his meal, with the gold, went to the palace, and sent a message that he wished to see the king. Having obtained an audience he went to the king.

"Why have you come?" the king asked.

"Lord, the land I ploughed today has all turned to gold. Take it into your treasury.[7]

"Who are you"? asked the king. The man said he was a poor man named Puṇṇa.

'Such a thing cannot happen without a reason or some cause,' thought the king and said, "What did you do today?"

"The only thing we did today was that when the Captain of the Doctrine came toward our field I gave him some teeth-cleaning twigs. My wife offered him the rice she was bringing to me in the field. Apart from that, the only other thing we did was that I ploughed the field and she cooked rice twice over."

Hearing that the king said, "Just as the mango named *gadaṁba* sprouted and bore fruit the same day, so you have this very day seen the good effects of the offering you made to the Captain of the Doctrine." Pleased he asked, "What should we do now?"

---

7. Puṇṇa makes a wise and expedient decision to hand over the vast wealth to the king. The king on his part accepts it "in trust" as it were and confers nobility on him.

"Send thousands of carts, collect, and bring the gold and use it," said Puṇṇa.

The king sent carts. Those who went under the king's orders promptly declared it state property, but when they picked up a lump of gold it turned into a lump of earth. As they put it back it turned again to gold. The king's men returned and informed the king of what had happened.

The king asked them, "What did you say when you took the gold?"

"We gathered it saying that it all belonged to Your Majesty."

"Was it we who made the offering to the Captain of the Doctrine today? What right have we to that gold? Go, and when you get there announce that this gold all belongs to Puṇṇa, the poor man. Then collect it and bring it here." Thus he commanded. They did as he ordered. Whatever they took then remained gold. They brought the gold and stacked it in the royal compound. It was a heap about eighty *riyan* in height.

The king called all the citizens and asked, "Who else is there in our city who owns wealth equal to this?"

"How can others have so much gold. Only Your Majesty has such wealth," they said.

The king then said, "Should not someone who owns so much wealth also have the status of a wealthy nobleman?"

So saying he made Puṇṇa a nobleman and placed the banners of office over him, and conferred great gifts, and named him Bahudhana Sitāno [nobleman of great wealth and generosity]. The king then gave him a piece of land that had formerly belonged to a noble merchant but that had now gone to seed and said, "Clear the land and build yourself a house here."

Puṇṇa cleared the land and while preparing the site his workers discovered great pots of treasure so he also obtained the blessing of having a large group of retainers and workers. The house was completed in a few days. He celebrated his going into residence and his elevation to the rank of a noble merchant together, and for a whole week entertained the Buddha and his monks in a vast Feast of Alms.

The Buddha preached to them and at the end of the sermon, the noble merchant Bahudhana, his wife, and his daughter Uttarā unequaled in goodness, all three received the blessings of the Path and the Fruits and became *sōvān*.

Sometime later, Sumana, the wealthy citizen of Rajagaha proposed that the wealthy nobleman Bahudhana's daughter should wed his son. Bahudhana was reluctant to give his daughter to the noble merchant Sumana's son because he was not a follower of the Buddha, while his daughter had already attained the Path and the Fruits and was fully committed to her faith.

Sumana the wealthy nobleman then said, "Do not refuse. All these years you lived as part of our establishment so because of those ties marry your daughter to our son." The wealthy nobleman Bahudhana was still reluctant, anticipating future unhappiness for his daughter. However, many pleaded with him and gave many reasons why he should marry his daughter to Sumana's son. Therefore, acceding to their requests, on the second moon of the month of *äsala* [August] he gave his daughter in marriage.

From the day of her marriage Uttarā lived among those who were not devotees [of the Buddha] and so she could not perform any Alms Feasts nor listen to sermons. Apart from anything else she could not even visit a temple. Since no monks came to her house she did not so much as set eyes on a monk. She spent two and a half months in this way. Then she inquired of those around her, "How many days more before the *vas*[8] period is over?"

"About two more weeks," they replied.

She sent a message to her father thus, "On the grounds of making a marriage, why have you put me in this prison? If you intended to do this, no matter that I was your daughter, it were better if you had branded me and sold me, because in a buyer, one does not check whether he is a devotee. By coming into this family of unbelievers I am unable to perform a single Act of Merit."[9]

Bahudhana was very upset. He sent fifteen thousand gold coins and said, "Child, listen to me. There is a courtesan named Sirimā in this city. She charges a thousand gold coins a day for her services. Send the fifteen thousand to her, bring her, and give her to your husband to perform the duties of a wife. During those fifteen days you engage in Acts of Merit."

Uttarā then invited Sirimā and said, "Sister, take these fifteen thousand gold coins and spend fifteen days looking after the needs of this wealthy nobleman." Sirimā saw the gold and agreed. Uttarā then led her to the noble merchant and said, "My Lord, for the next two weeks this person will perform the duties of a wife. I will spend those two weeks engaging in Acts of Merit that I have not performed and listening to sermons that I have had no chance to hear." The noble merchant saw the beautiful Sirimā, was attracted, and agreed.

Uttarā invited the Buddha and his monks saying, "Your Reverence, it would be good if you spend the next two weeks of the *vas* season coming to our home for food. Please do not go anywhere else." Thus happy at the thought, 'From now till the end of the *vas* season I can attend on the Buddha

8. [s. *vas*] from *vässa* (rains) was the season of the rains during which monks were expected to take up residence in a temple or home and preach to the people, not travel on missionary work.
9. It was considered the duty of parents when arranging a marriage to consider all factors that would contribute to a daughter's happiness. Uttarā thus rightly feels her parents have failed in their duty in marrying her to a nonbeliever.

and hear his sermons,' she busied herself in the kitchen organizing the Alms feasts.

"What is that foolish woman so busy about?" thought the noble merchant as he looked out one day through his chamber window at the kitchen quarters. It was just before the end of the *vas* period. He saw Uttarā, looking very ugly, her clothes covered in soot and ashes, busy organizing the cooking. 'Alas, what an unfortunate creature. Instead of enjoying all this wealth and all these comforts, she imagines that giving rice to these shaven monks is more important and busies herself obsessed with that thought!' He smiled to himself and left.

Sirimā happened to be standing by and as he moved away, thought, 'What did he smile at?' She looked through the same window at the kitchen. She saw Uttarā and thought, 'It is at her he smiled. Without doubt he has some earlier intimacy with her.' She, the outsider, just because she happened to be living in this house, believing that she was the owner of that wealth (because riches often make people arrogant), regarded Uttarā as the intruder, and decided 'I will make her suffer.' She left the palace, entered the kitchen quarters, took some boiling oil off a pan in which Uttarā was frying oil-cakes, using a spoon since the oil was too hot to touch, and walked toward Uttarā.

Uttarā saw her come and thought, 'If the favor that my friend has done me were given concrete form, all of *sakvala*[10] would not be wide enough nor the distance to the Brahma heavens long enough to contain it. What my friend has done for me is very great. Because of her for these two weeks I was able to achieve what I wished, and perform Acts of Merit. If there is the slightest anger in me toward one who has helped me so much, then may the hot oil burn me. But if I am free of anger and have only compassion toward Sirimā, then may the cooling water of compassion quench the heat of that oil and may it not hurt even the dead skin on my body. Thus she extended compassion toward Sirimā as if using a fire-quenching *mantra*. By the power of that compassion the hot oil poured on her head cooled as if it were cold water.

Sirimā, unaware that the transformation was the result of the power of Uttarā's goodness, thought, 'This oil has already cooled off.' She rushed to get another spoonful of the boiling oil and once more ran to Uttarā with it. Uttarā's servants saw her come and said, "Impertinent woman, you are barely fit to kiss the feet of our mistress let alone throw oil at her head. When did you, wretch, become better than one of us?" So they threatened her with angry words, rushed at her from all sides, and since looking for sticks would

10. [s. *sakvala*] Buddhist cosmology refers to systems of universes that include the sun, moon, and all the worlds as far as the light of the sun extends, as well as a series of heavens and hells. Such *sakvalas* are thought to be innumerable and infinite.

take time, they beat her with their hands and feet and threw her to the ground. Uttarā shouted to them from where she was but could not stop their beating and kicking. She then ran up to them, stopped the crowd of young women and said, "Why do you do this Sirimā? To you, who were engaged in the lowly profession of a courtesan,[11] I gave so much, even if it was only for two weeks. Is it fit that you do this to me who has done so much for you?" So saying she got hot water, bathed her, and rubbed medicinal oils all over her body and since the bruises were not made by a stick but by their hands and feet [they were not serious].

At that moment Sirimā realized from how the serving maids had acted that she was but an outsider and said, "Alas, what I did was wicked. This woman's husband saw her and smiled. The oil that she should have poured on my head had he seen me and smiled, I tried to pour on her. What right had I to pour the oil that was being heated in her pans on her head? Besides, when she should have beaten me she stopped the servants from beating me and instead did all she could for me. Therefore if I do not obtain her forgiveness for the wrong I have done her, my head will split into seven parts. She fell at Uttarā's feet and said, "Mistress, please forgive me."

Uttarā replied, "I am not like you. I have a father.[12] Did you not see from my actions that I'm one who has grown up under the loving care of parents? If you can get the forgiveness of my father I will forgive you."

At that Sirimā said, "Whatever I have to do, I will get your father, the wealthy nobleman Puṇṇa's forgiveness."

"The wealthy nobleman Puṇṇa is my father in *saṃsāra*. Getting his forgiveness is no use. If you win the forgiveness of the father born to the clan of the noble *Āryas* then I will forgive you," said Uttarā.

"I know that the wealthy nobleman Puṇṇa is your biological father but I do not know of an *Ārya* clan and so do not know your *Ārya* father. Who is he?" she asked.

"If you don't, let me tell you. The father born of the *Ārya* clan is the Buddha, Teacher of the Three Worlds."

"We are not believers and do not go to the temple. We are not servants of the Buddha so how will we obtain his forgiveness?"

"That can be done. The Buddha and his monks will come here tomorrow. You should prepare a food offering and come to our palace and obtain forgiveness."

---

11. Uttarā's words and that of the servants suggest that the profession of courtesan was not considered of high status. However, the earlier story of Sirimā, which showed her as well connected, wealthy, and with her own retinues, suggests the contrary. The ambivalence possibly resulted from shifts in attitudes over time.
12. Uttarā is speaking metaphorically but the implication is that parents teach one and put one in the path of goodness.

Sirimā agreed, returned to her home, and since she too was not poor, she ordered five hundred attendant women to prepare an offering of food with great care and cleanliness. On the next day she took the food offering, went to Uttarā's house, and stood unable to offer it.[13] Uttarā took it all into her charge and offered it to the Buddha and to the monks.

After they had eaten Sirimā sat worshiping the Buddha and the attendant monks. The Buddha knew that she wanted forgiveness so he asked, "What wrong did you do?" Sirimā related to the Buddha how the previous day she had taken a spoon of hot oil and tried to pour it on Uttarā, her failure, and how Uttarā had saved her.

"Master, in consideration of her goodness, I worshiped her and begged her forgiveness. She said she would forgive me only if Your Reverence forgave me."

"Is this true Uttarā?" asked the Buddha.

"It is true, My Lord," she replied.

"What thought passed through your mind when she came to throw the boiling oil on your head?" he asked.

"Master the help she has rendered me is such that if it could be expressed in concrete terms, all *sakvala* would not be wide enough, or the distance to the Brahma world not long enough to contain it. She has been of very great help indeed. Because of her I could engage exclusively in Acts of Merit for these several days. Thus I thought, 'If I have the slightest anger toward her may the hot oil burn me. If I'm free of anger may the hot oil not burn me. So I thought and evoked compassion toward her."

The Buddha acclaimed her action by thrice saying "Blessed!" He then preached a sermon.

"O Uttarā, if someone is angry, to retaliate with anger is but to add fire to fire. It will not subside. But if one is calm, the other also stops and as water puts out fire so one is able to conquer anger. If someone is not good one must overcome them by being good to them. Victory is to make the other good like you. If a person is very miserly one should shower gifts and make the other generous like oneself. If someone were to speak falsehoods, one should speak the truth and win the person over to speak the truth like you." At the end of the sermon Sirimā and her five hundred attendants also became *sōvān* because of their association with a good person like Uttarā. Thus the wise should consider the evil effects of anger, give up anger, and desirous of the eleven or more benefits of compassion, develop thoughts of compassion to all.

---

13. Sirimā probably felt that as an outsider she did not have the right to walk in and make the offering.

22

The Daughter Puṇṇā

Moreover, when an offering is made with a full heart it is never trivial. To illustrate this we will relate the story of the daughter Puṇṇā.

One day they [her employers] gave her a great amount of rice to pound and husk. It was too much to complete during the day so she lit a lamp and continued to work after dark. She then stepped out of the house to take a brief rest and stood letting the breeze play on her body. About that time the Elder Dabbamallaputta was organizing the sleeping arrangements for the monks. After the sermon he had to guide them to their sleeping place. He did not want to go up and down several times to light the way for each one. He magically created a monk whose fingers turned into tapers and who walked ahead lighting the way for them. Puṇṇā saw the monks walking back and forth by that light and thought, 'People like me, because of past Acts of Demerit such as ordering virtuous people around, have to toil and don't get to sleep even at this late hour. But why don't these monks sleep? Surely one of them must be sick.'

She was given work but was not provided a meal so she took a handful of the powdered rice-bits, wet it with water, moulded it in a pan, and set it on the fire to cook. Either because she was not permitted to eat it there or because servants are reluctant to eat in front of their superiors, she thought, 'I will eat this rice-cake on my way to fetch water.' She picked up the waterpot and set off to the ford in the river.

The Buddha, on his alms-rounds in the village, happened to be on that road. Puṇṇā[1] who was full, not just in name but also full of faith saw the

1. s. [*pun*] means "full."

Buddha. She thought, 'On all past occasions whenever I saw the Buddha I had nothing to offer him, and when I happened to have something to offer I never got to see him. Today I do have something to offer, though it is coarse, and I have met the Buddha. So even if it is not good enough for him I shall offer this cake of broken rice-bits.' Thinking thus, she put down the waterpot and bowed reverentially to the Buddha, and indicating that though she was full of faith she was poor in all else, said, "Your Reverence, this cake, because it is made mainly of broken rice-bits and has neither oil nor flour in it, may not be sweet, but if you will be kind enough to accept it, it will enable me to obtain the sweets of *nirvāṇa*." The Buddha accepted the offering of the cake of broken rice-bits. Puṇṇā made the offering and worshiping the Buddha said, "Your Reverence, just as this cake, by being offered to you, became flavorful and worthy of you, so may I who am a slave to others but have now come to you, be freed of the enslavement of desires."

"May it be so," responded the Buddha and went on to preach a sermon.

Puṇṇā thought to herself, 'The Buddha accepted this cake of broken rice-bits out of compassion for me, in order that I may obtain divine cakes. But will he ever eat it? Can he eat it? He will surely take it to some far place and throw it to the dogs. Then he will go begging for alms to the dwellings of rich men such as kings and regional rulers and partake of their sweet food offerings.' The Buddha knew what she was thinking and so he looked at the Elder Ānanda and indicated that he wished to sit down. Since they were outside the city limits the Elder Ānanda spread his double robe folded into four. The Buddha sat down and ate the cake of broken rice-bits that was transformed now into a divine cake.

This was why it became divine. On the day the Buddha attained Enlightenment and on the day of his death, the gods, as if squeezing honey out of a honeycomb, had poured all the best flavors in the universe into the food that was in his bowl. On other occasions, anything he took in his hand was similarly flavored. Thus, on that day too, though hardly fit for consumption, the moment the Buddha took the cake of broken rice-bits all the flavors of the universe soaked into it.

Puṇṇā looked on. After the Buddha had finished eating, the Elder poured water for him to wash his hands. When the Buddha had completed his meal he called Puṇṇā to him and asked, "Why did you say what you did about my monks Puṇṇā?"

"Your Reverence, I said nothing," she replied.

"What did you say when you saw my disciples returning at night after listening to a sermon?"

"The likes of us, since we are the slaves of others, have to work day and night and so get no sleep. I wondered why the monks walked about, sleepless? I said that surely one of them must be sick."

The Buddha listened to her and said, "Puṇṇā, you labor day and night and do not sleep because you get no respite from work. My disciples do not sleep because they do not wish to sleep, because they know that there is no Merit to be gained by sleep. If a person fulfilling the Three Rules of Discipline[2] in his or her desire for *nirvāṇa*, stays awake whether by day or night, his or her vigilance increases. As a result, just as darkness disappears when the sun rises and as dew dries as the sun gets hotter, so all Impurities are destroyed."

At the end of the sermon, Puṇṇā, who offered the cake of broken rice-bits obtained the divine cake of the Fruits of a Stream-Enterer. This sermon proved of great benefit to many others too.

The Buddha partook of the cake of broken rice-bits and then retired to the monastery. Monks in the assembly were very surprised that the Buddha had accepted the cake of broken rice-bits given by Puṇṇā and that he had eaten it. They began to talk about it. The Buddha heard their discussion and declared that not only after Enlightenment but even during the period when he was cultivating the Ten Perfections,[3] he had eaten cakes of broken rice-bits that she had offered. He recited the following verse:

> bhutvā tiṇaparīghāsaṃ bhutvā ācāmakuṇdakaṃ
> etaṃ te bhojanaṃ asi kasmādāni na bhuñjasi
>
> [Formerly you ate coarse grain partook of cakes of broken rice-bits.
> That was your food in the past. Why don't you eat that now?]

and related the *Kuṇḍakasindhava Jātaka Tale*.[4]

Therefore, just as the Buddha ate the coarse cake of broken rice-bits as a favor to Puṇṇā, good people in their desire for *nirvāṇa* should follow the observance of austere practices and win praise similar to what the Buddha won.

---

2. The Rules of Discipline are *dāna* (generosity or giving), *sīla* (morality), and *bhāvana* (meditation).
3. To become a Buddha one has to practice the Ten Perfections. The Buddha did so through many hundreds of births in *saṃsāra*. They are generosity, morality, selflessness, wisdom, energy or effort, patience, truthfulness, resoluteness, compassion, and equanimity.
4. Jataka No: 254:ii, 267–291.

23

The Nun Khemā

To illustrate the evil of being obsessed with color we shall relate the story of the nun Khemā.

How does it go?

[Queen] Khemā was one who had made a Fervent Wish in the time of the noble Buddha Piyumuttarā [Padumuttarā] to obtain the status of the chief disciple among the nuns. The Fervent Wish she had made was noble and so also was she noble in complexion. She was so beautiful that she became intoxicated with the color of her complexion. She was reluctant to go to the Buddha wrongly believing that since the Buddha preached against attachment to beauty he would find fault with whoever was beautiful.

The king knew that because of her wrong belief she was reluctant to go to the Buddha so he wrote songs about the beauties of the Vēluvana park[1] and gave it to poets to recite. Just as King Chūlani could not recognize his own wife Queen Nanda when he heard the descriptions extoling her beauty so when Queen Khemā heard the poets sing those songs [of the beauties of that park] she felt she did not know of such a place.

"What kind of a park do you describe?" she asked.

"O Queen we describe your own park, Veluvana," they replied.

Just as one acquires a desire to see some strange new thing one has heard about so the queen wished to go to the Veluvana park.

1. The Vēluvana monastery where the Buddha resided for periods of time was located in the Vēluvana forest or park.

The Buddha was aware of this and as he was seated, surrounded by his followers preaching a sermon, he created the phantom of a beautiful woman to stand beside him fanning him with a palm fan.

On her way to the Veluvana monastery Queen Khemā saw this woman and thought, "They say the Buddha finds fault with the beauty of form however lovely it may be. Now here is a woman beside him fanning him. I cannot hold a candle to her. I have never seen anyone so beautiful. It is as if she is there to stop anyone else coming near the Buddha.' Not listening to what the Buddha was preaching she stood gazing at the woman. The Buddha knew that Queen Khemā's mind was focused only on the woman and he transformed the figure from that of a sixteen-year-old young girl into a middle-aged woman and then into a woman at the end of her life. Finally he transformed her into just skin and bone, ugly as a *prēta*.[2] Since Queen Khemā had been looking fixedly at the phantom she thought, 'Such a beautiful form decayed in one instant. It is no use being misled by one's ideas [of beauty]. Just as there is no inner pith to a banana tree so there is no point to such thoughts.' The Buddha was aware that her thoughts were leaning toward the Doctrine of the Triple Gem and recited the following verse:

āturaṃ asūciṃ pūtiṃ passa kheme samussayaṃ
ugghrantaṃ paggharantaṃ bālānaṃ abhipatṭhitaṃ'

[Khemā, behold these Aggregates, diseased, impure, decaying, trickling, oozing, and desired only by fools.]

Describing the evils of the physical body he said, "When born of a mother's womb with its thirty-two Impurities, not pure like Manel or Ipul blossoms, nor created with gems by gods and Brahma, the very source is evil. So is it with all beings.' As he completed the stanza Khemā gave up her intoxication with color as well as other Impurities and became a *sōvān*. It was as if she did not go to the Buddha until her intelligence had matured. She now achieved the state of *sōvān* but had not yet become an *arahat*. In order to make her an *arahat* the Buddha addressed her thus:

"Listen Khemā, just as a spider constructs a cobweb and sits in the center of it and when a fly or a mosquito or some such creature is caught in a corner of it and the cobweb shakes, by that sign it instantly runs along that thread, captures it, sucks its sap, and then returns to sit in its place. Even so, if a being is trapped in Lust, made evil by Rage, and led astray by Delusion that

2. Spirits (often dead ancestors) who dwell in hell or in a state of perpetual punishment. They are wasted in appearance and look like dried leaves.

being of a spider constructs a net of Desire not to capture others but to trap himself. Such persons when trapped cannot escape by themselves. They can only be released by the advice of another, compassionate, person. Thus the wise should burn such a web of Desire with the fire of the Noble Path of *arahats,* rid themselves of all sorrow, and spend their days happily.

Like a flower that is about to open blooms when the suns rays hit it so, at the end of the sermon Queen Khemā became an *arahat.* And just as a shower of gems rain on persons of great Merit and benefit many others too, so the rain of the Good Doctrine that was triggered by Queen Khemā was of benefit to many. Many people picked up those gems and attained the blessings of the World and the Blessings of the Path and the Fruits.

Thus the wise should not be intoxicated with color, with good health, and other Impurities. They should bite them off and destroy them and attain the undying state of *nirvāṇa.*

The Buddha said to the king, "O king, Queen Khemā must now join the Order or she must die and attain *nirvāṇa.*"[3]

The king replied, "Your Reverence, how can she die and achieve *nirvāṇa* if she is destined to live for a longer time? Let her become a nun." The Buddha sent her to the nuns and she was ordained as an Elder. Because of the Fervent Rebirth Wish she had made one hundred thousand aeons ago she became the chief disciple among the nuns.

3. Since she has become an *arahat* she cannot continue the lay life. Were she to die she would attain *nirvāṇa.* Alternatively she could live the life of a renunciate.

24

Maha Prājapatī Gōtamī

Moreover, if anyone is free of Hindrances he is a Brahmin. To illustrate this we will tell the story of Maha Prajapātī.

How does it go?

She, [Prajapātī] like a pure person accepting a scented garland, accepted the eight rules such as that which said "a hundred year old nun should worship a monk who had only that day been ordained"[1] and together with five hundred others she obtained ordination.

However, her ordination did not carry with it the status of 'Elder.' As a result the talk later arose, 'This person's ordination does not carry with it the status of 'Elder.' Nor was she given the robes of ordination. Her ordination and her status as an elder are both in question.[2] Since the nuns had not questioned the Buddha, they expressed doubts, refused to have any association with her and informed the Buddha about it.

The Buddha learned of it and said, "O nuns, by observing the Eight fold rules she obtained ordination and the status of 'Elder' from none other than me. It is I who gave her the status of 'Elder.' " In order to squash their murmurings he preached thus: "O nuns, if a person does not engage in the three wrongful acts that enter from the three entrances [eyes, nose and ears],

---

1. The image emphasizes the monks' acceptance of the correctness of the rule establishing the hierarchical position of the nun vis à vis monks.
2. An indication perhaps of the kind of dissension and internal conflicts that seems to have surfaced quite early and might have undermined the Order of Nuns at a later date.

if they observe the Three Virtues[3] they are faultless. Though you may have expressed doubts because you did not know the facts, in future do not do so." At the end of the sermon many achieved *nirvāṇa*.

Thus good people should avoid the wrongful acts that occur through the three doors and should attempt to make their minds tranquil.

3. The Three Virtues [s. *tun susiri*] are Generosity *[dāna]*, Moral Discipline *[sīla]*, and Contemplation *[bhāvanā]*.

25

The Elder Sundarasamudda

To illustrate that harm does not come to those whose thoughts are pure we shall relate the story of the Elder Sundarasamudda.[1]

How does it go?

There was a young nobleman named Sundarasamudda who lived in the city of Sävät. He was the son of a rich man whose wealth amounted to about four hundred million. One afternoon he saw crowds going to the monastery at Deveramvehera to listen to sermons and asked, "Where are you going?"

"We go to listen to sermons," they replied.

"I'm coming with you," he said and went with them and stood at the far edge of the listening crowd. The Buddha knew his intentions and in order to excite his interest he preached the Doctrine in progression. Sundarasamudda heard the sermon and thought, 'Just as one can not be a world conqueror without being born a king so it is impossible to practise the Doctrine by remaining a householder. I will become a monk,' he firmly decided.

When the crowds left after hearing the sermon he asked to be ordained but learned that the Buddhas did not ordain those who had not first obtained permission from their parents. He went home and after much pleading, like the young noblemen Sudinna and Ratthapala, he too obtained permission from his parents.

He received ordination from the Buddha but decided 'I cannot pursue the Discipline as I wish in a place where there are hundreds of my relatives. I

1. I decided to include this story because once again a woman plays a major role in it.

will go far away.' He left his home, traveled over one hundred and eighty leagues to the city of Rajagaha, and there begged for alms.

One festive day, his parents who were living in the city of Sävät saw their son's friends all dressed up and enjoying themselves. They thought, 'Alas our son is deprived of all this,' and they grieved and wept. At that moment the daughter of a courtesan happened to go to that house and saw Sundarasamudda Thera's parents crying.

"Why do you weep?" she asked. They said they wept because they were reminded of their son.

"Where is he now?" she asked.

"He has become a monk," they said.

"Rather than weep and not see him isn't it better to see him by making him give up his robes?"

"That would be a good thing," they said. "But he does not want to give up the robes and thinks we might pressure him to do so and because of that he has gone to the city of Rajagaha that is about one hundred and eighty leagues away."

"Now if by some means I make him give up his robes what will you do for me?" she asked.

"If you do that we will make you, none other, his bride and you will then be heir to our wealth," they replied.

"In that case give me food and provisions for the journey," she said and obtaining all that she needed went to the city of Rajagaha with a big retinue.[2]

After two or three days of inquiries she found out on which street the monk begged for alms. She then took up residence on that very street and early morning prepared sweetly flavored food. When the monk came for alms she made the offering.

After several days had passed in this manner she said, "Your Reverence it is inconvenient to eat when it is all served together in the begging bowl. It would be better if you partake of the food within this house," and asked for his bowl. Not knowing her intentions he gave her his bowl.

She seated him that day on the outer porch and said, "Your Reverence, are you not tired out by walking, begging for alms?" For several days she served his meal on the porch. Thereafter, she gathered together some children who were playing in the vicinity, coaxed them with sweets and oil cakes and said, "Children, when the monk comes to eat on the porch, raise a lot of dust. Do so even if I try to stop you." She instructed them in this manner.

---

2. The following account shows that the woman is extremely resourceful and very clever. Her plans to entice the monk are carefully and intelligently made and indicate a good knowledge of the habits, inhibitions, and weaknesses of monks.

The next day when the monk was taking his meal seated on the porch outside the house they [the children] raised a lot of dust and even when the courtesan's daughter asked them to stop they ignored her, acting according to her instructions. They caused great inconvenience to the monk.

The following day the courtesan's daughter said, "Your Reverence, when you sit here to eat, these undisciplined sons of widows raise up a lot of dust in spite of all I do to try to stop them. Do sit inside and have your meal." For several days she made the alms offering inside the house. Then once again she bribed the small children with sweets and cakes and said, "Even if I try to stop you [ignore me] make a big commotion while the monk is eating. They did as instructed.

The following day the courtesan's daughter said, "Your Reverence, there is too much commotion out here. These disobedient children will not stop in spite of what I say or do. They are other people's children so one can't bash their heads[3] to stop them. However, they can't come upstairs with their fights can they? It will be good if you were to take your meal upstairs."

When he agreed she sent him on ahead and followed behind locking the doors below as she went upstairs. The Elder was in the process of observing the ascetic practice of walking to beg for alms. However, caught up in the desire for flavored foods he climbed to the upper story to eat his meal. They climbed to the very topmost floor of the seven-storied building.

In the beginning he had neither eaten nor accepted what was brought from inside the house, had walked from house to house in progression, and all he had done was to open the lid and present his begging bowl. He had not stepped beyond the outer porch. But what good was that to the woman? Even after that, it was because of the woman's words and because of the dust outside that he had gone inside without considering past or future consequences. It was tiresome to accept alms all mixed up together. [Thereafter,] it was because he could not escape the commotion even when seated inside that he had climbed up to the top story. Not yet being an *arahat* he had not guessed her intentions.[4]

The daughter of the courtesan now invited this monk, who was overcome by his desire for good food, to sit down. She had made all these offerings and

3. The original says [s. *marā navattantat bäriya*] literally "I cannot stop them by killing them" but it is a manner of speaking and not to be taken literally. Hence the idiomatic translation.
4. The author-translator of the SR is at pains to excuse the monks actions so that he is seen as in no way to blame for the situation he found himself in. The DA makes no such excuses but states "So firmly bound was he by the bonds of craving of taste that he complied with her suggestion" (Burlingame, vol. 3, p. 310).

done all this not from any faith or devotion but purely to arouse him, and all these days the offerings had been for this monk alone, none other. Therefore, now in order to arouse him and to display her femininity, she began to talk in a voice louder than his. All this is but a simplistic performance for the wise. She twisted and turned and bent as if writhing with the pain of desire. She picked her nails as if cleaning the dirt that had got under them. She rubbed one foot against the other. She rubbed her calves against each other. Then she carried the little children. She set them down. She got them to play with her. She ordered them to play with others. She fondled the children. She got them to fondle her. She began to eat in his presence. She fed the others too with rice. She gave away something she owned. She asked for something back. She did whatever they did. She spoke in a loud voice. She spoke softly like someone just off a sickbed. She spoke at great length. She spoke lucidly. She danced. She sang. She played the drums. She wept as if chili powder had got into her eyes. She adorned herself in his presence. She laughed a great deal. She gazed at him. She shook her hips. She shook her private parts. She displayed her thigh. She turned and hid it. She took off her upper garment and exposed her breasts and waist. She raised her arm and displayed her armpit. She winked.[5] She twitched her eyebrows. She put out her tongue and licked her lips. She loosened her clothes, then again tightened them. She let down her hair then tied it up again. Thus as if performing a magic show suggesting the pleasures that could be had from more such feminine graces, she stood before the monk saying,[6]

> alattakakatā pādā pādukāruyha vesiyā
> tuvampi daharo mama ahampi daharā tava
> Ubhopi pabbajissāma pacchā jiṇṇā daṇḍaparāyaṇā

> [Dyed in lac and clad in slippers are the feet of a harlot. You are young and you are mine. I am young and I am yours. we will both retire from the world later and lean on a staff.]

---

5. [s. *äs maranava*] literally: "kill the eye." However it is an idiom meaning "to wink." Burlingame has translated it as follows: "to bury the pupils of the eyes," indicating that idioms are probably the hardest aspect of a language for a non native speaker to translate.
6. Burlingame notes that this section of the DA "is taken bodily from *jātaka* v. 433–434 (Burlingame, vol. 3, p. 311). The SR is a fairly close translation of the DA except for little touches like the images where "she wept as if a fistful of chillie had been put in her eyes." The whole scene is presented as a performance—not very different from that of a modern nightclub performer who goes through similar seductive motions and gestures.

meaning: 'You and I are suited to each other in age. Enjoy the pleasures of the householder's life with me now and later, when we are old, let us both become renunciates.'

Thc monk thought, 'Alas what have I done unthinkingly,' and was very upset.

At that moment the Buddha who was one hundred and eighty leagues away at the Deveramvehera monastery, though not visible to those in *saṃsāra,* saw with his Eye of Wisdom the many antics of the courtesan and saw also that the monk had not been affected by them. As if such antics were only worth smiling at, he smiled.[7] The Great Elder Ānanda saw the Buddha smile and asked why he did so.

"Ānanda, in the city of Rajagaha in the topmost floor of a seven-storied house there is a debate going on between a monk named Sundarasamudda and the daughter of a courtesan.

"Has he won or lost the debate?" asked Ānanda.

The Buddha said that the monk Sundarasamudda had won and that the daughter of the courtesan had lost both in this world and the next world. As he sat there he sent forth a ray of light and indicating that he was close at hand he preached the following sermon:

"If a person regards the five sensory pleasures such as beauty of form and sound, and the Impurities of sensuality as being injurious, renounces both, enters the *sāsana* and lives as a monk observing the Discipline, and while so living seeks to become an *arahat*, such a person who has escaped the cycle of being I consider noble." At the end of the sermon the monk became an *arahat* and when he acquired the Path he also acquired Supernormal Powers. By those powers he rose up to the sky and came to the Buddha and worshiped him, thanking him for what he had done.

The monks gathered in the discussion hall said, "Fellow monks, the Monk Sundarasamudda was very nearly destroyed because of his addiction to the pleasures of taste. He was saved because the Buddha saw him." Thus they talked. The Buddha heard them and said, "Monks, this is not the only time I have been of help to him who was about to be destroyed because of addiction to the pleasures of taste. In the past too he was about to be destroyed just like this and I helped him." And since that was not enough to make them understand he added:

na kiratthi rasehi pāpiyo āvāsehi ca santhavehi cā
vātamigaṃ gehanissitaṃ vasamānesi rasehi sañjayo

---

7. It is important to note that the Buddha too sees it as a performance and his reaction is not a moralistic diatribe against such women but to smile at the woman's futile "antics."

> [There is nothing worse than the seduction of taste whether at home or among friends. Attracted by taste the deer was enticed into Sanjaya's house and captured.]

and described the *Vātamiga Jātaka* story. In the past the deer who came up to the palace door, attracted by the desire for tasty foods was this Sundarasamudda. The minister who saved him from death was me," he said concluding the story of the past birth.

Thus the wise, if they are inclined to do Acts of Demerit such as the taking of life in order to satisfy the sensation of taste, should avoid such acts, lead a good life, and try to destroy that desire by all possible means.[8]

---

8. This final admonition against killing animals for food was no doubt added for the benefit of his local rural audience who, on occasion, must have hunted.

26

Soreyya

In order to illustrate that a mere thought can have evil consequences we will relate the story of Soreyya.

How does it go?

At the time when the Buddha, Teacher of the Three Worlds, was living in the city of Sävät, there lived in Daṁbadiva, in the city of Soreyya a young noble merchant named Soreyya. [One day], he drove through the streets in a carriage and together with a friend and a large retinue, headed out of the city to the river for a bath. At that very moment the Great Elder Kasayin [Elder Kaccayana] intending to go to the city of Soreyya to beg for alms, stood at the city gates and was retying his robe. The Great Thera's body was very handsome. He had done much merit [in the past] so his body, like a mass of gold, was exceedingly lovely. The noble merchant Soreyya saw him and instead of thinking, 'Would that I could possess his virtue' was consumed with lust and thought, 'O if only His Reverence were my consort. If not that, would that my wife were endowed with the beauty of His Reverence.' Thinking evil thoughts is indeed a sign of immaturity. He [Soreyya] immersed himself in these wishful thoughts.

With that thought his masculinity left him and as if he had died and been instantly reborn he became a woman. Then, overcome with shame he got down from the carriage and fled. His companions, unable to recognize him asked, "What is this? What is happening?"

The nobleman Soreyya, now a woman, as if demonstrating the sufferings of *saṃsāra*, set off on the road to Taxila like one going to study with learned scholars, the culinary arts.[1]

The friend who had accompanied Soreyya searched far and near but did not find him. Then, all of them completed their baths and returned home. When asked where the noble merchant Soreyya was, they replied, "We thought he had bathed and returned ahead of us so we came back." Thereafter his parents seached for him but they too failed to find him. Believing him dead, they wept and mourned and performed the Merit-giving funeral ceremonies.[2]

The noblewoman [Soreyya] saw a caravan of merchants going toward Taxila and followed them. People saw her and said, "Come along with us [even though] we do not know whose daughter you are. What kind of a journey is this that you make?" they asked.

"Don't question me. Drive your carts. I will follow," she said.

However, when she had traveled some distance her legs ached so she took a ring off her finger, gave it, and obtained permission to travel in the caravan. The merchants traveling with her then had an idea. 'Our noble merchant in Taxila does not have a wife. We will tell him about this woman and we might be rewarded for it.'

They went to the city of Taxila and said to the noble merchant, "We have a young woman who seems well suited to you."

The noble merchant had her brought to him and seeing that she was all that he had wished for, he made her his wife.

---

1. Taxila was a city famous in ancient times for its scholarly institutions. It was a tradition that young noblemen went to Taxila to study with famous teachers and to acquire learning in all manner of arts and sciences. The reference in the text can be read as the author's ironic jibe at this woman on her way to Taxila, the famed seat of learning where only men of noble families went. There is no record of women studying there. The author ironically implies that if this woman was headed for Taxila it must be to study the culinary arts!

   One of the six extant Sinhala manuscripts however, has the word as *silpa sāṣtra* (scholarly studies) and not *sūpa sāṣtra* (culinary studies). It is possible (though unlikely) that the original text read as follows: "Soreyya the noblewoman . . . set off on the road to Taxila like one going to acquire *learning* from famous scholars." Later scribes, ignoring the fact that the reference was intended as a simile, may have changed the word *silpa sāṣtra* to *sūpa sāṣtra* as being more suited to Soreyya since she was now a woman. The reverse is equally possible. That one scribe changed the original *sūpa sāṣtra* to *silpa sāṣtra* as he missed the irony and did not think "culinary arts" were a part of the scholarly studies engaged in at Taxila!
2. Rituals performed at funerals are intended to convey Merit to the dead so they can be reborn in "good" circumstances.

The journey in *saṃsāra* is long and therefore it is not unusual for men to be reborn as women or women to be reborn as men. Men who commit adultery and suffer for hundreds of years in hell, when they are reborn in the human world are born as women for a hundred more times. Even the Great Thera Ānanda who, over a period of one hundred thousand aeons, made Rebirth Wishes [to attain Enlightenment] yet, when he was journeying in *saṃsāra* he was once born in a goldsmith's family, indulged in adultery, suffered in hell for a long period, and because the consequences of that Act of Demerit were not fully over, he was born a woman for fourteen more births. In seven more births he suffered castration. Women who do not wish to remain women but wish to be men, perform Acts of Giving and other meritorious acts, make Rebirth Wishes, and are born as men. Others who may not perform any special Acts of Merit but remain chaste wives and do not indulge in adulterous conduct are also reborn as men.[3] However, the nobleman Soreyya who indulged in unseemly thoughts about the Thera Kasayin was transformed into a woman in that very life without having to go any further.[4]

Cohabiting with the noble merchant of Taxila the noblewoman Soreyya became pregnant. In ten months she gave birth to a son. When that child was taking his first steps she gave birth to yet another son. In this manner, as a woman, she bore two children carrying them in her womb each for a period of ten months. As a man s/he[5] had fathered two other sons so s/he now had four sons.

Around this time, the noble merchant who was [formerly] Soreyya's friend filled five hundred carts with merchandize, left the city of Soreyya, and headed for Taxila. He drove into the city in a luxury conveyance. The noblewoman Soreyya happened to open the window of an upper story to look out onto the street and saw the noble merchant. She recognized him instantly,

---

3. Gender hierachy is clearly formulated here. A man who commits adultery is punished by being reborn as a woman. Women who perform Acts of Merit are rewarded by being born as men. This is tied to the Theravada Buddhist belief that while anyone can attain *nirvāṇa*, if one wishes to become a Buddha one must be born a male.
4. Gender change was not an unknown phenomenon. In parts of South India even today, there is a group called *hijras* who are invited into a home when a child is born to examine the genitals and declare the sex of the child. If the sex of the child is "ambiguous" they take the child for adoption among their group.
5. I have decided to use this form where the gender distinctions are blurred. In Sinhala gender is indicated in the agreement between the subject and verb. Some manuscripts use a feminine ending to the verb "bore" others use a masculine ending suggesting the author's and transcriber's confusion.

sent a maid to invite him in, seated him on the balcony, and entertained him graciously. The noble merchant enjoyed her hospitality and said, "Noble lady, we have not met before yet your hospitality is most gracious. Why do you do this?"

"What makes you think I do not know you? I do know you. Don't you live in the city of Soreyya," she responded. When the friend said that he did indeed live there s/he asked him about her/his parents and about the wife s/he had had as a man and about her\his two children.

The noble merchant replied that they were all well.

"Do you know them?" he asked.

"Yes I do," s/he replied. "The old couple had one son. Where is he now?"

"I do not wish to be asked about him. One day he and I drove off in a carriage to have a river bath and he disappeared; I do not know where. Not finding him I reported the matter to his parents. They too searched for him and did not find him. Believing him dead they have wept and mourned and performed the funeral rites of Merit Transference."

The noblewoman listened to it all and said, "In that case, [let me tell you] I am indeed that noble merchant."

"What are you saying? My friend was a man, handsome as a divine being," he said and did not believe her.

"Whatever you may think, I am he," s/he replied.

"If that be so, what then happened to you?"

She asked him if he remembered seeing the Great Elder Kasayin on that occasion.

"Yes I did see him," he replied.

"That day, when I saw him, I committed a great Act of Demerit. I thought, 'Would that his Reverence were my wife or that my wife had his great beauty.' By thinking such an impure thought about such a pure being it was as if I threw garbage on one who was fully adorned, or hurled something against the wind that flew back in my face. I became a woman. I was very ashamed, so without saying anything even to you I fled and then came here."

"What you did was very wrong. Whoever else you may not have told was it right that you did not tell me? Are friends not for times like that? If you had only asked forgiveness of His Reverence such a thing would not have happened. Did you or did you not ask his forgiveness?" he asked.

"My lord, was there such a possibility? I did no such thing." Then s\he asked, "Is there anyone who has had any news of the Thera?" When told that he was now in this very city the noblewoman continued, "If he comes this way when begging for alms, I shall give him alms."

Prepare a great Feast of Alms and I will arrange to get his forgiveness, he [the friend] said.

He then went to the Great Thera Kasayin, worshiped him, and stood on one side.

"Your Reverence. The invitation for tomorrow's meal is from me," he said.

"Aren't you a newcomer to this town?" asked the Great Elder.[6]

"I do not wish to be called that. But tomorrow I will provide the alms."

The Great Thera did not refuse. The noblewoman then prepared alms in her home and the Great Thera came there for alms. Thereafter, they seated him, gave him food, and at the conclusion [of the meal] the noble merchant led the noblewoman to the Great Thera, worshiped him, and said "Your Reverence, please forgive a wrong done by this person."

When he asked what it was she had done the noble merchant related the full story of her past.

"If that be so, stand up, I forgive you," said the Thera.

The moment the Great Thera declared his forgiveness her feminine form vanished and she became a man.

When his manhood returned the noble merchant of Taxila [her husband] said, "Friend, because these two children were born of your womb and from my seed we are both responsible for them. Let us therefore continue to live together."

At that the noble merchant Soreyya replied, "What are you saying my friend? In this one birth I was first a noble merchant, then became a noblewoman, and now for a third time I have been transformed into a nobleman. Must I stay on and become a nobleman's wife again? I have two sons born to me when I was a nobleman. Now I have two sons by you, born of my womb. When so much has happened in a single lifetime and when I do not know what the future holds, is it not enough to make one give up the life of the household? I will now join the Order under this great man who raised me from my lowly position to this noble status. If that eminent status (being a noble monk) is what everyone should aspire to, should I not also wish for that? To obtain that, I will become a monk. These two children I place in your charge. Look after them well." So saying, he comforted the children, handed them to their father, and left. He became a monk under the Great Elder.

The Great Elder made him a monk with full ordination and took him with him. In their wanderings they came to the city of Sävät. He who was formerly known as the noble merchant Soreyya, then [subsequently] as a noblewoman, was now finally known, not as a noble merchant but as the

6. The implication here possibly is that were he not a newcomer he would have had an assigned day for giving alms. His making a special invitation suggests that he was not on such a roster.

Monk Soreyya. People living in the area heard about him and were amazed. They came asking, "We have heard such stories. Are they true?"

When told that they were, they asked, "Can such things be? In such a short space of time Your Reverence was the parent of four sons. Which of them do you love most?"

"I love most those who were born of my womb when I was a woman," he replied.[7]

Whoever came to see him would ask him that same question. The monk replied in the same manner. Then ashamed, he stopped entering into conversations, went to live alone, engaged in meditation, and before long attained the four full Analytic Powers, achieved the Four Paths and the Fruits, and became an *arahat*.

Even after he became an *arahat* those who came would question him as to which of his four sons he loved most.

"I love none of them," he now replied.

Monks who heard him said, "Up to now this monk said he felt most affection for the children born of his womb. Now, perhaps in order to indicate that he has become an *arahat* he says he loves none of them." They informed the Buddha about him.

The Buddha replied, "Monks, that is not what my son says. From the moment one becomes an *arahat* one does not feel affection for anyone. A mind that has been weaned away from thoughts of Demerit and is established in the way of Righteousness, has no special affection for anyone, be it parents, relatives, or children. Thus in whatever way one can, one must discipline and control one's mind. Parents can give their children wealth that can only last one lifetime, not more. Even Viśākhā's parents who had so much wealth could only give her what could be of use in this one lifetime, not more. There are no parents who can give their children the wealth of a *Sakviti* or Universal Monarch. They cannot give their children the joys of heaven. They definitely cannot give them the joys of the Path and the Fruits or of Spiritual Attainments. Only a pure mind can give one all of this." Thus he spoke. At the end of the sermon many people attained the state of *sōvān* and the other Fruits and the Path.

Thus good people should make every effort to discipline their own minds and attain the joys of *nirvāṇa*.

---

7. It is a poignant admission of the power of a mother's love. For a Buddhist it also suggests the powerful tie of affection that one must overcome if one joins the Order.

Bibliography

Altekar, A.S. *The Position of Women in Hindu Civilization,* Delhi: Motilal Baranasidas, 1938.

Burlingame, Eugene Watson. *Buddhist Legends: Translated from the original Pali Text of the Dhammapada Commentary,* Parts 1, 2, 3, London Henley & Boston: Pali Text Society, 1979.

Church, Cornelia Demitt. "Temptress, Housewife, Nun: Womens Role in Early Buddhism," *Anima: An Experiental Journal* 1: 2, 1975, pp. 53–58.

Duley, Margot I. & Edwards, Mary I. *The Cross Cultural Study of Women: A Comprehensive Guide,* New York: Feminist Press, 1986.

Falk, Nancy. "An Image of Women in Old Buddhist Literature: The Daughters of Mara" in *Women and Religion,* Janet Plaskow and J. Arnold eds. Montana: Scholar's Press, 1974, pp. 105–112.

Gross, Rita M. *Buddhism After Patriarchy,* Albany: State University of New York Press, 1993.

Gupta, Kaushalya. *Women in Buddhist Literature,* Germany: Tubingen, 1990.

Horner, I.B., *Women Under Primitive Buddhism,* London: Routledge & Sons, 1930.

Law, Bimala. *Women in Buddhist Literature,* Varanasi: Indological Book House, 1981.

Murcott, Susan. *The First Buddhist Women: Translations and Commentaries on the Theri Gatha,* California: Parallax Press, 1991.

Obeyesekere, Ranjini, & Obeyesekere, Gananath. "The Tale of the Demoness Kali: A 13th Century Text on Evil" *Journal of the History of Religion,* vol. 29, no. 4, May 1990, pp. 318–334.

Obeyesekere, Ranjini, tr. *Jewels of the Doctrine: Stories from the Saddharma-ratnāvaliya,* Albany: State University of New York Press, 1991.

Paul, Diana. *Women in Buddhism: Images of the Feminine in the Mahayana Tradition,* Berkeley: University of California Press, 1985.

Richman, Paula. *Women, Branch Stories, and Religious Rhetoric in a Tamil Buddhist Text,* Syracuse, NY: Maxwell School of Citizenship and Public Affairs, University of Syracuse, 1988.

Rhys Davids, Caroline. *Psalms of the Sisters,* London: Published for the Pali Text Society by Oxford University Press, 1909.

Sponberg, Alan. "Attitudes toward Women and the Feminie in Early Buddhism" in Cabezon, Jose Ignacio, ed. *Buddhism Sexuality and Gender,* Albany: State University of New York Press, 1992, pp. 3–36.

Van Esterick, Penny, ed. *Women of South East Asia,* De Kalb Illinois: Center for South East Asian Studies, 1982.

Index